M000160212

The Idea of the Union
Great Britain and Northern Ireland –
Realities and Challenges

edited by
John Wilson Foster
William Beattie Smith

BELCOUVER
PRESS

Published 2021
by Belcouver Press

info@belcouverpress.com

ISBN 978-0-9935607-2-9

Publication of *The Idea of the Union* has been made possible through the generous financial aid of pro-Union individuals and organisations in the United Kingdom.

Designed by April Sky Design, Newtownards

Printed by GPS Colour Graphics Ltd, Belfast

CONTENTS

Foreword

Baroness Hoey

Occasionally a book is published just at the opportune time to ensure it is read widely. *The Idea of the Union: Great Britain and Northern Ireland – Realities and Challenges* is such a book. It is in our bookshops just when the debate on how to strengthen the Union is widespread throughout the United Kingdom, and in Northern Ireland at a time when the Irish republican case for a united Ireland separated from Great Britain is being pushed by the media at the expense of any equivalent pro-Union argument.

For too long, many pro-Union Northern Ireland citizens have got on with their lives and – whilst quietly shocked at how much credence is given to nationalist commentators – have stayed silent. That can no longer continue.

The Northern Ireland Protocol has shown that when it comes to the crunch a Conservative and Unionist government is willing to sacrifice Northern Irish loyalty and leave us under European Union rules and European Court jurisdiction whilst dividing the UK with a trade border at Larne, Belfast and Warrenpoint. The consent principle enshrined in the Belfast Agreement (1998) has been ignored. As Lord Trimble says (and he should know, as one of its constructors) the Agreement has been entirely broken.

During my 30 years as a London MP I would meet many Northern Irish living in Great Britain. It was always the same story when they were pressed as to whether they spoke up for Northern Ireland. Their unionism was still firm but they kept quiet, usually making some reference to it being easier to say nothing.

For many years, particularly since the signing of the Agreement, young people have had instilled into them the idea that Protestants or unionists rode roughshod over downtrodden Catholics. So it is good to read Graham Gudgin's article on alleged housing discrimination which paints a truer picture.

There are so many incisive chapters in this book, some specifically relating to "Our Wee Country" but others looking at the wider Union, including Scotland. The relationship with the Republic of Ireland is examined in a brilliantly articulated chapter by Ray Bassett, a former Irish Ambassador to Canada. He forecasts the difficulties faced by Ireland now that they are the last English-speaking EU member. The Republic's refusal to speak up for the UK during Brexit negotiations could well backfire when the EU no longer sees it as useful.

Living in London, I had hundreds of Irish-born constituents and I was always struck by how the longer they had lived in Great Britain the more they seemed to have forgotten the anti-English rhetoric so loved by many back home. Rejoining the Commonwealth is one way the close links could be furthered, suggests Bassett.

The long-running disputes over legacy are brought up to date by Jeff Dudgeon who shows how "lawfare" is now the favoured method for republicans to continue their grievance cases against security forces.

In every chapter there is something really worth reading. Overall, by the time you have finished the book I hope you will understand even more clearly why the Union is threatened and why all of us who care about the future of Northern Ireland as an integral part of the United Kingdom need to do more to face the challenges.

In Northern Ireland's centenary year, we are reminded of our history and of the threats we have withstood over the past 100 years. The next 100 years will see even greater threats. Our resolve must be to strengthen the Union we are part of by being proud of Northern Ireland and proving that the Union works for all who live here. This book should play a big part in this task.

The Idea of the Union

Introduction

John Wilson Foster

The Idea of the Union: Statements and Critiques in Support of the Union of Great Britain and Northern Ireland appeared in 1995. It was a modest affair, avoiding an academic look. It offered itself as a practical handbook of arguments to counter the campaign to sunder Northern Ireland from the United Kingdom and annex this portion of a constitutional monarchy to a neighbouring republic. That republic was founded in profound hostility to that monarchy and has maintained ever since a low-intensity version of that hostility, which the recent Brexit negotiations revealed. This campaign had been waged in one form or another since the island of Ireland was partitioned in 1920–21 in order to prevent an all-island civil war but was renewed as an armed insurgency in the 1940s and 1950s and most seriously in the late 1960s which lasted until 1998 with a seventeenth-month ceasefire from autumn 1994. Most of us know at least the rough statistics of the damage done to human flesh, human minds and human hearts and to the social fabric, during thirty years of bombing and shooting.

The Idea of the Union seemed timely in 1995 because a recent series of political initiatives, manifestoes and agreements had seemed to many unionists to have qualified, diluted or endangered the status of Northern

Ireland inside the United Kingdom. These included the New Ireland Forum (1984), the Anglo-Irish Agreement (1985), the Downing Street Declaration (1993) and The Framework Document (1995). One of the acutest decoders and interpreters of the resulting documents was Robert McCartney QC whose analytical bravura was one of the energisers of the 1995 book. Yet another stimulant that produced the book was the widespread feeling among many in Northern Ireland that their wish to remain citizens of the UK was not being clearly and forcefully articulated. I was one of those who felt this puzzling deficit, which is why I edited a collection of essays by articulate fellow (mostly small-u, i.e. non-party political) unionists and whom I knew as reasonable and moderate colleagues whose motive was not triumphalism or sectarianism but the desire to retain their Britishness in constitutional as well as cultural terms.

Whether *The Idea of the Union* was of practical use is difficult to gauge. It didn't seem to have encouraged a greater number of pro-Union commentators whose sparseness of number is one of the parallels between 1995 and 2021 and which has prompted this updating of the 1995 book as *The Idea of the Union: Great Britain and Northern Ireland – Realities and Challenges*. It is extraordinary that in the year 2021, Gail Walker, former editor of the *Belfast Telegraph*, should have to tell her readers that "Unionism must spell out a clear case for the Union" (1 May). However, at least one observer, David Hoey, thought a few years ago that the book warranted a reprint; after all, sadly the defence of the Union is always timely. Then some months ago, William Beattie Smith, author of *The British State and the Northern Ireland Crisis, 1969–73* (2011) suggested a co-

edited re-vamp of *The Idea of the Union*. I agreed, with that
reluctance (I whimsically imagined) displayed by the aged
gunslinger in the westerns who reaches for his holster only
out of inescapable necessity before his muscle memory
kicks in and he knows what he has to do! And I recalled,
too, what the narrator of George Birmingham's witty
novel *Gossamer* said: "It has been the great misfortune of
my life that I have never been able to escape from the
Irish question. It was discussed round my cradle by a
nurse whom my parents selected for her sound Protestant
principles. The undertaker will give his views of the Irish
question to his assistant while he drives the nails into the
lid of my coffin". That was written 106 years or three
generations ago.

Another parallel between 2021 and 1995 is a series of
events since the book appeared that likewise qualify, dilute
or endanger the Union. The Belfast Agreement of 1998
seemed to many at the time a breakthrough and a kind of
constitution for a prosperous, peaceful and stable Northern
Ireland. Some unionists opposed it, while others, some
albeit reluctantly, resolved to give it their vote. For a while
many people began to think of themselves as Northern
Irish, an identity that transcended nationalist and
unionist, Protestant and Catholic. This was heartening
but alas the Agreement was for republican diehards not a
destination but a signpost to a united Ireland severed from
Great Britain that they were sure they could see on the
horizon, no mirage but a terminus reachable as the "peace
process". The collapse of Stormont in January 2017 and its
suspension until January 2020; the deteriorating relations
between the chief power-sharing parties, Sinn Féin and the
Democratic Unionist Party (DUP); the ongoing fall-out

from Brexit, including the infamous Protocol mandating a trade border down the Irish Sea between GB and Northern Ireland – these freshly painted the signpost pointing south. The Nobel Peace Prize-winner, Lord Trimble, was instrumental in bringing the Belfast Agreement to fruition and tells our readers why the Protocol violates the spirit and the letter of that hard-won agreement.

Since the Brexit referendum, the campaign for a united Ireland has reinvigorated itself, to the extent that the old idea that unification of the island entirely independent of the neighbouring island is predestined and thus inevitable has taken hold even of nationalists with letters after their names. This is a deeply entrenched mindset and can be an unconscious bias. When the *Belfast Telegraph* reports on its own canvass – "Our poll finds major barriers to a united Ireland still remain" (3 May 2021) – it is the words "still remain" that betray predestinarian pro-unification thinking; what is posited is a shrinking and residual opposition to what is coming your way; when a newspaper tells you that where a united Ireland is concerned "there is still some way to go": Go where? you ask the paper. To a united Ireland, of course.

For some, this inevitability idea means that where we want to get to is already mapped out and all we have to do is adapt our means exclusively to the end which pre-exists us. In reaching that end, some, such as Sinn Féin, reject as unnecessary the requirements of open-ended debate, consensus, gradual change and reform; at most, Sinn Féin will accept only reform or change that in their eyes hastens the end – and certainly no debate, only dogma.

Others such as the current Fianna Fáil Taoiseach, Micheál Martin, may also think a united Ireland is inevitable: indeed, a belief in its inevitability might readily sponsor the tactic of "take it easy but take it", to borrow a Sixties counter-culture advisory; chill out, it's coming anyway. That is the meaning the journalist Ben Kelly in the *Irish Independent* reads into the Taoiseach's new Shared Island Unit. Kelly, wishing to reverse the partition that he fondly imagines was foisted by the never-failing source of all our woe on an innocent, unified island ("100 Years after Britain partitioned our island, we must prepare for a united Ireland", 23 December 2020), welcomes Martin's initiative: "In October, the Irish government presented its new Shared Island unit, which is designed to increase island-wide projects to bind north and south closer together". At least the cards are on the table.

But this echoes sentiments that create another historical parallel. I wrote the following in one of my 1995 chapters: "An expatriate Fianna Fáil stalwart, who travels often to Dublin, narrated to me in Vancouver during Gerry Adams' visit [1994] the likely sequence of events as he claimed southern constitutional nationalists saw them. First we unify tourism, he said, then agriculture, energy, transport and telecommunications – 'the soft economic targets and infrastructures'. Then we go for the sturdier structures and agencies, consent and cross-borderism in the same breath. Fianna Fáil and Sinn Féin grow intimate, Fine Gael and Labour recede. The British don't want you, he said, but we do – we'll keep 70 seats warm for you in the Dáil. The Alliance Party of Northern Ireland will be the first unionist party through its portals. Fantasy? I told him so, and he chuckled at my naivety". I have heard those same thoughts (and even the same number 70) reported recently in the papers. Tourism Ireland, issuing from the Belfast Agreement, indeed promotes abroad an unpartitioned island. (The *Belfast Telegraph*'s "Staycation 2021" holiday guide (4 June) assumes that holidaying at home means holidaying in the Republic of Ireland, not in Britain.) The electricity grid of Northern Ireland is now owned by Electric Ireland (Cork). When I phone my First Trust Bank branch in Belfast I am put through to Dublin: it is now, seamlessly, Allied Irish Banks. In the imminent future, much more "consensual" cross-borderism is on its way, courtesy of the Protocol.

We should remind ourselves of what is claimed to be the heart of the problem: that there is an enlarging minority of Northern Irish who sincerely wish to live in an expanded Republic of Ireland without leaving home. This aspiration became a crisis when there was agitation on their behalf since just before the thirty-year IRA terrorist campaign from the 1970s and which now takes vigorous social and cultural forms. It has never been precisely known how representative is this campaign of the feelings of non-political Catholics or even nationalists, some of whom at least are professedly if privately content to live in the Northern Irish part of the UK.

The immediate target of this campaign is British administration in Northern Ireland, but the collateral damage in the event of success is to the roughly known number of those Northern Irish who wish to stay where they are, at home with their British postal code. They and their parents and grandparents have always lived under the British monarchy and have never lived with their Catholic friends or nationalist neighbours in an Irish republic. Indeed, their grandparents and great-grandparents watched while the Irish Free State, founded in 1922 on liberal-conservative principles, turned itself into an ethnic, nationalist Catholic theocracy hostile to unionists, Protestants, socialists and atheists, who either left or uneasily assimilated. The transformation was mirrored in the constitutional reincarnations of Éire (1937) and the Republic of Ireland (1949). In 1998, the name of the country quietly became Ireland, simultaneously dropping its constitutional claim to Northern Ireland and nominally arrogating to itself the whole island (I have been told that government departments in the South do not accept the phrase "the Republic of Ireland" in documents, official or otherwise). Notwithstanding the recent liberalisation in the Republic of social policy, the growing ethnic plurality, and the decline in the power of the Church, the national narrative which is the Republic's Story of itself, and which infuses every important aspect of society, is sadly still anti-British and anti-unionist; of late, fuelled by Brexit, that Story has become greener.

The campaign for a united Ireland is diverse – historical, current, and future-orientated – and its restless activity in various walks of life unavoidably suggests fronts. For the legacy front, readers are directed to the chapters below by Jeff Dudgeon and Ben Lowry: it is now "lawfare", as Dudgeon puts it, instead of warfare. It is on this front that the battle between historical truth and republican ideology and politics is being joined. Several of our contributors, including Patrick Roche, Brian Barton, Owen Polley, Graham Gudgin, William Beattie Smith and the late Edgar Haslett (whose 1995 chapter we have reprinted) have felt the need firmly to set the historical record straight. The historical record on the origins of partition, unionist discrimination against Catholics, abolition of the Stormont Parliament and prime responsibility for the violence of the Troubles, is especially important to set straight. Others contributors, including the late Arthur Green, the former Irish ambassador Ray Bassett, Geoff Sloan, Graham Walker, Graham Gudgin and myself, remind readers of other realities (economic, geopolitical, cultural) inconvenient, to say the least, for any campaign for an imminent united Ireland.

For the human rights front, they are directed to the chapter by Daphne Trimble. On the medical front, there is a north-south nexus of medical researchers and consultants whose declared aim is to create an all-Ireland research and treatment culture and practice in oncology, independent of Great Britain. There have been even more strenuous medical efforts to bend response to the coronavirus crisis to an all-Ireland agenda; one distinguished doctor employed in England but originally from west Belfast has been particularly energetic in pushing an all-Ireland agenda for the application of rules and restrictions in combatting the virus and pops up in Belfast and Dublin to do so, and receives considerable coverage in the local newspapers. One Dublin medical consultant and teacher wants us to go far beyond an all-Ireland response to Covid-19. He wants to see an all-island collective, a new all-island health policy, a new form of government, a new kind of post-national (but conveniently 32-county) economy (Professor S. McConkey, *Belfast Telegraph*, 13 April 2020). The economic front – the argument for an integrated island economy – is examined below and found wanting by Graham Gudgin.

In terms of what is good for the native tongue, the Irish language front is regrettable and even the Dublin-based journalist Ann Marie Hourihane has described the Irish language as "the nationalists' weapon of choice" (*The Times*, 15 February 2018). It may begin with street signs but through an Irish Language Act is bound to progress to much else. I know this from my experience of the career of French in the province of Quebec whose majority, having failed politically to achieve secession from Canada in the 1970s and 1980s, resorted to a successful programme of extracting political concessions from the federal government and enacting language laws aimed at culturally de-anglicising the province; any renewed calls for independence (and they have begun) will have a stronger cultural rationale than ever before. What we are talking about is public culture reassignment, likely to be rapid in Northern Ireland. "In the Republic," writes Hourihane, "almost a hundred years have been spent on a regime of compulsory Irish, bilingual road signs, civil servants who have to be able to limp through public business using a travesty of Irish, and a lot of politicians who can start and end a speech in Irish while being unable to answer a simple question in that language... In the South Irish has been used to exclude non-Irish speakers from official jobs, and from feeling entirely Irish..." After a century of promotion, 1.7% of the southern population speak the Irish language daily; that figure would be considerably lower in Northern Ireland. "The Irish language", writes Hourihane, "has indeed been weaponised – by republicans, for generations". An ILA, *qua* Act, has little really to do with linguistic respect or protection: the language was recruited in 1982 by Sinn Féin as a front in the campaign for ultimate political hegemony. An Irish Language Act will serve to further divide the citizenry into Irish and British, territorially by district and neighbourhood through signage and language initiatives. The momentum will be with the Irish language activists.

Lastly, the political front is, of course, broad and venerable and its strategists are unsleeping.

These fronts may not add up to a consciously concerted effort: there are party-political and other kinds of rivalry among those who want a united Ireland. And there are on any given front activists who sincerely wish to see a united Ireland and believe that their method to achieve it is legitimate (which it is), nonsectarian and benign. But the co-existence of multiple ways of promoting an all-Ireland agenda ironically invites unionists' suspicion, rightly or wrongly, on any specific way, even when it might be for the good of all. The shared goal of a united Ireland lends to these various fronts a synergy that daily harasses and unsettles unionists, many of whom supported the Belfast Agreement because they were told it would achieve stability for generations to come.

What swells unionist alarm is the absence of influential support for the pro-Union cause from anywhere outside the Northern Irish pro-Union political parties. Irish republicanism (by which I mean nationalism that actively seeks a united separate Ireland) suffers no such political privation; it enjoys assent and promotion around the world even from those who know nothing about Ireland north or south. A united Ireland has the impersonal force of a meme or folk belief rather than of a convincing argument, even when it obviously goes against the grain of contemporary inclination and tendency, including anti-nationalism.

Reviewing a Sean O'Casey autobiography in 1945, George Orwell asked: "Why is it that the worst extremes of jingoism and racialism have to be tolerated when they come from an Irishman?" His answer was "England's bad conscience... It is difficult to object to Irish nationalism without seeming to condone centuries of English tyranny and exploitation". Northern Irish unionism has unjustifiably inherited this dilemma.

It is presumably that bad conscience that prohibits the British government – the natural primary defender of the Union, one might have thought – from being other than neutral on the question of Northern Ireland's place in the Union, while its counterpart, and partner in political oversight in Northern Ireland, the government of the Irish Republic, along with all the political parties in the Republic, energetically pursue the dismantling of the United Kingdom. But in being neutral on the Union in the context of a near-universal desire to see Northern Ireland amputated from the UK, the British government is *in effect* pro-united Ireland. Neutrality conveys complaisance and emboldens republicanism. This geographically and politically specific neutrality over the Union might explain Britain's failure to object strenuously to the anti-British stance of the Republic during Brexit negotiations, perhaps with the thought at the back of British negotiators' minds that in the endgame Northern Ireland could be deserted and the Republic (a potentially useful stayer-behind in the EU) appeased.

Whatever the role of conscience, there seems to be an unconscious English bias at work. We see it in the title of Robert Tombs' recent robust defence of Brexit, *This Sovereign Isle*, unfortunately ignoring the UK portion of the neighbouring isle in order to achieve an understandable patriotic flourish. His title's generic echo of Dorothy Sayers' 1940 patriotic poem "The English War" – "The single island, like a tower/Ringed with an angry host" (as though we in Northern Ireland – and indeed Scotland – were not fighting Hitler from our industrial arsenal!) – threatens to betray the apparent English inability to process something as simple as partition on the island to the west. Those in Scotland and Wales who care for the Union might not care if Northern Ireland is cast adrift, but I can't believe that the behaviour of the British government as a defender and promoter of the Union is reassuring to them.

Nor does significant support for the Union come from where one might reasonably expect it: the two provincial universities, Queen's University Belfast and the University of Ulster. Little of comfort to unionists in the way of scholarly intervention and public debate emanates from these campuses but there is enough to give comfort to nationalists, and there are outspoken republicans who are unfazed by any tradition of a cautiously political academy. Orwell's explanation may well hold true here as well: educated bad conscience, plus, perhaps, the political incorrectness that sadly has always tainted Ulster unionism. It may not be the fault of the university administrations. Is it lack of intellectual self-esteem among pro-Union professors and lecturers? I'm receptive to any explanation of the low level of public support for the Union among academics who are, I am certain, privately in favour of the Union of Great Britain and Northern Ireland continuing.

What of business? Occasionally one reads about a member of the professions or business community "of unionist background" who declares that he or she (usually he) could change his view of the Union under certain business or professional circumstances. Under the circumstances, he is declaring himself, as a businessman, neutral. One might be more inclined to accept the neutrality if it were balanced by a businessman "of nationalist background" questioning the wisdom of a united Ireland from a business point of view; but I haven't heard such a voice. If one is in the business of selling, then a divided market for one's wares, based on the political affiliation of seller and buyer, is a smaller market, which good business by definition wants to avoid. And there is a built-in neutrality in commerce which puts its business first even at the expense of the civic order. In any case, I have yet to hear a firm declarative embrace of the Union from Ulster businesspeople, even though we know many are in fact unionists, possibly very firm unionists if push came to shove, i.e. in the event of a border poll.

But it's clear that we shouldn't repose our hopes solely in the unknown eventualities of the polling-booth. In Scotland there is Scottish Business UK – "the voice of pro-Union business people operating in Scotland", but as far as I know there is no Northern Ireland equivalent. One is not asking for businesses, *qua* businesses, to declare themselves pro-Union (business, after all, is business), but rather for an articulated sense of UK-wide business enterprise and professional membership. In the years between 1970 and 2000 there was every justification for business-owners to keep a low profile personally and commercially, as businesses and business-people were targets of the terrorists, and some were kidnapped, but those circumstances no longer obtain.

And the professionals – the doctors, lawyers, dentists,

Church of Ireland ministers, scientists, ex-civil servants (constrained, of course, before retirement by professional protocol)? One has little sense of pro-Union voices among the professionals. For example, I have yet to read a spirited public defence of the UK medical system (its infrastructure, funding, logistics, models, research, best practice) by a prominent medical practitioner in Northern Ireland, and a rejection of any suggestion of an all-island medical system independent of the UK's. Again, perhaps it's that peculiar inhibition and embarrassment that afflicts pro-Union academics and professionals. There are one or two pro-Union legal minds applying themselves to cases involving the Union, whereas it is easy to name Northern Ireland-trained lawyers, solicitors and law lecturers who are professed republicans and who write and lobby to that end.

In this matter, the contrast between today and, say, fifty years ago and more is extraordinary; back then the Union was moored by business and the professions. Specifically, unionist leadership was almost synonymous with the linenocracy and captains of industry in Northern Ireland. Admittedly, this was in part because the sound and stretch of Northern Irish business was politically univocal and monopolistic; big Ulster business and Unionist politics were interwoven and together they ran the whole shebang. Such monopoly could breed incompetence and even corruption. In any case, and for whatever reason, big local business, the higher professions, and the inhabitants of the Ulster big houses have fallen silent on the constitutional question. In 1991 on the death of Sir George Clarke, Josias (Joe) Cunningham was elected President of the Ulster Unionist Council. His Wikipedia entry tells us that he was "one of the last remainders of Northern Ireland's moneyed families to remain involved in politics in the most recent instalment of The Troubles".

For some decades, public defence of the Union has cascaded down the social scale. It has now fallen through classless academia and come to rest mainly with loyalists (i.e. working-class unionists), whose reflex is to assert rather than articulate the Union. And they are targets for those who wish to denigrate the Union and dismiss the culture of unionism as all bonfires and marching bands. Meanwhile, the descendants of the linenocracy and engineering dynasties have, like Elvis, apparently left the building.

There may be some precedence for this. Jonathan Bardon in *Belfast: An Illustrated History* (1982) writes: "During the first quarter-century after the [Act of] Union the middle-class Protestants of Belfast, disillusioned and shaken by the [violent] events of 1798, tended to avoid contentious politics; instead they re-directed their public spirit towards improving the intellectual, cultural, and social life of the town." Our own middle classes may have abandoned contentious politics but what they have not done is follow their early 19th-century forebears in turning from politics to culture. There has been no compensating philanthropic or cultural activity; the Union has not benefited from any displacement of energy into activity that can serve the Union (at least that I'm aware of).

Indeed, the very notion of culture has shrunk among unionists, along with the industry, education and business that once underpinned it. Political unionism seems to have little idea that culture in our society is as important as politics. (One example is its opposition to the official-bilingualism campaign exclusively on the basis of the financial cost rather than the predictable cultural cost to unionism.) According to W.B. Yeats, the fall of Charles Stewart Parnell in the 1890s caused those who promoted Irish independence to abandon politics and divert their energy into culture. This, Yeats claimed, energised the Irish cultural revival (which produced among other things the Irish Literary Revival) and which in turn reinvigorated the next political phase which resulted in the Easter rebellion (led by cultural activists), the war of independence, and the creation of the Free State (and Northern Ireland). Sinn Féin have also seen the profit in turning from failed extremist politics to culture, including the culture of legacy, rights and language.

As for the mainstream media, they are in Britain on balance at best indifferent, at worst hostile, to Ulster unionists and by association to the Union of GB and NI. There is certainly no warmth or enthusiasm from the BBC or ITV, nor even from the *Times*. And are we even certain the *Daily Telegraph* (in the absence of Charles Moore) would declare as energetically for the GB-NI Union as for Brexit, say, or for the Scotland-England Union? (This makes it unclear how these media outlets will respond to the next Scottish independence referendum.) Locally, there is the unionist *News Letter*, balanced by the nationalist *Irish News*. Until recently an important pro-Union organ, the *Belfast Telegraph* is increasingly neutral on the constitutional question. It was recently bought by Independent News & Media, a Dublin organisation, itself a subsidiary of the Belgian-Dutch Mediahuis (with its own Dublin ties) and is edited by a Dublin journalist. The paper increasingly reports stories from the South of Ireland with tenuous Northern Irish connections to justify them. Ruth Dudley

Edwards, the historian, crime novelist and anti-Sinn Féin political columnist, has departed the *Belfast Telegraph* and now writes for the only unambiguously pro-Union major Northern Irish newspaper, the venerable *News Letter*.

Seamus Heaney was famously taxed by an Irish republican with writing for the nationalist cause and put the encounter into verse: "'When, for fuck's sake, are you going to write/Something for us?'/'If I do write something,/Whatever it is, I'll be writing for myself.'" But when Andrew Motion and Blake Morrison asked to represent Heaney in the *Penguin Book of Contemporary British Poetry* in the early 1980s, Heaney agreed until cultural politics intruded and he remembered his people. After publication, in *An Open Letter*, Heaney famously versified his reason: "Be advised my passport's green, / No glass of ours was ever raised / To toast the Queen". Why is it difficult to imagine a Northern Irish poet or novelist, nurtured in the magnificent English literary tradition, writing "Be advised my passport's blue"? (John Hewitt of 40 to 70 years ago would have come close.) Your answer will epitomise the unionist plight.

Obviously one doesn't wish Northern Irish artists and writers to push constitutional positions or take crude sides, as that republican expected Heaney to do. Nonetheless, such a cultural reality as Northern Irish Britishness in times of crisis might have been expected to find a cultural and literary defence, even if only at the level of essay and polemic. Moreover, as became clear in the Irish Literary Revival, artists and imaginative writers, even when they do not embrace a political identity, do in their work offer a broad politico-cultural inclination. Would anyone mistake St John Ervine for an Irish republican or Daniel Corkery for an Irish unionist? Nor would anyone mistake Seamus Heaney for an Ulster unionist, regardless of his religious identity.

Northern Irish artists and writers seem restrained by the demonstrated excellence and coherence of the Irish artistic and literary tradition. Most pro-Union artists and writers wish to belong to this tradition, presuming it (I suspect) to be apolitical. But in the end it isn't. Northern Irish artists and writers, even if they vote UUP, DUP or (most likely) Alliance in the privacy of the polling booth, do not offer much succour to unionists who feel their cultural place in the UK to be under grave threat. A Scottish political historian tells me that there's an analogous situation in his home country, where the SNP own, more or less, the writers and artists and the artistic milieu. Scottish unionism faces the same problem as Ulster unionism: the lack of any real or imagined cultural backup for the constitutional cause.

The noisy energy of nationalism, the neutrality of the British government, the inability of Northern Irish unionist parties to articulate with eloquence and feeling the idea of the Union, the silences of business, the professions and the academy in the cause of unionism – these have enabled republicanism to appear to be the Zeitgeist, to represent the tide of history, to express the popular will. But it is all by default and not by very much intrinsic merit or force of argument as *The Idea of the Union* seeks to demonstrate. And there are two further, potentially crucial, silences in the campaign to wrest Northern Ireland from the UK, one silence on each side of the Irish Sea, and both skewing the apparent politics of our predicament.

To say that I have Northern Irish friends and acquaintances who were born into the Catholic faith, and thus "from a nationalist background", but yet who wish to remain in the UK where they are happy, is to risk saying something self-deriding akin to "Some of my best friends are…" Only after a border poll by secret ballot, and an analysis of the results, might we get a sense of how many from a nationalist background prefer known life in the UK to an unknown life in a new unified island republic. That witty and acute observer Malachi O'Doherty made an ironic pun when he described Northern Irish Catholics happy enough in the UK as "provisional unionists". But that might undersell them by assuming that no Northern Irish Catholics can be contented full citizens of the UK. We have little evidence to go on because those from a nationalist background do *not* publicly defend life in the UK. Much of Northern Irish life (like southern Irish life) being tribal, there is an unspoken taboo on a Catholic declaring allegiance to unionism. The concept is inadmissible and the word most assuredly is, "unionism" being synonymous with historical anti-Catholicism and anti-Irishness. So the political position of someone of a nationalist background contented with living in the UK cannot be identified and named. The taboo is an ancestral instinct (unionism has its equivalent) but I wonder if it is not also something unspokenly imposed by muscular republicanism, Irish nationalism's superego. But the breaking of the silence is not encouraged by unionists either, who have been derelict in the matter of trying to bond with Catholics in a Union for all. Former leader of the Ulster Unionist Party, Mike Nesbitt, and William J.V. Neill, back from a distinguished university career in Aberdeen, lay out what unionists and moderate nationalists, Catholics and Protestants, need to do to renew the Union. And Henry Hill wonders if there is now a turn against the divisiveness and disappointments of devolution in favour of a larger common vision across the islands and constituent nations.

The other silence emanates from those successful or contented southern Irish living in Great Britain, the subjects of one of my chapters below. Their very existence, let alone their immense contribution to British life, and the equally immense benefit they derive from living in Britain, should confute and discredit the Irish republican Anglophobia that serves to distort Irish–English relations. That Anglophobia functions as a wholly unwarranted justification for anti-British republican separatism and which indirectly destabilises Northern Ireland and the Union of which it is a part. Sean O'Casey might have been castigated by Orwell for being a deep-dyed Irish nationalist, but in fact the famous playwright, former member of the Irish Republican Brotherhood and James Connolly's Citizen Army, spent the last 37 years of his life happily in England, in London and Devon. Special 1943 issues of *Picture Post* on "Changing Britain" even carried no fewer than four letters from him, followed by his printed response to the "A Plan for Britain" issue: a far cry from the Dublin Lockout and the Easter Rising.

What a different picture we would have of the political landscape if these two unrepresented constituencies of opinion had their fearless spokespersons! For many decades, the Irish, and the Irish across the water, have lived with what the advanced and increasingly multi-cultural western democracies are being painfully introduced to today: community censoriousness, tactical self-censorship ("whatever you say, say nothing"), tribal requisitions – in short, an unhealthy culture of cancelling not just after the fact, but before the fact.

It is the huge numbers of northern and southern Irish living in Great Britain that should remind us that the Union of Northern Ireland with Great Britain is only a portion of the larger Union that is the United Kingdom. Arthur Aughey's keynote chapter from the 1995 version of this book, and which gave it its title, we have retained since it (like its new companion chapter) is eloquent on the meaning of the Union and unionism, and unionists across the water should read it. And the specific NI-GB Union is only a portion, too, of that unofficial union that is the entire archipelago that some still call the British Isles, others (if they stand on the archipelago) These Islands, and others still, the North Atlantic Isles. For a heartfelt and cultural companion to Aughey's constitutional elucidation, British unionists should read the Scottish archaeologist and TV presenter Neil Oliver's eloquent paean to the British Isles printed in These Islands, the UK-wide online forum. We have kept Graham Walker's 1995 chapter on the Scottish dimension of Northern Irish culture to which he has added a postscript. Scotland's threat to secede from the Union has drawn attention to the imperilled value of the United Kingdom and the intimacies the two islands share. *The Idea of the Union* (2021) has thus a broader geographical purview of the Union than *The Idea of the Union* (1995), though the editors have retained from 1995 the late Arthur Green's even timelier chapter, "The British Isles: A Cliché for Rediscovery". Geoff Sloan gives a geopolitical inflection to Green's archipelagic perspective.

Perhaps the looming Scottish crisis is timely for Northern Irish unionists, disturbing though the coincidence is. For nearly a century and a half, Ulster unionists have been explaining and defending their constitutional place in the United Kingdom but also explaining and defending the Kingdom itself. Perhaps Ulster unionists can come in from the cold in an ironic fashion: perhaps English, Welsh and Scottish unionists can exploit our experience in the matter and draw profitably on some of our seasoned arguments. And perhaps in doing so – this is devoutly to be wished – they can see the similarities between the challenges they face and realities they need to reaffirm and those challenges and realities unionists across the narrow water have been grappling with against the odds for a very long time.

Realities

The Idea of the Union

The British Isles:
A Cliché for Rediscovery

Arthur Green

One

Because it is inconvenient, the concept of the British Isles has almost disappeared from public language, or is veiled by meaningless references to "these islands".[1] It took a Dutch scholar to demonstrate what should be a basic presupposition for everyone in Great Britain and Ireland. There are only about 200 pages in Marcus Heslinga's *The Irish Border as a Cultural Divide* (1962), but it is written with elegant concision and great intellectual drive. Since it is in itself a short summary of Irish history within the British Isles there is a risk of distortion in reducing it to a paragraph; but I shall try to do so as a starting point and then use its general approach as a touchstone for some literary and historical themes.

Heslinga's subject is the Irish border between the United Kingdom and the Republic of Ireland. By this he means both the sea and the land borders, both, in his view, problematic. Historically sea has allowed easier communication than land. There are, and always have been, great barriers and contrasts within Ireland. On the other hand, there are and always have been great linkages and similarities between the two parts of Ireland and Great Britain. Heslinga explains the separation of the Irish state from the United Kingdom mainly by Catholic religious considerations, and the separation of Northern Ireland from the Irish Free State mainly by Protestant religious considerations. In his opinion the Irish land boundary could be interpreted as a cross-Channel extension of the Scottish border, marking off, in a very arbitrary way, the "scoticized" part of Ireland from the most anglicized part. He finds the separatism of the Republic harder to explain than the unionism of Northern Ireland.

Heslinga writes as a physical as well as a human geographer. He sees Ireland as historically without a political focus, and with the central Ulster lowlands and the Foyle valley standing apart. Physiographic conditions favoured separate communities rather than any form of central authority. Great Britain and Ireland are both extensions of the European mainland, rather than oceanic islands, and he quotes a geographer who says that "the physical geography of Ireland is so closely related to that of Great Britain that to the imaginative eye the intervening seas exist only as a geological creation of yesterday". There is a case, Heslinga says, for thinking of the British Isles as a major natural region standing on its own. "From Snaefell, the peak which rises from the Irish Sea to form the highest summit of the Isle of Man, the mountains on all four sides of the sea are visible". The uniqueness of Ireland's position is that, though an island, it has in fact only one neighbour. Thus Heslinga rejects the traditional nationalist proposition that because Ireland is an island it must be a separate political entity. In terms of human geography Heslinga argues that Ulsterism is a form of nationalism, but a nationalism which, like Scottish and Welsh nationalism, is fulfilled not by political independence but by the maintenance of the constitutional link with the British Crown.

Under Heslinga's inspection the major tradition of Irish historiography melts away. He provides a sharp analysis of the historical divisions within Ireland and the historical connections between Ireland and Highland Britain. This includes an account of the movements between Ulster and Scotland and back; the Viking incursion as a phenomenon of the British Isles; the to- and froing between Wales and Ireland. Over the whole medieval period he shows that the area called Ulster fluctuated in extent but the links between Ulster and Scotland remained close. The English king was accepted as a kind of high king in most of Ireland and there was far more warfare between the English and the Scots, than between the English and the Irish. What did however survive until the Tudors in the sixteenth century was an archaic Gaelic civilization in both Ireland and the Scottish Highlands.

Next he describes the "regional contrasts and contacts of post Reformation Ireland". This includes a striking account of population movements in seventeenth–century Ulster. Government plantation was relatively unimportant. In essence he sees the continuation of a population movement from Scotland into Ulster which had been going on for a much longer time. Some of the settlers from Galloway were Gaelic speakers. The Lagan valley first began to be cultivated by English settlers. There was a shift from Irish chief to Scottish or English landlord. The Act of Union with Great Britain was initially supported by Catholics and opposed by Protestants. The failure to respond fairly to Catholic demands was the essential cause of later separatism. Heslinga notes the absence of racial divisions between people living in the different parts of the British Isles.

In his Foreword to the book, Estyn Evans, the most distinguished geographer of the last generation in Ireland, praised Heslinga's objectivity and excused the fact that Irish scholars north and south had neglected the subject of the border because of its political sensitivity. Evans refers to the myth of Ireland as a "natural geographic unit", the superficial view that the Ulster problem was created by English politicians and militarists, and also to the myth of "the historic Irish nation", commenting that it is a myth Irish scholars have long ceased to defend. Finally Evans remarked on the paradox that essentially religious frontiers came into existence, even though the nineteenth-century Catholic church stood for established law and authority, and was by definition "the antithesis of a nationalistic faith".

Two

Evans and Heslinga were writing during the peace of the early Sixties. Their precision and breadth are badly needed today. Irish liberalism is in retreat, and distinguished scholars lend themselves to racism and reaction. Yet in doing so, such writers also indicate their own despair; Ireland and Irish people, they feel, are not prepared to fulfil their unique cultural destiny; instead most Irish people seem prepared to lead Anglo-American lives and have Anglo-American attitudes. You and I might say that by this route Ireland may discover it has at last a common culture, and that Irish cultural separatism, an example of early twentieth century micro-nationalism, belongs in the dustbins of history. But so far, that vision is left to Irish unionists, and has nothing to support it but the strength of reason and the appeal of broader sensibility.

Such strictures may seem harsh. But consider Professor Lee's *Ireland 1912–1985* (1989). It ends with 175 pages on "perspectives". Here Lee's history becomes a personal manifesto, not only for the social sciences in Ireland but for Irish cultural separatism. He says that Ireland once had an identify forged by "an independence". He concludes that "as circumstances normalize only the husk of identity is left without the language", so he goes so far as to advocate Gaelic revival "if only to create a bi-lingual society", and adds: "Despite all the mundane pressures to the contrary, despite the apparently imminent and inevitable victory of the big battalions" [meaning, I insert, the United Kingdom and the United States of America], "even cultural history may still have many futures".

Professor Lee is so obsessed with Ireland versus England that he cannot grasp the reality and attractiveness of the British Isles as related communities. Instead, he reckons that if only Ireland were Gaelic-speaking it would produce intellectual innovation of greater distinction.

Another well-known cultural nationalist is Denis Donoghue. In his autobiography *Warrenpoint* (1990), he too clings to themes of Irish cultural separatism. Against such revisionists as Roy Foster, he insists on the traditional version of Irish nationalist history, from Devorguilla to the 1916 GPO, as taught fifty years ago by the Christian Brothers in Newry. Also, he still adheres to the Roman Catholic Church of his youth. It is as though on these topics he has never grown up. The book is wonderfully candid about his own predispositions, including as they do his wartime neutralism vis à vis Nazi Germany, his inability to speak the word "Chorister" because it has Protestant associations, or the fact that he cannot enjoy oratorios because most of them are Protestant. There is more, and much much worse, about Ulster society as he thinks he knew it.

Warrenpoint may be contrasted with Max Wright's *Told in Gath*, another autobiography which came out the same year. *Told in Gath* relates the self-emancipation of a member of the Plymouth Brethren in Ulster. It does not whine. It is very funny. It moves from the local world of the sect to the universal world of the professional philosopher. There is great naturalness about Wright's spells of teaching in Canada, Australia, and Belfast. He takes for granted Ulster's place in an English–speaking world. It is a book which enlightens and which will live. *Warrenpoint* by contrast is the work of a pure critic, elegant but crippled. If anyone wishes to explore the stunting effect of hibernianism it is a classic case study. Denis Donoghue, like Professor Lee, recognizes that his causes may be moribund, but sees that the unthinkable alternative would diminish Irish uniqueness. "Unfortunately Ireland without its story is merely a member of the EC, the begging bowl our symbol". So, the story, however unhistorical, must be adhered to.

Lurking behind both Lee's history and Donoghue's *Warrenpoint* is the belief that Ireland has a unique destiny, which is obtainable if only Irish people would be faithful.

Separatist Irish thinkers are inhibited from facing up to their part in the society of the British Isles. When Richard Kearney writes about Ireland in the Nineties in *Transitions* (1987), and explores its post-national dimension, he feels it is necessary to explain specifically that he is not anti-national, and when he develops the theme of Irish links with Europe he concentrates entirely on the Continent, merely saying that Irish links with Britain "are so intimate as to require no further mention". This is a very remarkable cop out. No Irish nationalist has attempted to trace at length Ireland's permanent involvement with British society, although Desmond Fennell, quoted by Heslinga, did say many years ago: "Though the life of the people in Ireland – and in particular the Republic of Ireland – has characteristics of its own, these characteristics do not make Irish life more than a regional variant of life within the British Isles. The flavour of Yorkshire life is very different from that of the Scottish Highlands or the English South-East: the 'local flavour' of Irish life is not any greater in degree". Generally, it is as if Irish separatism were a sacred faith, and the writer is seeking to avoid blasphemy.

Deliberate insularity has so far not been conventional in Northern Ireland. But it is very remarkable that United Kingdom cultural policies now concentrate on narrowing its broader perspectives. Local history and local studies are heavily supported. The core school history syllabus will not deal, for example, with the indispensable themes of British constitutional development, the Industrial Revolution, or British Isles expansion overseas but will focus in the nineteenth century on the Irish Home Rule controversy and the emergence of a separate Northern Ireland. As for the twentieth century, the core focus will be on "Northern Ireland and its neighbours", a non-topic since Northern Ireland is not a constitutional, economic, or cultural entity. Still more striking perhaps is that there will be no core study of European history before the twentieth

century, while for the twentieth century there will be
some core study of European history, but there will not
be any core study of American history. The programme
is anti-educational because it derives from the mindset of
Irish localism.

Three

These examples suggest that Irish cultural separatism is still
very much alive among scholars and governments, however
much it is threatened by popular indifference and common
sense. As you read Professors Lee and Donoghue or study
the proposed Northern Ireland syllabus you recognize
echoes of excited old scholarly nationalisms. When in
The Betrayal by the Intellectuals (1927), Julien Benda wrote
his famous denunciation of Barres, Maurras and the rest
for their willingness to sacrifice their intellects to French
nationalism, there was a live tradition of cultural nationalism
throughout Europe. In north-west Europe that tide has
probably ebbed.[2] We tend to see our governments as more
like local authorities than as a complete focus for loyalty.
But in Ireland cultural nationalism remains important.
The Dublin state has nothing to rely on except cultural
nationalism, since without it, and without a separate Irish
language, the whole enterprise of Irish separatism becomes
a will o' the wisp.

Historians are free to impose their own preferred
patterns on the past. It is possible, like Sir Francis Hill,
to write an immense history of the single small city of
Lincoln, and Thoreau made it clear, once and for all, that
someone who had travelled a great deal – in Concord –
could be a citizen of the world. That may be the hope
of Irish scholars. But local history is mindless without

the perspective which Hill or Thoreau possessed, and it is, no doubt the day by day boundaries set by social communication that determine what is an intelligible field of study. The proposition Heslinga suggests is that the British Isles forms such an intelligible field of study, both now and in the past.

The Irish separatism which finally triumphed was the product of pressure generated from Catholic loyalties and the Gaelic League. The impulse was carried forward – and anyone interested should read Tom Garvin's *Nationalist Revolutionaries in Ireland* (1987) – by people who narrowed their vision to Ireland, who were *petit bourgeois* to the marrow, and who left a legacy to Ireland of anti-intellectualism, puritanism, and xenophobia, as well as unquestioned Catholic mores and Gaelic cultural tyranny. It is not surprising that their state was disowned by Yeats, Joyce and AE, not to mention Beckett, nor that a large proportion of the Protestants there left, or were forced to leave.

In very modern times the whole of Ireland shares *de facto* in the north-west Atlantic cultural world. The de-Anglicizing dreams of Hyde and Pearse have been mercifully by-passed, yet because those dreams led to a separate Irish state there is perpetual unease that its cultural basis has gone. Hence our intellectual Luddites, the Lees, the Donoghues, and (I fear) the drafters of the Ulster history syllabus.[3]

There has been one very remarkable modern re-interpretation of Irish history. It is that historically Ireland is best seen as a colony. This concept is now used by many good historians, for instance Oliver McDonagh, and has become almost a cliché among literary critics. It would provide a more solid basis for Irish separation than alleged cultural differences, were it well founded, and no one doubts that there were colonial aspects to Irish society in the sixteenth, seventeenth, and eighteenth centuries. But after 1801, with Irish representation in Westminster, with free trade, with common citizenship, with better social communication, the idea becomes far-fetched. Certainly the colonial world described by Albert Memmi or Frantz Fanon with its absolute racial distinctions and economic exploitation, is utterly different from nineteenth-century Irish experience. By the early twentieth century Ireland was even a net gainer from the United Kingdom Exchequer.

But the basic objection to the colonialist interpretation is that it ratifies an ill-founded Irish racism. It suggests that there were Irish people in Ireland – implicitly Catholic, Gaelic and poor, set against British people in Ireland – Protestant and relatively rich, and that Ireland, and truly native Irish people, were predestined for separatism. This is historicism with a vengeance. Besides, the model is not valid at all in Ulster, where it is obvious that today's "two communities" are not racially distinct, and where there is great economic overlap.

Ireland on its own cannot sustain massive cultural significance. But if we accept, as rationally we must, that our environment is the entire British Isles, the Irish reader is free to think of Ireland as a region like the others. This releases him from the dreary limits of the Irish territorial imagination. The Dorset reader, for example, is free to like or dislike the work of William Barnes, the county's nineteenth-century poet; or he may be more attracted (say) to Ettrick's James Hogg or the Potteries' Arnold Bennett, or for that matter to Wexford's John Banville.

In turn the bi-insular Irish reader is in no way obliged to follow ethnic or collective prescriptions. He, too, is free to value Barnes, Hogg, Bennett or Banville or Bloomsbury, or New England's Literary Renaissance or Dublin's or eighteenth-century Scotland's. He can accept or reject at will from a galaxy of minds across the English-speaking world, including minds only accessible in translation. It is masochism to suppose that our intelligences and our imaginations are uniquely fed by people with Irish birth certificates; and even more self-destructive to treat the rest of the British Isles as alien.

There is no imaginative compulsion to focus on Ireland. We live in a multi-cultural world and can choose our own identities. In Heslinga's spirit I have suggested that the most immediate environment in Ireland is the entire British Isles, whose newspapers we read, whose television we watch, and which we understand and share in more intimately than anywhere else. We cannot help belonging to the English speaking world and most of us must encounter other worlds in translation. Beyond the British Isles the same facts of social communication involve us in North America. United States hegemony is cultural as well as political, and everyone in the British Isles is under its umbrella.

It is true that there are large sub-cultures within the English-speaking world. Canada and Australia are examples. But Australians do not need an ideology to justify having independent government. To some extent Canada does, in its resistance to the United States, but the larger justification for Canadianism is the size of the country, the distinctive lives of its provinces, and its governmental mode, more collective than that of the USA.

Nationalist Ireland's problem is that it is trying to invent a full-scale culture to shore up political separatism. In today's world that is a ridiculous ambition. To solve the problem by stressing Europeanness is unreal for a monoglot English-speaking island. The enlivening alternative is to face up, after all this time, to being varieties of Briton, and within that, not English, Scottish, Welsh, but varieties of Irish, although Irish as minor variants rather than as isolated societies. Before Garrett FitzGerald succumbed to the coerciveness and insularism of the Anglo-Irish Agreement (1985) he used to hint that his preferred model would be a confederal Ireland, with two heads of state, evidently the Queen and the President of Ireland. The notion was fanciful but it had imaginative power.

This enrichment is understood by some modern writers who bridge the two islands. Among modern novelists I think of William Trevor, J.G. Farrell, Patrick O'Brian, Anthony Powell and of course Iris Murdoch. Professor Marcus Heslinga lifts us to these broader perspectives by his cool empirical survey. His book must be a classic of Dutch scholarship, penetration and integrity. It is also a dazzling linguistic feat to have written such beautiful academic English. Anyone interested in the tangled relationships of the British Isles is deeply in his debt. (1995)

Endnotes

1 "These Islands", however, is now an online forum dedicated to promoting the union of countries that make up the UK and culturally embracing the Republic of Ireland too. The phrase has been used by Irish nationalists in Ireland to avoid their having to use the term "British Isles" when talking of the archipelago. (Eds. 2021)

2 The situation is more fluid and complex than in 1995, and mass immigration, changing power relations in the EU, financial crises, multiculturalism, the growing salience of Islam, and the Coronavirus pandemic have stirred nationalist feelings in Europe. (Eds. 2021)

3 There has been a recent resurgence of cultural nationalism in Ireland, inspired by certain international cultural developments and, closer to home, by what might seem mere pretext and yet to be explained: the decision of the UK to leave the EU. (Eds. 2021)

Down to Earth:
Geopolitical Realities

Geoff Sloan

Geopolitics and the Union

It was the American writer Samuel Huntington who observed that the job of the political scientist is not to improve the world, but to say what he thinks is going on in it. Huntington demonstrated this ability in his 1996 classic, *The Clash of Civilisations and the Remaking of World Order.* The book was badly reviewed at the time by the elite he had the temerity to criticise, but his geopolitical themes eventually achieved a heightened reality. He is now dead, but regarded as a "startling clairvoyant".

I do not claim this characteristic. However, I am going to aim for a heightened reality by applying some concepts to the idea of the Union—the geopolitical realities. Firstly I will identify the conditioning influence of geography on the British Isles and its relationship to Europe; secondly I will explain how geographical configuration has conditioned Northern Ireland's integral place in the United Kingdom. Northern Ireland's relationships within the British Isles predate the 1801 Act of Union by hundreds of years. These geopolitical realities have been obscured or insufficiently acknowledged by successive Irish and British governments, and by Irish nationalism.

Understanding the idea of the Union through the lens of geopolitics is not a partisan enterprise—it is a vital one. It will critique the narrative of geographical determinism, which falsely assumes that because Ireland is an island, it must be a unitary state. But geography does not determine political outcomes; it merely conditions other factors that unfold within a geographical framework. The fact that Ireland is an island creates no presumption that it should be one state.

By geopolitics, I do not mean a synonym for international strategic rivalry: classical geopolitics is a confluence of geography, history, and strategy. It can do two things: draw attention to geographical patterns in political history, and formulate explanations which suggest the political relevance of geographical characteristics. It fuses spatial relationships and historical causation. Geography conditions but does not determine political actions, relations and outcomes. Classical geopolitics helps us to assess practical conduct. It does not obey the artificial boundaries of academic disciplines, but embraces a synthetic approach to address interdisciplinary policy issues.

Britain and Europe

Sir Halford Mackinder formulated key concepts in understanding the geopolitical realities of the Union. He was that rare beast in British public life, a polymath. He set up the School of Geography at Oxford, and founded what was to become the University of Reading in 1926. In 1919, he was appointed British High Commissioner to South Russia. Between 1910 and 1922 he served as Scottish Unionist MP for a constituency in Glasgow.

In a book published in 1902, *Britain and the British Seas,* he identified an important geographical pattern in the history of the political relationship between the British Isles and Europe. His starting point was the southeast coast of England. This area lies on what he called the "linguistic frontier of Europe", a confluence between the Teutonic and Romance peoples. This confluence had geographical expression in the form of the Rhine and Seine rivers. Both had shaped Britain: "To the Teutonic – Easterling and Norsemen – England owes her civil institutions and her language; to the peoples of the west and south, her Christianity and her scholarship."

Mackinder saw this as a unique geopolitical paradox: "Britain is part of Europe, but not in it." It framed political and strategic relationships: "Great consequences lie in the simple statements that Britain is an island group, set in an ocean, but off the shores of the great continent; that the opposing shores are indented; and that the domains of the two historic races come down to the sea precisely at the narrowest strait between the mainland and the island." Britain was able through sea power and freedom from land frontiers to defend and expand its economic and political influence. This analysis still stands. Terms change, but— whether we say France and Germany, or the prosperous North and the debt-burdened South or, like Mackinder, the Teutonic and Romance peoples—the great ports and hinterlands of the Elbe, the Rhine, the Scheldt and the Seine and the British archipelago still impact on each other.

Much has changed in the relationship between Britain and Europe since 1902: Mackinder would acknowledge the importance of the European Single Market for the UK. Unfortunately, Boris Johnson has failed to understand the nature of the geopolitical relationship between Britain and Europe, and that it has at its heart two enduring qualities that are difficult to align: paradox and mutability. They constitute the essence of the policy challenge that successive Conservative governments have struggled to resolve.

The paradox is, as I have said, that Britain is part of Europe but not in it. History illuminates the mutability of the relationship. It was not until the Tudor period that the English Channel became an effective strategic boundary. Before then, Mackinder argued that "London was more closely connected on the tide ways with Paris, Flanders, and the Hanseatic cities than with Scotland or Ireland or Wales."

Northern Ireland

The primary function of any nation state is to integrate its diverse regions into a cohesive organizational unit, assimilating regional differences. This raises the question of the nature of the boundaries that separate these regions. The differences between Northern Ireland and the Republic are extensions of variations in Britain. Much of the previous literature (including that by N.J.G. Pounds, J. Anderson and F. Gallagher) focuses on the "disputed" nature of the land boundary. This is despite the fact that the international boundary was confirmed in a tripartite treaty between the Free State, the British government and the Northern Ireland government in 1925. This did little to impede the development of a narrative by Irish governments that the Irish Sea and the North Channel constitute a "natural" boundary. Implicit in this is the assumption that the whole of Ireland and Britain constitute two distinct cultural regions, the geographically deterministic rationale being that they are both islands.

In *The Irish Border as a Cultural Divide* (1962), the Dutch political geographer, M.W. Heslinga studied regionalism in Ireland in the context of the British Isles, and comes closest to a valid understanding of the geopolitical realities of Northern Ireland. Heslinga's thesis consists of three propositions that are all grounded in the methods of geopolitics. Firstly, political boundaries that have no relation to conspicuous geographical configurations are not necessarily unworkable. Secondly, Heslinga challenges the assumption that the sea constitutes a natural boundary separating political entities: in the context of the British Isles the sea actually brings people together. Thirdly, he builds on the concept of human associations as articulated by the American political geographer Richard Hartshorne. A consequence of these associations is that regions can have ties with one another which do not conform to the boundaries arising from physical geography. There are three types of human associations: historical, socio-economic and cultural.

These three associations provide the core of Heslinga's thesis: the Irish border not only delineates the limits of political jurisdiction, but also conforms to one of the most important regional divisions in the British Isles as a whole. Firstly, it marks off, in a geopolitical sense, the Scottish part of Ireland from the Anglicized part. These human associations were conditioned, not determined, by two aspects of Ireland's geographical configuration. In a geographical sense there is little evidence of "national unity": "The general physiographical plain, a central basin surrounded by group of mountains and hills is repeated on a smaller scale in the north-east of the island" (p. 43).

The central Ulster lowlands clearly stand apart, as does the Foyle valley in the north-western part of Northern Ireland. Secondly, this dividing line between the north and the south of the island conditioned political outcomes: "… it may be said that the often-repeated Nationalist argument, that the natural unity of Ireland should have imposed a natural unity from an early date, is one very hard to sustain in the light of historical geography. It was relatively easy to gain a foothold on Irish soil; it was very difficult to establish an effective supremacy over the whole island" (p. 45).

Heslinga's analysis focuses on how relations between the northern sub-regions of what he called Highland Britain were conditioned, but not determined, by two geographical configurations. First is the geographical isolation of Ulster from the central Irish lowlands, due to the features that have been described. Second, the geographical proximity of Ulster to Scotland. The North Channel at its narrowest point, between Fair Head and the Mull of Kintyre, is less than twelve miles wide. It was in this sub-region encompassing Scotland and Ulster that human associations achieved the greatest frequency of interaction, and where this frequency had the greatest effect. These human connections give Northern Ireland its unique geopolitical nature.

Scotland and Ulster
The socio-economic associations between Scotland and Ulster have a number of strands. In Ireland outside Ulster an inefficient system of land tenure existed. This resulted in the sub-letting of small holdings for short periods, usually one year with six months grace. In Ulster there existed a

system of tenant right, which guaranteed Protestants and Catholics alike security of tenure, a fixed rent and the right to sell their stake in their holdings. This accounted for Ulster's relative prosperity during the eighteenth and nineteenth centuries. The Irish Land Act of 1870 extended it to the whole of Ireland. The origin of the Ulster tenant right predated the Plantation, and can be traced to the settlement of Scots in Antrim and Down.

Commentators in the early nineteenth century such as William Parnell – landlord, Liberal MP for Wicklow (1817–1820), father of Charles Stewart Parnell and an opponent of the Act of Union in 1801 – recognised the effect that this type of human association had on Ulster: "The six northern counties of Ireland are so very differently circumstanced from the rest that they very well deserve a separate consideration, if there be really any intention of restoring the tranquillity of the country."[1] According to Parnell, the advent of the industrial revolution and the geographical scope of its application were products of geographical configuration and the frequency of interaction: "The industrialisation of Ulster is by no means remarkable when it is seen in its proper perspective, in the context of the 'northern half' of the British Isles. Indeed, industrial Ulster is a province of the industrial empire of north-west England and south-west Scotland. There was a constant flow of capital and machinery from across the Channel. The industrial development of Ulster merely epitomizes the historical intertwinement of the north of Ireland with the north of Great Britain" (pp. 188–89).

In terms of historical human associations, the frequency of interactions conditioned by geography had an effect that was long, complex, and deep. Hugh Shearman in

Ulster (1949) indicates its long lineage: "For thousands of years the inhabitants of north-east Ulster and south-west Scotland have been aware of each other's existence and have looked across at each other's territory with a view to exploration, conquest, refuge or trade. There have been comings and goings between the two since the earliest periods of human occupation".[2] What this description lacked was a geopolitical analysis. Heslinga provided this and more: "For the colonists from east Ulster gave Scotland her name, her first kings, her Gaelic language and her faith. It is often suggested that modern Ulster is an extension or projection of Scotland, but the first concept of Scotland was really an extension or projection of Gaelic Ulster" (p. 118).

This conception of Scotland had a number of different geographical iterations that preceded the formation of a Scottish state. The most surprising was a chiefdom that straddled both sides of the North Channel. A.T.Q Stewart tells us in *The Narrow Ground: Aspects of Ulster 1609–1969* (1977) that "In 1399 the heiress of the Norman Lordship in eastern Antrim married John Mor MacDonnell, the Lord of the Isles. The son of that union became Lord of Antrim and Lord of the Isles; thus Antrim was absorbed in the MacDonnell kingdom... The combined Lordship lasted throughout the fifteenth century, resisting the hostility of the Scottish kings until the Scottish part was overrun and the MacDonnells defeated by James IV" (p. 36).

The final human association is cultural. It has both tangible and intangible dimensions. Today the colloquial language you hear people using throughout Northern Ireland is the same that you would hear in Girvan, Ayr or Glasgow. Heslinga articulated the intangible and claimed that Protestants and Catholics in Northern Ireland have more in common with each other than with their co-religionists south of the border: "Many a southern Catholic regards his northern co-religionists as being 'sharper' and more business-like than himself. The northern Catholics may be as hospitable and charitable as their co-religionists but they have a 'hard core' which is not found in the south. These opinions are, to some degree, paralleled by the views expressed by Protestants from the south. As they see it, their northern co-religionists are on the whole more dogmatic and pugnacious" (p. 74).

In summary, these three different human associations show convincingly that cross-channel contacts between Scotland and Northern Ireland have been a sustained feature of Highland Britain long before the Anglo-Norman invasion of Ireland. Geographical proximity meant that these contacts were pronounced and continuous.

England, Wales and southern Ireland

There were also human associations between England and the south of Ireland. They were fewer, and lacked the historical complexity of those between Scotland and Northern Ireland. Again, geographical configuration conditioned political outcomes, as identified by Mackinder. The lowland gap between the southern end of the Pennines and the northern part of the Welsh uplands is often called the Cheshire Gap. He gave it a new name, the Midland Gate, as it gave access to the English plain. This configuration is one of the most significant in the geography of British Isles. He drew attention to the fact that there existed, mirror-like, a similar configuration in Ireland: "The Midland Gate, affording an exit from the English plain may be correlated with the Dublin Gate opposite, which gives wide entrance to the Irish plains of Meath. It was by this way that the Goidels, and afterwards the English, succeeded in thrusting a colony into the midst of Ireland ".[3] This resulted in the Anglicization of large parts of southern Ireland. The Irish Republic was a product of secession from the United Kingdom in 1922. Geopolitically its origins go back to the medieval English settlement in southern Ireland. The French geographer Pierre Flatres applied a synthetic analysis to these geopolitical realities and argued that the British Isles can best be understood by recognising the existence of what he called 'two pairs of countries'[4]: southern Ireland, Wales and England; and Northern Ireland and Scotland.

Irish nationalism and geopolitical determinism

These geopolitical realities have been consciously obscured by Irish nationalists and insufficiently challenged by successive British governments since the formation of the Irish Free State. They are displayed in the mentality of extreme nationalist Éamon de Valera. Between July 1921 and the signing of a treaty in December 1921, the British Prime Minister, Lloyd George, and de Valera engaged in an extensive exchange of letters. Lloyd George's willingness to engage with the realities that he hoped would frame the forthcoming negotiations was notable for its geopolitical insight: "The geographical closeness of Ireland to the British Isles is a fundamental fact. The history of the two islands for many centuries, however it is read, is sufficient proof that their destinies are indissolubly linked … when you as the chosen representative of Irish national ideas, come to speak with me, I made one condition only, of which our proposals plainly stated the effect—that Ireland should recognise the force of geographical and historical facts. It is those facts which govern the problem of British and Irish relations. If they did not exist there would be no problem to discuss" (13 August 1921).[5] De Valera's response was evasive: "I shall refrain therefore from commenting on the fallacious historical references in your last communication" (30 August 1921). As his fellow Irish republican Kevin O'Higgins observed, "… de Valera hated facts like a cat hates water".

When de Valera took power in 1932 as leader of Fianna Fáil, he immediately embarked on a five-year campaign to destroy the agreed provisions of the 1922 Anglo–Irish Treaty. By 1937 he had replaced the agreed constitution with one containing the phrase "the island of Ireland". It was evasive, deterministic, and designed to fulfil three political objectives. Firstly, to deny the political implications of the geographical configurations and human associations that Lloyd George had mentioned. Secondly, to enshrine a "blood and soil" nationalism which excluded Protestants throughout Ireland. Age did not wither de Valera's extremism. In 1962 he stated, "If in the north there are people who spiritually want to be English rather than Irish, they can go and we will see that they get the adequate, right compensation for their property".[6] As Liam Kennedy has remarked, "The crudity of the terminology—English instead of British, the exclusiveness of the idea of Irishness—is consonant with the sinister undertones to the proposition itself."[7] Thirdly, to build geographical determinism into a constitutional document. As Len Hochberg, a leading geopolitical analyst, has remarked, this kind of exclusive nationalism can have toxic implications for those who are excluded from the chosen racial group: "Ethnicity and nation are often confused in the social scientific literature. This is a regrettable source of considerable confusion. What distinguishes a nation from an ethnic group is the assertion of territorial exclusivity by the ethnic group. Nations are human communities that believe they have the exclusive right to given territory, over which their state should enforce laws derived from a particular ethnic group's traditions and folk ways."[8]

The Irish demand to have exclusive rights over the territory of another sovereign state, and to enforce the laws of a particular brand of nationalism, was candidly set out in de Valera's constitution. Article 2 stated, "The national territory consists of the whole island of Ireland, its islands and the territorial seas." Article 3 was evasive as to how this territorial appropriation would be achieved: "Pending the re-integration of the national territory and without prejudice to the right of the Parliament and Government established by this Constitution to exercise jurisdiction over the whole of that territory, the laws enacted by that Parliament shall have the like area and extent of application as the laws of Sáorstat Éireann and the like extra-territorial effect."

The strategy de Valera used to legitimize this illegal claim was to hold a referendum, and thereby coat it with a veneer of democratic credibility. The result provided him with only 38.6% in favour: no votes, abstentions and spoilt ballot papers amounted to 61.4%. These two articles represented a frontal assault on one of the central doctrines of international politics: that states should respect and acknowledge the sovereignty of other states. This in turn produces legitimacy, a vital coinage in sustaining peaceful and co-operative relationships.

The reaction of the British government, led by Neville Chamberlain, was pitifully weak: "His Majesty's Government in the United Kingdom has considered the position created by the new Constitution … of the Irish Free State [and] cannot recognise that the adoption of the name 'Eire' or 'Ireland', or any provision of those articles [of the Irish constitution], involves any right to territory … forming part of the United Kingdom of Great Britain and Northern Ireland".

De Valera's geographical determinism has not gone away. In 2018 the Sinn Féin MP Paul Maskey underlined the continuity of this unfounded claim of ownership: "For 100 years now, Irish republicans have refused to validate British sovereignty over the island of Ireland by sitting in the parliament of Westminster. As an abstentionist Sinn Féin MP, I can provide an Irish republican perspective on this issue".[9] By 1969 the idea of geography as political destiny, and the constitutional claim of ownership over Northern Ireland, was deeply embedded within the ideological parameters of Irish republicanism.

"Powersharing with an Irish dimension"
In 1972 it gained further traction from the British government itself. In October, seven months after devolved government in Northern Ireland had been suspended to take the blame for the events of "Bloody Sunday", the Northern Ireland Office produced a discussion paper titled "The Future of Northern Ireland" (HMSO, 1972). A new strategic narrative was created by the use of the phrase "The Irish Dimension". Instead of defending the integrity of Northern Ireland's territorial boundaries as part of the British state, a distancing process was set

in motion: "A settlement must also recognise Northern Ireland's position within Ireland as a whole ... it is a fact that Northern Ireland is part of the geographical entity of Ireland". There was a sense that the British state in future would become what Richard Rose had characterised as a "qualified state", and it would just carry out administrative tasks in an integral part of its territory. The discussion paper went on to assert: "Whatever arrangements are made for the future administration of Northern Ireland must take into account of [sic] the Province's relationship with the Republic of Ireland; and to the extent that this is done, there is an obligation upon the Republic to reciprocate". Unfortunately this reciprocity has never been forthcoming.

Perhaps the most egregiously erroneous geopolitical statement to come from a British Prime Minister was that made by John Major. It was a neutralising proposition designed to distance Northern Ireland from its rich, long and complex geopolitical relationship with the rest of the British Isles. The "Joint Declaration" of December 1993 stated "... on this basis, he [Major] reiterates, on behalf of the British Government, that they have no selfish strategic or economic interest in Northern Ireland".[10] The weasel phrase in this statement was "selfish strategic" as it deliberately obscured the fact that the territory of Northern Ireland has since 1949 been an integral part of the North Atlantic Treaty Organisation.

In 1998, Article Two of the Irish constitution was replaced by the Irish government in return for endorsing the Belfast Agreement. However, the new Article Two remains geographically deterministic and regards geography as political destiny. "It is the entitlement and birthright of every person born in the island of Ireland, which includes its islands and seas, to be part of the Irish nation. That is also the entitlement of all persons otherwise qualified in accordance with law to be citizens of Ireland. Furthermore, the Irish nation cherishes its special affinity with people of Irish ancestry living abroad who share its cultural identity and heritage." The Belfast Agreement uses the phrase "the island of Ireland" ten times. Since then it has performed a dual function. For Irish republicanism— and successive Irish and indeed British governments—it provides a mechanism for keeping alive the issue of the future ownership of Northern Ireland. By contrast, it gives only trifling recognition to the geographically conditioned human associations that exist within the British Isles as a whole.

The geopolitical realities show that the United Kingdom's only international land boundary conforms to one of the most important regional divisions in the British Isles. It marks off the Scottish part of Ireland from the English part. Geography must underpin democratic aspirations and policies if democracy is not to become subservient to sectarian politics.

As Northern Ireland celebrates its centenary, we see the recurrence of a politically motivated attempt to obscure these geopolitical realities of the Union. The Conservative Party has again qualified its support for the Union, prioritising its own electoral interests. On 14 December 1921, after the signing of the Anglo-Irish Treaty, Carson launched an excoriating attack on Lord Curzon, the Foreign Secretary, and on the Conservative Party: "I think he is a very proper person to pronounce the funeral oration over all that has been said and done by that misguided party … for the last 35 years, dead and buried from today, with all the engineered splendour to cover up defeat and humiliation you have had in Ireland; dead and buried, strangled, without consultation with their followers, by the leaders and trustees who were sent into the Government to protect them".[11]

Fast forward one hundred years and this political trickery remains in rude health. The imposition of the Northern Ireland Protocol has meant a Conservative Prime Minister walking away from the vital and eternal challenge of statesmanship: maintaining the unity and integrity of the state that you govern. The imperative to "get Brexit done" has resulted in the Union being sacrificed again on the altar of office. This has totally discredited the Democratic Unionist Party, now revealed as the victim of its own naïve faith in the Conservative Prime Minister. This was summed up in the woeful comment made by its former leader Arlene Foster on 2 October 2019, when she described Johnson's proposals as a "serious and sensible way forward". Her party has been reduced to playing the role of the Judas Goat of Ulster unionism.

Despite this reverse, all unionists can take comfort from the conditioning effect of geography and human associations. The geopolitical realities which I have outlined have endured for centuries and remain resilient. The false proposition of the "island of Ireland" is still viral, but the vaccination of geopolitical understanding is available and ready to be used. It provides a pathway to show that Northern Ireland is and will remain connected to the larger tapestry of the British Isles through the geopolitical phenomena of "Highland Britain".

Endnotes

1 W. Parnell, *An Enquiry into the Causes of Popular Discontents in Ireland* (London: Wallis, 2nd ed., 1805), p. 22.

2 H.Shearman, *Ulster (*London: Hale, 1949), pp.181–2.

3 H.J. Mackinder, *Britain and the British Seas* (Oxford: Clarendon Press, 1902), p. 227.

4 P. Flatres, *Geographie Rurale de Quatre Contrees Celtiques* (Rennes: Plihon, 1957), p. 38.

5 Lloyd George to de Valera,13 August 1921, Lloyd George papers, F/14/6/15, House of Lords Library.

6 Quoted in J. Bowman, *De Valera and the Ulster Question: 1917–1973,* Oxford :Oxford University Press,1982 p.318.

7 L. Kennedy, *Who was Responsible for the Troubles?* (Montreal: McGill–Queens University Press, 2020), p.77.

8 Interview with Professor Hochberg, 16 April 2021.

9 www.theguardian.com/commentisfree/2018/mar/06/sinn-fein-mp-british-parliament-irish-republicans-brexit Accessed 14/8/18.

10 The Downing Street Declaration, 15 December 1993, paragraph 4.

11 Hansard, House of Lords Debate, 14 December 1921, col 36.

The Scottish Dimension of the Union

Graham Walker

For Irish republicans it has always been a simple matter: the object was, and remains, "to break the connection with England". Following this dictum, they have equated the Union with the English connection specifically. For republicans, and indeed most constitutional nationalists, "Britishness" means "Englishness". Thus they are at a loss fully to comprehend what unionists fear they will lose if the Union is broken. This is not just the sentimental ties of crown and flag; for many Ulster unionists their "British heritage" means a significant Scottish link, both historical and contemporary.

This perception of a Scottish bond is proclaimed clearly in aspects of Protestant culture in Ulster which range from Presbyterian church traditions through to murals of a paramilitary nature in working-class areas. In a recent television programme the Presbyterian minister, the Reverend John Dunlop, attempted to impress upon Sinn Féin spokesman, Mitchel MacLaughlin, what the Scottish link in particular meant to him, and how unionists fear the implications of the breaking of the Union for the survival of such cultural affinities. In a bracing critique of *The Field*

Day Anthology of Irish Writing (1991), Ivan Herbison has protested about the exclusion of "Ulster Scots" writing and the attempt by this very political cultural organisation (Field Day Theatre Company) to marginalize Ulster–Scots culture.

The episode can, indeed, be viewed as illustrative of the republican/nationalist tendency to discount cultural influences from any part of Britain as irredeemably "imperialist". Ulster–Scots language, as well as literature, has been largely ignored; as the Scottish writer and broadcaster Billy Kay has argued, it is in Ulster today that the only recognizable Scottish cultural communities outside Scotland can be found, and Scottish regional dialects are spoken in several parts of the Province.

The political sterility of the "anti–imperialism vs. loyalism" dichotomy has carved needless and arbitrary boundaries through the cultural mosaic of Northern Ireland. The Scottish link, according to the political logic of this dichotomy, is identified almost exclusively with Loyalists as being part and parcel of the Union. However, this belies the considerable Scottish associations past and present of Catholic communities in Ulster, epitomised perhaps by the people of the Antrim Glens. The extent to which Gaelic culture in Ulster has been influenced by Scotland is well documented. Ulster Catholics, it might be said, have been discouraged by the dogmatism of the republican anti–imperialist perspective from appreciating and expressing more fully the influences in their cultural makeup across the water, particularly from across the North Channel.

Overall, the Scottish–Ulster relationship is a notable example of the cultural cross-fertilisation which is both a distinguishing feature of the British Isles as a whole, and a powerful argument in favour of the Union.

The Union as an idea, however, has to be radically re-thought. At present it constitutes a political structure which cannot adequately give voice to the increasingly rich cultural mix within the UK. Arguably, one symptom of its decay is the impoverished level of debate on the British mainland about Northern Ireland. This is as true of Scotland as it is of England and Wales, and in Scotland's case, given the wealth of historical interaction between the two places, it is even more depressing. By and large Scotland has gone along with the interpretation and the conceptualization of the Northern Ireland problem as a matter simply for governments in London and Dublin to resolve. Scots have not notably objected to the way "Anglo-Irish" has become such an accepted term in relation to the Northern Irish debate. As the Scottish journalist Robbie Dinwoodie has argued, the Scottish media have not challenged the essentially Home Counties perspective of the English media on Ulster. He has contended that Scots commentators are better placed to get beyond the clichéd images and the simplistic commentary which characterise much of the London coverage of the Province. It seems that, just as the issue has provoked widespread despair, resignation or indifference in England and Wales, such attitudes can equally be attributed to most Scots. Certainly, opinion poll evidence increasingly indicates that in answer to basic questions about Northern Ireland, Scots do not differ much from the rest of Britain.

It might be the case that Scots are too acutely aware of, and sensitive to, the "Ulster" type of problems and tensions in their own midst, to wish to risk the exacerbation of them by getting involved in debates about Northern Ireland. The recent political row over alleged corruption and sectarian bias on the part of the local council in Monklands in Lanarkshire, has revealed the depth of religious loyalties and orange-green sectarian friction in certain parts of Scotland. It may also have indicated the potential of such factors for political division along sectarian/ethnic lines in the narrower political context of an independent Scotland. Whatever about this, enough sectarian tension already exists to give weight to the argument that the "distancing" of Northern Ireland is sensible.

On the other hand, such an attitude could also be interpreted as a failure to confront one of Scotland's major social and cultural divisions leading to an inability to contribute something distinctive and possibly constructive to the Northern Ireland question. Certainly, it is somewhat anomalous that, as a confident and assertive national consciousness has been in evidence since the 1960s, Scots should have been apparently willing to allow all things "British" in respect of matters Irish to be reduced to "English". Against a background of a cultural nationalism on the upswing, it is ironic to observe that many Scots nowadays are largely in ignorance about the cultural affinities between Scotland and Ulster, a phenomenon which could and should be regarded as eminently non-sectarian.

In contemporary Scotland, a proper appreciation of the Scottish influence on Ulster has fallen victim to the kind of fear of contamination by the Northern Ireland Troubles mentioned above, or to a hostility to the perceived negativity of unionist/loyalist politics, which fosters a reluctance to contemplate past, present or future Scottish involvement in any part of Ireland. Put more baldly, many Scots have been persuaded that their historic connection with Ireland is now something of an embarrassment; there is little recognition of the positive features of it.

The poverty of the feedback from the rest of the UK has led the debate in Northern Ireland to turn in on itself with depressing consequences. Whether the current ceasefire [1994] will fundamentally change the terms of the debate remains to be seen. But much work has to be done to overturn the "exclusionary" politics which have been a hallmark of the conflict. Militant republicans, at an ideological level at least, have "anathematized" British influence and have fostered the facile equation of "English" and "British" in an attempt to present their project as one of resistance to imperialist oppression; militant loyalists, on the other hand, have repudiated influences emanating from the rest of Ireland and have engaged in a project to "de-Irish" Ulster, a perverse self-fulfilling acting-out of the extremist Nationalist belief that the "true" Irish identity is Catholic and Gaelic.

However, as the literary critic Edna Longley has famously said, Northern Ireland should be viewed not as a place apart, or in such a deadly introspective manner, but as a "cultural corridor" between the rest of Ireland and the rest of the UK. This is why it is important that Scotland, in the midst of its own debates on possible constitutional change and its relationship to the rest of the UK, takes account of the cultural diversity and history of Northern Ireland to which it has contributed so much, and learns lessons from it for its own situation and, perhaps, feeds back into it the fruits of its own deliberations about identity, political structures and social and ethnic division. Interacting with

Northern Ireland about the constitutional futures of both places might be the only effective way Scotland has of addressing the issue of its religious divisions and how they have shaped so much of the working-class culture of the lowlands. The debate on Northern Ireland, in short, has to be widened, and, indeed, connected up to other debates about such matters as constitutional reform for the whole UK, the meaning of "Britishness" and national and regional identity in the evolving European context.

The widening of the debate could mean many things. It could mean, politically, the involvement of the main British (and Irish) parties in an attempt to broaden the choices of the electorate beyond provincial parties of, for the most part, a "tribal" colouring. It can be strongly argued that the wider context of British party politics has had the effect of containing Scottish sectarian political redress for grievances in the past while allowing them opportunities to participate in public life – a glaring contrast to the situation in Northern Ireland. Neither did this political participation mean that they had to abandon their distinctive community identity. Many Catholics in Northern Ireland might participate in politics through the Labour party without feeling their Irish nationalist identity or aspirations diminished one iota. Given the security of the Union, many Protestants in Ulster might start to rediscover the radial dissenting traditions of some of their ancestors and put them to work in a politically dynamic fashion.

Moreover, as Labour MPs Kate Hoey (from Northern Ireland) and Calum MacDonald (from Scotland) recently pointed out while arguing for Labour organisation in the Province: "national identities are not mutually exclusive.

One can feel both Scottish and British, perhaps even British and European. There is certainly no illogic in feeling both Irish and British". A healthy concept of the Union would seek to maximise interaction between the two islands, something which would carry with it a will to foster joint actions between the north and the south of Ireland. Progressive ideas of the Union make room for all such initiatives: between north and south, and also between east and west in the widest sense. They can help to make the border in Ireland, and all borders, irrelevant.

New ideas of the Union might embrace a "federalized" UK as the best means of reflecting the multicultural nature of the State. Most Scots want constitutional change but only a minority as yet demand separatism. It is quite feasible that the Scots could be encouraged, perhaps with the right example set from Northern Ireland, to work for a new negotiated Union which entailed autonomy without endangering fundamental constitutional links and cultural affinities. In the Scotland of the late twentieth century, it would make a lot of sense to ethnic minorities such as the Pakistanis and the Chinese to remain with the many other ethnic communities of the English cities in a union which would be genuinely pluralist. Notwithstanding the robustly nationalist atmosphere of Scottish politics since the early 1980s, most Scots might still be persuaded to acknowledge the benefits of a revamped Union especially if it is one in which complacent notions of English cultural and political dominance and of "Britishness" being reduced to "Greater Englishness" can be convincingly dispelled. In striving to achieve this the Scots and the Northern Irish could pull impressively together: both have been resentful, from a range of different political viewpoints, about various iniquities of London rule over the years.

Both communities in Northern Ireland have felt alienated for different reasons. Culturally, the rest of the UK and Ireland have largely contrived to isolate them. In the case of the Ulster unionists, for instance, it might be worth pondering whether they would have behaved in a less narrowly sectarian fashion if they had not been so politically and culturally distanced from the rest of the UK. Part of the problem might be that the Unionists have been offered a positive role only by the people they distrust and fear, an offer they feel they could only accept by "surrendering". They have not been offered anything positive by successive British governments over the years. Is it possible for a reformed and decentralized UK (with a strong and meaningful all-Irish dimension) to offer both communities a positive role? A new approach must demonstrate that the Union, anathematized by republicans and celebrated by loyalists, can amount to much more than the symbols of static world views.

As Hoey and MacDonald have argued, a divided sense of identity should not be viewed as a problem. Those who argue for the Union must stress that such phenomena are eminently in tune with the new language of pluralism. A "Scottish-British" or "Irish-British" identity is very much in the spirit of the post-nationalist thinking of our times, particularly in relation to matters European.

Northern Ireland and Scotland are drawn together by an agenda which stresses constitutional reform and the need to recognise a plurality of identities. The case for the Union in Northern Ireland must be beyond the traditional loyalist insistence on it as security against a perceived antagonistic Catholic nationalism, in order to formulate a truly inclusive project. This would have the potential of fitting both unionists and nationalists into new structures while allowing them to be positive about their identity. In Scotland, arguments for the Union might attempt to tap into strains of the "civic" nationalism which has been a significant feature of Scottish political and cultural life, and which is responsive to the language of citizenship regardless of race, ethnicity or creed. Not the least of the objectives of a movement to refashion the Union would be to nullify the dark currents of "ethnic" nationalism in Scottish life, recently expressed through shadowy organisations such as "Scottish Watch" and "Settler Watch", which foment blind anti-English hatred and encourage a Scottish version of "the politics of exclusion".

Scotland and Northern Ireland, in short, are at the heart of contemporary constitutional debate in the UK. They should help each other to steer that debate in a mutually beneficial direction to ensure that the Union truly reflects national, cultural and regional diversity. Those in Scotland and Northern Ireland who desire a revitalized Union can combine to ensure that the English recognise the need to make it a genuinely reciprocal and interactive organism.

One of the most powerful arguments in favour of the Union as it stands is the cultural breathing space that its broad context supplies. This should now be accompanied by a greater political flexibility and clear evidence of a capacity for structural renewal. (1995)

Postscript (2021)
Shortly after the Labour government came to power in 1997, an interesting exchange took place in the House of Commons. In a debate over the legislation to bring

devolution to Scotland, there was an intervention by the Ulster Unionist MP for East Londonderry, William Ross. He suggested to the Scottish Secretary of State, Donald Dewar, that he (Dewar) was being remiss in not pointing out that "the only party in the House that has direct practical experience of devolved government and its operation is the Ulster Unionist Party". "Is he aware", Ross continued, "that we know that the Scottish Parliament and the Westminster Parliament must work together to strengthen and to maintain the Union because, inevitably, the politics of Scotland, like the politics of Northern Ireland, will be increasingly nationalist and unionist?" Ross then went on to add: "In these circumstances, is the Labour Party in Scotland, which will have members in a devolved institution, going to be a Unionist party?" Dewar replied that it was because he wished to avoid "the polarisation of politics into two choices at the extreme" and to provide better government, that the Government was pushing forward with devolution (House of Commons Debates, Vol. 298, 14 July 1997).

Ross turned out to be prescient and Dewar (who died in 2000) too sanguine. Scottish politics did indeed become increasingly nationalist and unionist and thus closer to those of Northern Ireland. The very language of politics in Scotland – the everyday use of the terms "nationalist" and "unionist" – ensured that the Labour party became primarily a Unionist party along with the Conservatives and Liberal Democrats. The degree of polarisation in Scotland over the question of independence or Union was deepened and not lessened by the holding of a referendum on the issue in 2014. Despite the 55–45 per cent verdict in favour of the Union, the question only gained political traction in the aftermath.

The Labour Party made a commitment to devolution for Scotland and Wales and a constitutional shake-up upon which it could not renege on taking office. There were indeed cogent reasons to believe that such a re-structuring was necessary to strengthen the Union and to thwart nationalist challenges. Coincidentally, as part of the Belfast Agreement of 1998, devolution – on a power-sharing basis – was restored to Northern Ireland. By 1999 the UK State had undergone significant de-centralisation. Northern Ireland was woven into this new pattern, and was no longer a constitutional "outlier". On the face of it this was good news for unionists in Northern Ireland.

However, to the detriment of the Union as a whole, the Labour government took its eye off the ball. It did not seem to appreciate the size of the task involved in simultaneously loosening and sustaining the Union. Back in the 1970s, when devolution was being debated for Scotland, one of its Labour champions, the MP John P. Mackintosh, who was a mentor to both Dewar and to Gordon Brown who became Prime Minister in 2007, had warned that if devolution was to lead to a healthier form of politics and a stronger UK Union then certain things had to happen. There had to be a proper partnership between central and devolved governments and parliaments; there had to be an effective system of inter-governmental relations; there had to be flexibility about the best use of power across the different responsibilities; there had to be greater citizen participation; and there had to be an end to unitary state assumptions that belonged to the era of A.V. Dicey (author of *England's Case Against Home Rule*, 1887, and who believed that Home Rule would infringe upon Westminster sovereignty). None of this happened. Instead,

Labour was guilty – as successive central governments have all been – of a "devolve and forget" approach. Too little attention has been paid to striking a balance between providing for diversity and autonomy on the one hand, and maintaining a set of solid commonalities and UK-wide identity markers on the other.

In Scotland the Labour party – which governed along with the Liberal Democrats between 1999 and 2007 – allowed the new political context of devolution to become too nationalistic and too geared to regarding the central government as a rival or worse. It was complicit in allowing an "us versus them" paradigm to develop. Labour allowed the ground of Scottish politics to shift from class-based politics – as the Ulster historian Alvin Jackson put it in *The Two Unions: Ireland, Scotland and the Survival of the United Kingdom* (2012): "class politics were unionist politics" – to the identity and grievance politics that the Scottish Nationalist Party thrived on. After taking office as a minority government following the highly dubious and hairsbreadth electoral victory in 2007, the SNP prioritised temporarily the task of being seen to govern competently and so win over many who had dismissed it up to then as a mere party of protest. Their success in this, amidst Labour losing its grip on its heartlands, was evidenced in their outright victory in 2011, thus paving the way for an independence referendum and the "one issue" politics of the constitutional question. In this sense Scottish politics has been "Ulsterised".

The 2014 referendum outcome appeared to avert calamity, and unionists in Northern Ireland, as much as in Scotland itself, were relieved. However, the breathing space to review and renew the case for an expansive, pluralist, outward-looking and progressive Union was squandered. Moreover, Brexit has had the effect of making the pursuit of such a case in both Scotland and Northern Ireland much more difficult.

In my original contribution to *The Idea of the Union* in 1995 I called for more positive interaction and dialogue between those in favour of the Union in both Scotland and Northern Ireland. I do so again. William Ross's point back in 1997 about the way Northern Ireland had been marginalised within the broader debate over constitutional change in the UK still holds to a considerable extent. Those in Scotland who wish to see the Union survive need to be persuaded that Northern Ireland is an asset and not a liability; they need to be reminded of what Northern Ireland brings to the overall social and cultural mix of the UK and to the Union's capacity to enrich through positive interaction. Scottish Unionists should recognise that there are many things to learn from Northern Ireland politically, not least the way the SNP has adopted the Sinn Féin playbook and is similarly set on "de-Anglicising" Scotland.

Correspondingly, unionists in Northern Ireland can learn from Scotland and perhaps start to own the arguments for the Union which are now among the most compelling, namely the preservation and strengthening of the NHS and wider Welfare State, and the "social insurance" aspect of the Union which has long addressed so impressively the needs of people in all walks of life across the UK.

Why I am a Unionist

John Wilson Foster

One

The only hesitation I have in declaring myself a unionist is
that for many people the word stirs negative connotations.
But no other word as far as I know can replace it (it works
in tidy opposition to nationalism), and it seems wiser to
recuperate the word than resort to a less accurate one. I am
not, however, a Unionist, a member of the Ulster Unionist
Party, Democratic Unionist Party or Traditional Unionist
Voice; indeed, I belong to no political party whatsoever.
It is the constitutional union of the four portions of the
kingdom that best expresses the historic and contemporary
realities of my cultural and ethnic kinship, as well as
safeguarding the citizenship and civil rights I wish to
continue enjoying. My pro-Union position does not of
course erase the strong sense of neighbourliness I feel with
the southern Irish and with northern nationalists, nor the
many contexts in which I properly regard Ireland as an
unpartitioned island.

Opponents of unionism often make the deliberate or
ignorant error of assuming that it is merely a political
position (and a foolish one) and therefore vulnerable to
persuasion, be it by the rhetorical denunciations or dubious
blandishments of the more aggressive constitutional

nationalists; by the murder and mayhem of the IRA; or even, latterly and obliquely, by Britain herself (in order to placate those same nationalists). But it is instead a deeply embedded cultural identity and allegiance. It is hard to forget that the unionism of the Anglo-Irish was equally (and even more venerably) embedded and was effectively uprooted only through a prolonged policy of religious and – in the sentiment of Dr Noel Browne expressed in October 1994 – ethnic discrimination by the governments of the Irish Free State and Irish Republic. Many Irish nationalists who pride themselves on the undeviating, predestined, profoundly cultural nature of their own cause appear to entertain the belief that unionists are, by contrast, merely perverse and cultureless, resembling newly arrived settlers whose tiny repertoire of response consists of drawing wagons into a circle; a colony of Carsons and Craigs whose very names suggest cliff-faces of philistinism and willful obstinacy.

This is an insulting, racist and dangerous delusion. I am a unionist for reasons that have deep foundations in British and European history. I am a unionist because unionism is my culture. The reality is that the Union of Great Britain and Northern Ireland has been forged through innumerable decades of history and culture and if it is dissolved it will be so only through a policy of bureaucratic stealth emanating from Dublin with or without London's complicity, and not by consent freely given by the pro-Union citizens of Northern Ireland.

It is a grave error to assume that because the culture of unionist Ulster (mainly but not exclusively Protestant in its widest senses – religious, ethnic, and secular) is not a free-standing ethno-nationalist culture like that into which

Ireland consciously fashioned itself from the 1890s, then it must not be a culture at all. The ethnic idea of culture which originated with German romantic nationalism differs fundamentally from that secular, pluralist United Kingdom culture of which unionist culture – and, in unacknowledged fact, much of daily southern Irish culture – is a portion. The Republic of Ireland now rightly congratulates itself, after decades of Catholic theocracy and state and church censorship and constraint (which Ulster Protestants bravely and rightly rejected at the time of the Home Rule bills), on being a secular and pluralist society. (But I remind myself that 90% of primary schools in the Republic of Ireland in 2021 are still under the patronage of the Catholic Church.)

Besides, pluralism might be an increasing southern phenomenon but the *Story* of Ireland remains ethnic and intact. The stream of history books from Irish publishing houses confirms it. A handful of southern Irish historians attempted to revise the Story from the late 1980s but the Story has reverted to its original nationalist version as the extraordinary Irish hostility to Britain during Brexit, and President Higgins' recent diatribe against British imperialism, make clear. The Story is simply not for revision in order to make the Republic attractive to northern unionists: the imperative of republican teleology makes revision impossible. Perhaps behind the reiteration of the Story is anxiety. "Unfortunately," wrote Denis Donoghue in his memoir, *Warrenpoint* (1990), and opposing the revisionist historians and literary critics, "Ireland without its story is merely a member of the EC [EU], the begging bowl our symbol". The Story must therefore be told at all costs, including the radical distortion of reality and the estrangement of northern Protestants whom the Story purports to "cherish" but who in fact are destined to play the role of despised henchman to England, the Villain in Chief, as graphically as any such figure in a European folktale or Hollywood Marvel movie.

Two

What do I mean by the Story? In *The Cuchullin Saga in Irish Literature* (1898), Eleanor Hull wrote that patriotism "rests upon what we may call the historic imagination. It connects itself with certain events in the past history of our country, or with occurrences ... that have stamped themselves upon the mind of the nation". Hull was laying the foundation stone for what became the Irish Cultural Revival that in turn nourished the Irish war of independence. To this day, the nationalist Irish historic imagination suffuses everything of public note in southern Ireland. The flag, the anthem, the constitution, the proclamation, the speeches of the founding martyrs, the anniversaries, the Irish language, Gaelic sports and the GAA, the pantheon of heroes and the sin-bin of traitors and enemies. Southern Irish education, institutions, customs, values and worldview, government policies (especially when involving Northern Ireland and Great Britain) – these are all suffused. Ninety-Eight, the Great Famine, the Diaspora, Easter 1916, the founding of the Free State – these were the kilns in which Irish nationhood was fired. The Famine of late has been revisited repeatedly by Irish historians: it is now the chief narrative episode emblematic of national oppression, British cruelty, Catholic suffering. Meanwhile, Leo Varadkar has suggested that 18 April, 1949 – the day the Irish Free State became the Republic

– be annually commemorated each Easter Monday, when the Easter rebellion is already commemorated, thus unavoidably making the rebellion the state's symbolic founding event. Entitled the Irish are to tell their Story. But when the then Taoiseach said that "Our history shows that symbols matter, dreams matter", he needs to remember that unionists have their symbols and dreams, too, just as potent and no less legitimate.

The Story of Ireland is still, even in 2021, one of autochthonous identity, colonisation and unbroken resistance, catastrophes and emancipation. A story of chronic adversity and penultimate triumph pending guaranteed reunification of the homeland in an all-island republic and extirpation of unionism on the island. A story, once justified in its salience but inadequate and inappropriate in its linearity for contemporary Ireland, written, moreover, from the moral high-ground from an aggrieved minority perspective; it has gathered intensity in its multiple tellings. The Story, for example, wrote Fintan O'Toole's recent anti-Brexit book, *Heroic Failure* (2018), which is why it is an anti-English outburst, a work of bizarre ventriloquism. Brexit has been a convenient pretext for an oblique re-telling of the Story by the Dublin commentariat. That recent radical changes in Irish society involving divorce, gay marriage, abortion, EU membership, immigration and the emptying pews of the Catholic Church have not seriously altered or enlarged the Story that drives the politics is testament to its resilience. It is a Story whose denouement is embedded, in the manner of folktales, in the telling: a united Ireland is foretold and so everything that *can be politicised* (human rights, the legacy of the years of disgrace – 1969–1994 – medical research and treatment, the Irish language, the economy) *must be politicised* to make it happen.

The Story is a stirring and addictive narrative. In my youth I was attracted by it. But it is not my story, though I know it well and once was happy to tell it in my Irish literature classes. It is irrelevant that I prefer Dublin to Belfast and southerners to northerners. Mine is the British Story, and the Irish Story, as it is written, won't accommodate it. Mine is not just the Ulster Scots story (though that, too, is stirring if not addictive), but the entire British narrative. The fact is, Protestant Ulster and even middle-class Catholic Ulster are dialect versions of British culture. But enemies of the Union believe (or affect to believe) that the Protestant dialect – fifes and drums, political gable murals, the Twelfth of July demonstrations, bonfires – is the whole language of unionism and which by comparison pales beside the impressive culture of nationalist Ireland. This is a baseless comparison, but it might be a deliberate attempt on the part of some Irish nationalists to see unionist culture as subaltern and therefore ripe for absorption into Irish culture as a "cherished" minor tradition.

So naturally I resent the attempt to return me to a smaller jurisdiction, society and culture, however venerable and rich they may be (and I have engaged warmly with Irish culture in a dozen books). Sean O'Faolain in explaining why he felt stifled in the western island Gaeltacht of the 1920s said that "any sensible man naturally goes from smaller to larger islands, and ends up with continents, which are also islands within the popular definition". Unionists cannot be accommodated in a united Ireland and remain unionists; the Republic as we know it does not have enough cultural storage space. Should the UK break asunder and the skies fall, my primary kinship would still be across the narrow water. Distance is culturally irrelevant: try telling an Alaskan in a bar that his state, separated from the Lower 48 by the vastness of the Yukon and British Columbia, should become the eleventh province of Canada – then duck.

These Stories generate a deep ecology: they enter not just the hearts and minds, but the viscera. Like me, most Irish have internalised their Story and believe it to be indubitable. So what is the solution to the narrative deadlock on this island? What we might call the Anglo-Irish Solution, whereby the original colonisers left, or, if they stayed, reluctantly bought into the nationalist Story, would hardly appeal to northern unionists. Nor, given the steep attrition of the Anglo-Irish population after 1922, would their story reassure them. In the course of discussing newspapers in Britain, Geoffrey Wheatcroft in the 1990s permitted himself a casual, but to me, chilling aside. "The *Irish Times* is also an excellent paper at present, but a far cry from the voice of temperate Unionism which it was within living memory; an inevitable change, given that its old audience – not so much the landed Ascendancy as the Protestant professional and commercial middle class of Dublin and nearby – has vanished without trace". Vanished without trace! Why on earth would Ulster Protestants wish to follow these hapless into extinction?

Constitutional nationalists from around the 1980s until recently claimed that the new Ireland would be a rich one, consisting of two ethnic and religious traditions rather than one. Now the cultural welcome signs held up by southern nationalists have been lowered, as nationalism grows emboldened, in part through the changing demographics in Northern Ireland that seem to reassure nationalists that, as with the Story, no revision or expansiveness of Irish nationalism needs to take place. Even if the welcome signs stayed aloft, the same welcome was pledged in the 1922 Free State constitution, soon, however, to be replaced by De Valera's 1937 theocratic, irredentist and passive-aggressive document. So unification in the foreseeable future – even a campaign for a united Ireland in the event of a border poll – would be disastrously and dangerously divisive. And if it were declared, and imposed by the Irish or more likely by the British, unification would not be, could not be, unity.

Nor would what we might call the "British Columbia Solution" find favour with Irish nationalists, despite Ireland's pride in now being a multicultural society. It replaces national history in high schools with indigenous, Asian, or world history, in order to create the multicultural Euro-Canadian citizen who lives by diversity and has her own cultural history airbrushed out or denigrated. Would the southern Irish pay this price to achieve a united Ireland? I doubt it. No multicultural story has begun to emerge in Ireland as it has in Canada that would rewrite or radically revise the prevailing founding narrative or replace the prevailing founding fathers. Indeed, as southern Irish books on multiculturalism will demonstrate, Northern Irish Protestants are regarded as beyond the remit of Irish multiculturalism and thus do not qualify even for the fashionable nominal respect reserved for immigrant cultures.

The Irish response to Brexit has signposted me in the only direction of betterment I can think of: the Irish must revise and expand their Story to include their centuries'-

old intimacy with the whole archipelago of the British, or, if you prefer, North Atlantic, Isles.

Three

Unionism, then, is not just a "tradition" to be "accommodated" in a united separate Ireland like some quaint folk custom: it is a cultural reality which cannot breathe the air of Irish republican separatism than which it is bigger and to which it is diametrically opposed. Unionism has at base to do with breadth of thought and deed, with the capacity of the intellectual stadium in which the mind is exercised, and the size of community in which wishes, opinions and hopes can be respected and given legal and political expression. True unionism has no truck with trying to curtail nationalist expressions of their Irishness – unless such expressions disadvantaged unilingual unionists in government office or workplace, as an Irish Language Act, for example, might very well do, as such Acts have elsewhere, for example in Quebec and the Republic itself.

Unionism should not be judged by its flawed practice during the Stormont years when it was warped not just by its own internal failings and narrowness but also by northern nationalist abstentionism and Southern hostility. If it is to be so judged, then we must judge republican separatism by Michael Collins' covert war on Northern Ireland, the fate of the Mother-and-Child scheme, articles 2 and 3, *Ne Temere,* the birthday wishes to Hitler, censorship, the laws forbidding contraception and divorce, De Valera's sectarian vision of Ireland, and the fate of the Anglo-Irish.

The immense and perhaps impossible task for unionists

is to persuade nationalists that the Union, cooperative local government, and open acknowledgement of the close cultural ties between Ireland and Great Britain, better square with reality than a separate island republic. The nationalist aspirations of almost half of the population of Northern Ireland must be met as comprehensively as possible inside a Union newly and more expansively perceived. That can only happen if the Republic can be persuaded to allay its Anglophobia and come closer to unionists instead of demanding that only unionists move and then only in the direction of unification; I say: West–East first, then, and then only, North–South.

Surely wise nationalists (such as the late Seamus Mallon) who desire political unification of the island in amity more than they desire power over unionists or an island cleared of Protestants know that they should soft-pedal unification, cease harassing unionists on its behalf, since not to demand unification is obviously the only chance for it someday to happen by consensus. Republicans have turned Northern Ireland into an arena, into a forcing-ground, instead of the evolving society it was becoming.

I hope it is not just because I was born Protestant that I am a unionist. I rebelled against unionism at one stage. I travelled throughout Ireland and became a fan of Irish folk music. I wrote my doctoral dissertation on living Irish Catholic writers. But my later study of Irish literary culture in the crucial decades between the 1880s and 1922 convinced me of the superiority of unionism over republicanism.

I am a unionist as much despite England as because of her. Whether she wants me or not, I wish to remain British and will not permit England to redefine me for England's own expedient reasons. Like Enobarbus in *Antony and Cleopatra*, I have said to myself:

> Mine honesty and I begin to square.
> The loyalty well held to fools does make
> Our faith mere folly.

But I have persisted out of self-identify and the dictates of reason. It is not easy to be a unionist in these politically correct days (and my career as a professor and critic in Irish Studies would have benefited had I declared myself an Irish nationalist), but I cannot be otherwise and remain the person I have thought and felt my way to becoming.

Unionists have been fellow wayfarers in the kingdom's long trek – through the travails of the Glorious Revolution, the excitements of the Enlightenment, the hardships and achievements of the Industrial Revolution, the dubious pleasures of monarchs, the dangerous veldts, prairies and mountains of colonial settlement and imperial campaigns, the trenches and morasses of the Great War, the nobility of the welfare state, and latterly the fall from greatness, the collapse of northern industrialism, the decline of the Protestant faith, the discrediting of nationhood itself, Americanisation, Europeanisation. Recently, some of those experiences – the colonialism, the empire-making – have been decried and vilified. But the Scots, Protestant Irish and Catholic Irish must own their fair share of historical guilt in these historical ventures. Like others on the islands, I am a unionist out of comradeship and affinity, not out of triumphalism, sectarianism, separatism or anti-Irishness, and in foul weather as well as fair. (1995, 2021)

Britain and Ireland after Brexit

Ray Bassett

The post-Brexit relationship between Ireland and Britain is a conundrum, the eventual outcome of which is difficult to predict.[1] It is now the biggest challenge facing the Irish government. Because of its role in the first phase of the Brexit negotiations, the onus is on Dublin to improve it.

Ireland joined the EEC in 1973 because it was so intrinsically linked with Britain. Much has changed in the meantime, but it is impossible to change the past and geographical reality, the dominant factors in the relationship between the two islands. Ireland now faces an existential moment in its history. If handled badly (and to date it has been very badly handled) it has the potential to damage economic, political and cultural ties that have lasted centuries. This is a pivotal moment in Irish history. The decision of the Irish government to adopt a hard-line policy, which prioritised the country's Europhilia over any assistance for London, will have serious long-term implications. It will also have consequences for relations between the Irish government and the pro-Union community in the North. Naturally it affects the future of the Good Friday Agreement.

Before we get too excited about supporting our Government's devotion to Brussels, we in Ireland should be very cognisant of what we could be endangering in our relationship with our neighbours across the Irish Sea. We should weigh up the likely future direction of the EU and see whether it still remains in our interests to throw in our lot with Brussels.

With the departure of the UK from the EU, Ireland will be entering a new era in its relations with its neighbouring island and its most important economic, ethnic and cultural partner. The Brexit divorce process has been needlessly painful. Old passions and, in particular, anti-English feeling, have been stirred up again in Ireland. These are never buried too deep but in recent years have largely been confined to sporting rivalry. In addition, there has been a revival in English resentment of Ireland and a renewal of the old accusation that Ireland will never miss an opportunity to stab Britain in the back.

This is in neither country's interests. Both should be anxious to stop the deterioration and to allow a new relationship to bed down. There will be complications because the EU is pressing hard to take over responsibility for much of what was formally the preserve of the member states, particularly in the area of relations with third countries. The UK is now in that category. Brussels must not be allowed to interfere with the healing process. The EU has no interest in seeing the UK enjoy any bounce from Brexit and will not be helpful. Despite the acrimony of the Brexit procedure and the EU's interference, there are firm Irish-British foundations on which to build future cooperation. The Irish/British relationship is one of the closest between two sovereign countries. They share the Common Travel Area (CTA).

Neither country regards its neighbour's citizens as

foreigners. Both allow each other's citizens to vote in parliamentary elections and immediately access social benefits in each other's jurisdictions. Both follow common law and the Westminster form of government. They have a strong bilateral treaty, the Good Friday Agreement, which pledges each to support the other. Our security services enjoy a huge level of cooperation and mutual trust.

This special relationship will not sit well with the ideologues in Brussels who are not comfortable with such close ties between a member state and a third country. There will be increased strain on Dublin/Brussels relations, now that their common sparring partner, the UK, is out of the picture. Ireland's role as the EU's leading cat's paw in the first part of the Brexit process will soon be forgotten in Brussels. In these circumstances, Dublin will have to reassess its recent pro-EU policy and rebuild its links with London.

Of course, the relationship between Ireland and Britain has often been fractious. We had been joined in some form of political association for over 700 years. However, the old animosities had recently started to die away, especially since the signing of the Good Friday Agreement. The two governments worked closely with each other and with the political parties in the North to bring about that settlement. There needs to be a return to that type of interaction.

Apart from working together on issues relating to peace in Northern Ireland, our common membership of the EU played a crucial role. This was not always so. When I first joined the Department of Foreign Affairs, there was a conscious policy to emphasise our differences with the UK. However, after working together for many years, the interests of Ireland and the United Kingdom increasingly converged. Ireland's focus moved away from agriculture towards the promotion of free trade and cross-border services. Here the UK was a staunch ally along with the Netherlands. Ireland with its large multinational sector and the UK's traditional adherence to free trade ensured similar approaches, in contrast with the protectionist instincts of France, Belgium and Germany. On budgetary matters too, the Irish and British positions became more aligned. In 2013–14, Ireland moved from being a net recipient of EU funds to a contributor. The previous Irish position of always lobbying for extra resources for Brussels started to shift.

The personalities at the top of government in Dublin and London assisted in the rapprochement. In the period of Bertie Ahern and Tony Blair, Irish-British relations reached a level of cooperation which would have previously been unthinkable. Bilateral meetings were held before European Councils, phone conversations were frequent, draft speeches were exchanged in advance and there was the most detailed bilateral consideration of draft legislation at official level. It was an unprecedented period of harmony in Anglo-Irish relations.

The relationship has since declined sharply. This drift apart was apparent before Brexit, but the real damage has occurred since the 2016 referendum. Trust has been severely lacking over Brexit. In 2017, Theresa May unwisely turned down an invitation to address the Irish parliament, the first time a Conservative PM had been offered this honour. It was a good example of May's failure to appreciate the importance of personal relations with EU leaders, in this case Leo Varadkar. Ireland was going to be a key player in the first phase of the Brexit negotiations.

Brexit and its consequences now threaten the good work of the Good Friday period. Speeches by Varadkar and his deputy Simon Coveney have been needlessly provocative. Ireland's insistence on a backstop for the north made negotiations for the original withdrawal agreement, and its acceptance by the Commons, hugely more difficult.

The backstop

It is widely rumoured that the backstop in its original format was drawn up by the Irish delegation in Brussels, with enthusiastic assistance from the European Commission. It purported to be a position of last resort to maintain an open border on the island of Ireland, in the event of the UK leaving the EU without an all-encompassing trade deal. In essence, it involved detaching the North economically from the UK, should the British decide to operate an independent trade policy. It was later extended to cover the whole of the UK. In reality, it was never about the border or the peace process.

Essentially, its purpose was to keep the UK within the economic orbit of Brussels and to preserve the integrity of the Single Market. Given the poor economic performance of the Eurozone, the Commission did not want the UK to be able to adopt other and possibly more successful trade policies. The backstop was enthusiastically supported by Remainers in London, who quickly identified the border as a weapon to thwart Brexit.

The original backstop, which covered only the North, was hailed as a smart manoeuvre which gave Ireland and Brussels the whip hand in the Brexit negotiations. However, the Commons refused to stomach it. May then extended it to cover the whole of the UK, but again it hit the rocks. In reality, it proved to be a major strategic error. It scuppered May's premiership and left the pro-EU wing of the Conservative Party in retreat. Ireland attracted a large part of the blame.

The Irish and British authorities should have used direct bilateral discussions to resolve the border question. This could have been done with a mixture of exemptions of the type allowed by the World Trade Organisation (WTO), together with enhanced use of technology. The two governments could then have gone to Brussels with a solution, not a problem. It would have required some flexibility from the EU, but that would have been difficult to refuse. Instead the Irish government cooperated fully in misusing the border issue to maintain Brussels control, jettisoning its obligations under the Good Friday Agreement to display its euro credentials. The proposal to time-limit the backstop was rejected by the Irish side, even though this would have secured the Commons' assent to the withdrawal agreement.

The backstop's failure placed Varadkar in a dangerous position. To his credit he reacted swiftly as the possibility of the UK falling out of the EU without a deal loomed large. Suddenly dispensing with the EU embargo on direct negotiations with London, he met Johnson and agreed to drop the backstop. His volte face was breath-taking after years of intransigence.

Mutual interest

Despite the globalisation of the Irish economy, the UK is still Ireland's main trading partner, accounting for nearly 30% of the country's merchandised imports. However, the real cornerstone of the British–Irish relationship is the connection between its peoples. Irish and British settlers have moved between the two islands for millennia. There are about 600,000 Irish citizens in Britain, far more than in any other EU country, a powerful demonstration of the ethnic links between the two islands. Millions of Britons have at least one Irish grandparent. There is a huge commonality of citizenship as exemplified by the fact that many of England's most successful football internationals could have played for the Republic because of their Irish ancestry. After the Brexit referendum, many British people discovered that they could retain their EU citizenship by obtaining an Irish passport. It is vital for Ireland that this intimate relationship is maintained and that Irish people are able to travel and work freely in Britain.

Energy dependence

The trading relationship with the UK is particularly important in the energy sector, where Ireland depends heavily on the UK. In 2012, UK imports accounted for 92% of the gas used in Ireland and 93% of refined oil products. Any disruption to gas supplies has the potential to cause significant disruption to the Irish economy. If the interconnector failed, this would cost the Irish economy up to €350–€640 million per day. Ireland's 90-day reserve stocks of oil are held in the UK.

Energy supply is a key strategic element in any economy. It will be important for Ireland that the UK can remain as close as possible to Ireland on energy supplies. It would be better to keep as much of the present arrangements in place as possible. Here as right across the economic spectrum, Ireland needs to act in a way which facilitates EU–British cooperation on a mutually advantageous basis. The anti-

British approach of Ireland to the Brexit process will have to be replaced by a much more constructive policy. This is overwhelmingly in Ireland's interest.

Trade
While the USA has replaced the UK as the biggest single market for Irish exports, it is the nature of Ireland's exports to the UK that causes the greatest concern. The country's small and medium-sized enterprises (SMEs), tourism, food and drink (all employment-rich sectors) are the most heavily dependent on the UK. These companies are generally locally owned and source their raw materials in Ireland. Hence their activities have a bigger multiplier effect in the local economy than high-tech foreign direct investment enterprises. The SME companies are concentrated in less economically advantaged areas of the country, where alternative employment is not as readily available as around Dublin. They are vital for the health and balance of the economy. Many of Ireland's SMEs which export to the UK lack the linguistic skills and international business experience to diversify into new markets in Europe.

Bilateral migration
Migration to the UK has traditionally been an option for Irish people in economic difficulties. This has been a recurrent experience throughout Ireland's modern history. When I was growing up in Dublin in the 1960s, almost every family had relatives in England. Many working-class families were grateful for the chance to earn a decent living in British cities such as Liverpool. If the Brexit process leaves a sour taste, with long-term consequences for the Common Travel Area, this centuries-old "safety valve" could

be shut off. Where will young Irish people migrate to then? No Irish government would wish to see this connection disrupted. Mainland Europe is unlikely to be a viable alternative. This is not just because of a lack of linguistic skills but also because of historical cultural connections.

Ireland is now the only English-speaking country left in the EU apart from Malta, which also has English as one of its official languages. One of the reasons why Britain attracts so many immigrants is language; English is the main foreign language taught in many eastern European countries. While Ireland will never attract the same number, it will probably see a major increase in immigrants from eastern Europe once Britain is closed off to them. To date there has been little public opposition to immigration in Ireland, where it is still seen by most as beneficial. However, a large unplanned increase could change attitudes, with immigration becoming a major focus of discontent, especially where there is pressure on public services and housing.

Hopefully, the Common Travel Area will continue indefinitely. The EU Withdrawal Treaty recognises the right of the UK and Ireland to "make arrangements between themselves relating to the movement of persons between their territories". It is a pity that a similar bilateral approach to the problems of the Irish border was not taken by Dublin during the Brexit negotiations. However, the CTA depends on the goodwill of both governments and public acceptance. There is a danger that those seeking to immigrate illegally to the UK may see Ireland as a weak link in the UK immigration control system, with implications for the CTA in the longer run. Safeguarding against this will require deeper cooperation between immigration officials in both countries, including the positioning of UK immigration officials at Irish air and sea ports. The Republic's authorities will be anxious to ensure that the dreadful scenes from the "Jungle" refugee camp in Calais are not repeated outside Dundalk.

Further challenges

As the effects of Brexit take shape, Ireland will find itself on the extreme western fringe of the European Union. The centre of gravity of the Union will shift eastwards. The Republic will represent four fifths of an off-shore island, positioned behind a larger off-shore island that is no longer a member state. Ireland will suffer from a physical dislocation from the main centres of power in the EU. Brussels is hoping for further expansion to the east and south, thus giving greater influence to Germany and central Europe. This will be evident in the languages used in Brussels as the relative importance of English declines. With only five million English speakers in the Republic, English will no longer have a strong case to be the dominant language of the European institutions.

This peripherality will also affect Irish trade with the remaining members of the EU. Irish trade with mainland Europe overwhelmingly travels through Britain. Two-thirds of Ireland's total exports by value (and a much higher percentage by volume) pass through the UK transport system. No Irish authority has yet indicated how this can be maintained without the threat of some disruption at the point of entry into the UK, and later when the exports re-emerge into the EU Customs Union. Apart from the potential for huge time delays at either end, there will be extra administrative costs. Also, there will be inspections as no national customs regime can simply accept that goods travelling through its territory from a separate customs jurisdiction are completely safe from contraband solely on the basis of enhanced technology. There will always be the need for on the spot human inspections, even if these occur well away from the ports. This will disadvantage Irish trade and involve extra expense. Many of Ireland's seaports are not equipped to deal with cargo from outside the EU. The bulk of trade in our ports will now fall into that category. The change in the status of trade with the UK, Ireland's biggest trading partner, will therefore necessitate major change and new and financial outlays at those ports. Some will be unable to cope and may have to cease operations.

Every level of society is linked
At every level of society, there are huge interconnections between Britain and Ireland which dwarf comparable associations with any other country. Any impediment to these links would be extremely disruptive and, given their scale, almost incalculable. Even with good cooperation, tensions will arise. The national security implications of backdoor immigration into the UK from Ireland are bound to become an issue.

As the Brexit debate took place in Britain, many in Ireland openly boasted about attracting financial, insurance and legal firms from London to Dublin. Ireland's Industrial Development Authority was particularly triumphalist. However, these promised investment flows have not yet materialised. The over-enthusiasm of the Irish authorities was fanned by some of the most outrageous claims of what has been described as Project Fear in Britain. The Bank of England had claimed that London's financial sector could lose up to 75,000 jobs. This has proved completely wrong. It is now estimated that any job losses will be relatively low, and Brexit will not seriously impair the City of London's status as the world capital for financial and insurance service.

For Ireland and its Financial Services Centre, the presence of this global financial centre in London has represented a major plus. The fact that the UK and the USA recovered much quicker from the financial crisis greatly assisted Ireland's bounce back from that period. These two Anglophone countries are Ireland's most important economic partners. The Dublin–London air route is said to be the second busiest international inter-city air route in the world, a testament to the commercial closeness of the two capitals. London's Heathrow is Ireland's gateway to Asian, Latin American and African cities. Ireland has a huge stake in the continued success of the UK's economy. To listen to Irish Ministers speaking about Brexit, this salient fact seems to have bypassed them. The Taoiseach's hyperbole about the UK facing "decades of economic decline" post-Brexit is not in Ireland's interest, apart from its wild assertion. It demonstrated a mindset which was not focused on Ireland's interests.

The future

The Brexit process impaired the rapprochement across the Irish Sea which had been growing for over twenty years. Post-Brexit, how do these two island nations begin to rebuild their damaged relationship? At a political level, strong personal ties will ensure that good communications remain, but at the public level damage has been done. It is impossible to insulate government-to-government links from the popular mood. The failure of Ireland to assist the UK at its time of need was a bad error. The Irish government could have rescued Theresa May's withdrawal agreement by simply agreeing to the insertion of a reasonable time limit on the backstop. At that stage, this would have been a magnanimous gesture to our neighbour, and it would have been overwhelmingly in Ireland's long-term interests. However, that opportunity is long gone.

The Conservatives have been the natural party of government in Britain for the last century and it does not make sense to make them our enemy. Some of the arch-Remainers in that party encouraged and plotted with the Irish government to try to thwart Brexit. This was no excuse for Dublin trying to overthrow the democratic decision of the British people. Ireland has been cynically used by establishment elements in both London and Brussels. We should have seen this danger a mile away and shunned it.

Rebuilding British-Irish institutions

With Brexit finally done, Ireland needs to use the existing intergovernmental machinery to rebuild trust. The British government will also need to give a much greater emphasis to its relations with Dublin. The two administrations used regularly to meet in the margins of EU meetings: this opportunity will no longer be available. Our lack of serious engagement with organisations outside the Brussels bubble has made our politicians and officials too EU-centric. Regular consultations with the UK would help broaden their experience and outlook.

Therefore, there is a strong need to reactivate the

mechanisms of the Good Friday Agreement. I am glad that the British and Irish Governments have agreed to recommence meetings of the British Irish Intergovernmental Ministerial Conference, which has been a neglected part of the GFA in recent years. I was Irish Joint Secretary of that body from 2001–5, when it was functioning well. It is a useful forum where all matters of bilateral interest can be discussed. It should use its wide remit to meet in sectoral formats, not just the Taoiseach/ Prime Minister and Foreign Affairs/Secretary of State for Northern Ireland.

While I believe that in the longer-term Ireland should leave the EU, unfortunately this is unlikely to take place soon. The GFA could be used for close collaboration and consultation with the British government on EU matters. Since it is very much in our interest that the UK continues in a close relationship with the EU, Ireland should consider itself a close ally and friend of the UK inside the Council of Ministers. This would help restore some of the trust lost in the Brexit negotiations.

Hopefully we have entered a better and more realistic period. Detailed discussions should now take place between the Irish and British governments, in the framework of the GFA, to tackle the problems arising from the Northern Ireland Protocol. These would be informed by wider EU/ UK trade discussions.

All parties claim to be supporters of the GFA, which commits both governments to "come together to promote bilateral cooperation at all levels on all matters of mutual interest within the competence of both Governments." It is time to review the agreement and amend it in a way that reflects the new situation. It actually provides for such a review of "the machinery and institutions established under it." A successful refurbished GFA could reset the Dublin–London relationship in a positive direction.

Another institution which needs to be energized is the British-Irish Council (BIC). This brings together the Irish and British governments; the devolved administrations in Edinburgh, Belfast and Cardiff; the Crown dependency of the Isle of Man; and the Bailiwicks of Jersey and Guernsey. It is a curious body but has assisted in re-establishing relations among administrations which would not otherwise have cause to meet. The concept of a Council was suggested by the Ulster Unionists during the Good Friday talks as a counterweight to the North/South Ministerial Council. Most of those designated to be members of the Council were unaware of their inclusion until well after the signing of the GFA. It never got the same powers as the North/South council but in its own quiet way it has built up strong links between Ireland and the devolved British administrations, especially Scotland. Perhaps there should be an initiative to strengthen the British-Irish Council further. It has a permanent secretariat, based in Edinburgh.

The British-Irish Parliamentary Assembly is also a useful body, which includes 25 members each from the Irish and British Parliaments, five members each from the Welsh Assembly, Scottish Parliament and Northern Ireland Assembly, and one each from the Isle of Man, Jersey and Guernsey. This could be another vehicle for strengthening relations. In promoting stronger Dublin–London links, one issue which needs to be looked at seriously is Ireland's possible association with the Commonwealth. This is a sensitive matter and any Irish republican who raises the prospect is immediately labelled as a traitor. The link between the British Crown and the Commonwealth was the reason for Ireland's original departure and would remain a difficulty for many in Dublin and Belfast. However, it is something which would undoubtedly strengthen British-Irish links at a time when these are badly in need of positive development.

Endnotes

1 This chapter is a contracted version of chapter 3, "The British-Irish Relationship, Post Brexit", of Ray Bassett's *Ireland and the EU Post Brexit* (2020).

Ireland Out of England?

John Wilson Foster

One

Sharon Horgan, 49, grew up on a turkey farm in Meath and moved to London in her early twenties in pursuit of an acting career.[1] She worked in a job centre in Kilburn before recording sketches for a BBC radio pilot. Breakthrough success came when she wrote and starred in the BBC sitcom *Pulling*, after which she wrote *Divorce* for Sarah Jessica Parker. She married an English property developer and lives with her daughters Sadhbh and Amer in a designer house in Hackney, where in fact she was born to a Kildare mother and Irish-New Zealand father. The actress and ITV presenter Laura Whitmore was born in Dublin and educated by the nuns at Loreto Bray and now lives in Camden, wife of a Scottish comedian. Genevieve O'Reilly's family left Dublin for Australia when she was ten after years but now the 43 year-old actress of *Star Wars* and *Tin Star* fame makes her home in east London with her chiropractor husband. Niamh Algar, 27, left her Mullingar home in 2017, headed to London, and landed a starring role in the Channel 4 miniseries, *The Virtues*. She will better that with the English director Ridley Scott's big-budget series, *Raised by Wolves*. Algar is now house-hunting in London. Paul Mescal from Maynooth is not at the house-hunting stage quite yet, having moved to London just before the coronavirus lockdown to star in BBC's *Normal People*. Alex Murphy and Chris Walley, both from Cork, star in the BBC comedy series *The Young Offenders,* and its British audience proves, as it does with Channel 4's *Father Ted* and BBC Scotland's *Mrs Brown's Boys*, that it regards the Irish as culturally outlier versions of themselves. Keith Duffy from Dublin has copper-fastened that perception by playing an outlier character in that most British of television programmes, *Coronation Street*. Duffy's initial success came as a singer in Boyzone alongside Ronan Keating from Dublin who now hosts a show on London's Magic Radio. Keating was managed for some years by Louis Walsh from Co. Mayo who achieved his highest profile with ITV's *X-Factor*.

Horgan, Algar, Whitmore and Mescal are only the most recent aspiring southern Irish movie, stage and television performers trooping to London. The Wexford actress Charlie Murphy left for London in 2013 after success in a BBC drama; she was reported to be in a long-term relationship with Ciaran O'Brien, the Irish stage actor also living in London. They followed in the footsteps of Kate Binchy, Donal Donnelly, Richard Harris, Peter O'Toole (born either in Connemara or Leeds), Eddie Byrne, John Welsh, Cyril Cusack, Fiona Shaw CBE, Sinéad Cusack, Cillian Murphy, Andrew Scott, Killian Donnelly, and Daragh O'Malley who grew up in Limerick and became friends with Harris, a fellow Limerick-man; O'Malley found his place in the thespian sun by starring in *Sharpe*, the ITV series, after learning the ropes at the London Academy of Music and Dramatic Art; he married in London. Byrne was a congenial presence in British movies in my youth and whereas the usual sites have him born in

Dublin in 1911, his birthplace on PeoplePill.com is given as Birmingham, with his upbringing in the Irish capital. The doubling of Byrne's native countries, as in the cases of Horgan and O'Toole, is telling. And John Welsh played English characters so impeccably in *The Forsyte Saga*, *Vanity Fair* and *The Moonstone,* among numerous other dramas, that I was surprised to discover that he was born John James Walsh in Wexford in 1914.

The curve of actors' visibility goes north or south, but a select few entertainers become celebrities which means they settle in with the showbusiness equivalent of a professorial chair, and become national identities, in the Australian sense of the word. I grew up in the ubiquitous sunny presence of Eamonn Andrews CBE because my family in Belfast got a TV as early as 1953. He was born in Synge Street Dublin, educated by the Christian Brothers at Synge Street School, and was a sports commentator for Radio Éireann before graduating to the BBC in London. His most famous role was compère of the evergreen *This is Your Life.* Andrews was succeeded as a cheerful fixture in the British consciousness by Terry Wogan – (Sir) Terence Wogan KBE, DL (Deputy Lieutenant, a Crown appointment), son of a Limerick store manager. Now it is Graham Norton from Bandon, the third Irish star in the BBC firmament over the past continuous sixty years, subject of a 2013 *Daily Telegraph* profile, "The making of a national treasure", the nation in question being the UK. Meanwhile, Robert "Sir Bob" Geldof KBE and Freeman of the City of London, born and raised in Dun Laoghaire, is a kind of roving celebrity-campaigner who lives in Battersea but is too divisive to be a national treasure. He can affix KBE to his name but cannot call himself

Sir Robert because the Republic of Ireland is not in the Commonwealth; but others call him Sir Bob anyway, no doubt because they know that Ireland does not need to be in the Commonwealth in order to be in the British Isles; Sir Bob is one of them, even when ornery.

What does Irish talent's homing instinct that locks on to London like a heat-seeking missile tell us? Well, at least this: the performative genius of the Irish, if it also ambitious, needs a metropolis in which to take wing. London (not Dublin, Paris or Berlin) is the metropolis of Ireland. And London, metropolis or not, is in England.

The singer Róisín Murphy, born and raised in Arklow, moved with her parents to Manchester, stayed when her parents returned to Ireland, and has made a glittering career and life there, with a daughter by the English artist Simon Henwood. We are told that, like many thousands, and quite naturally, "Murphy shares her time between London and Ireland". Why didn't this give the Irish at home pause during their vocal anti-British sentiment during Brexit? Have Murphy and others felt reciprocal anti-Irish feeling in England? *Au contraire*: warm British-Irish relations in entertainment and the professions have for a century been deliberately bracketed off by Irish politicians and commentators so that British–Irish relations can be portrayed as inherently and exclusively hostile. We in these islands are in dire need of a candid exposure of those warm relations so that we can then consider how we might import empirical reality into Irish official and unofficial attitudes to the UK and the Union, and encourage a sea-change in Irish popular and political mindset. I believe that the peace of Ireland, the capacity to reconcile the peoples of the archipelago (and then, *and only then*, the people of Ireland itself), depends upon it.

And this is the case because, contrary to what is assumed, neither "the North" nor partition is the chief source of contention between Britain and Ireland. Northern Ireland, in reality, is the veronica that distracts the Irish bull from his real problem which is the British-Irish relationship itself. This schizophrenic relationship would rankle even if the Northern Irish disappeared. Edna Longley's eloquent notion of Northern Ireland as a corridor between Ireland and Britain once seemed hopeful, but ambitious Southerners prefer direct traffic with the British mainland and have no interest in the North as a detour, bridge or go-between.

Two

To kick-start this candid exposure, we might read the Irish historian Diarmaid Ferriter's contribution to a recent book, *Britain and Ireland: Lives Entwined. Shifting Borders, Shifting Identity* (2019), which despite its title does not even begin to build on Ferriter's revelations. "Over the last 30 years I have spent more time in London than Belfast and that is not unusual for my peers," writes Ferriter. Indeed; his peers' eyes are fixed firmly on England. Ferriter introduced me to an acronym for the Irish of his generation who live across the water: NIPPLE (new Irish professional people living in England). They are the latest instalment of a very old sequence but more likely than their immediate predecessors to share the culture of their host society. Some of Ferriter's historical statistics are startling. By 1830, Irish soldiers "were estimated to represent 42.2 per cent of the regular British Army … By 1878 a fifth of all British Army officers were Irish. More than 200,000 Irishmen fought in the First World

War and were volunteers rather than conscripts ... at least 60,000 Southern Irish citizens served [in the Second World War] ... Joining the British Army was a family tradition for many, and was not seen by them as either pro-British or anti-Irish". That became "an inconvenient truth", says Ferriter with some understatement. So inconvenient that President Higgins omitted to mention it in his recent diatribe against the British Empire in which by his account the Irish were exclusively victims of imperial oppression. He also forgot to mention that, as Mary Kenny reminded readers of *The Oldie* recently, the British Empire was very good for the Irish Catholic church; "the Irish missions often tended to follow where the British flag had led," she writes in *Goodbye to Catholic Ireland* (1997). In the 20th century, Ferriter tells us, "1.6 million Irish left for Britain, more than twice as many as went to North America". Roy Foster reminds us in *Paddy and Mr Punch* (1993) that the Irish-born population in Britain in 1861 was 805,000; the combined first-generation and their immigrant parents would have boosted the figure to several million. By 2001, the Irish-born population was 850,000; after all, by the late 1950s, nearly 60,000 Irish were arriving in Great Britain annually. (These last figures courtesy of Maurice Sweeney's moving 2009 documentary set in Birmingham, *The Forgotten Irish*.)

Obviously many of the descendants of the three million Irish who have emigrated to Britain since 1600 (Ferriter's figure), have simply dissolved into the mainstream of British society, helping to feed and propel that stream while, in many cases, keeping proudly alive at some level of acknowledgement their Irish ancestry. As we know from David Fitzpatrick's essential study, "A Curious Middle Place: the Irish in Britain, 1871–1921" (in *The*

Irish in Britain, 1815–1939, ed. Swift and Sheridan), by the turn of the twentieth century many Irish had escaped the Irishtowns of Liverpool, Manchester and other British cities and were moving to the suburbs; they also lived in Stafford, Stockport, Winchester, York, Dundee, Newcastle, Hull, Bristol and other smaller British towns and cities.

The alienation from British culture that first characterised Irish life in Britain accordingly diminished. Foster reminds us of the nineteenth-century Irish "who saw much of their focus and most of their career opportunity as lying across St George's Channel. But for many of the Victorian Irish middle class, life was spent travelling back and forth across the Irish Sea, observing and participating in British forms of Government, reading English books, attending British educational institutions, looking for employment within the structures of the British Empire and speaking English". He refers to those Irish "who went to England and made a good thing out of it"; but we don't need to trumpet the success stories that he tells: a mere reminder of the Irish educated middle-class presence in England is sufficiently novel, and the fact sufficiently unappetising ideologically to many Irish historians, politicians and journalists. But of course, high-profile success stories pack a greater punch than common or garden success stories, and both kinds can help to counterbalance the prevailing lazy image to this day of the Irish in England – exiled, unhappy, discriminated against, nostalgic for the old sod.

During the research for my study, *Irish Novels, 1880–1940: New Bearings in Culture and Fiction* (Oxford University Press, 2008), I was astonished to recover from obscurity so many popular Irish novelists, mostly women and middle class, Catholic and Protestant, who lived in England and set their fiction in either of the two islands, who frequented the Irish mail train and Holyhead ferry between Euston and Dun Laoghaire (or who travelled the Empire) and who wrote in blithe disregard for the nationalist stipulations of the Irish Revival culture-givers. They could be disapproved of ideologically (and have been by Irish critics for a century) *but there they were*, unembittered and ethnically more Irish than Patrick Pearse, Erskine Childers, Maud Gonne or Éamon de Valera. Even so, Irish scholars have no intention of dislodging the Irish Revival as the literary counterpart of the republican independence movement.

Fitzpatrick reminds us that Irishmen were indeed over-represented among casual and seasonal workers, dock labourers and coal heavers, and Irishwomen in domestic service: "In England, Paddy (and doubtless Biddy) remained proletarian". And they remained so into the 1950s. To balance the longstanding discrimination that these particular Irish suffered, Ferriter reminds us of the inimitable opportunities England offered to those who could find no work in Ireland. England was Ireland's missing construction site. Which reminds me. "Oh mother dear, I'm over here," sings the narrator of "McAlpine's Fusiliers", "I never will come back". The song lists what lightens the navvies' nights and induces them to throw their suitcases away: "What keeps me here?/The rake of beer,/The ladies and the crack". Pleasure and freedom, in short. But the image persisted of an oppressed workforce amidst an alien host population. Sweeney's *The Forgotten Irish* reveals how immigrant Irish workers were in fact often exploited by their compatriots who had become contractors in England. And in the song it is the Irish gaffer, The Horseface Toole, who when The Bear O'Shea is killed on site callously retorts "I'm a navvy short". Besides, the navvies weren't press-ganged and trafficked to England. If they were forced to emigrate to Great Britain from Ireland, by whom were they forced? In the cases of the Birmingham Irish that Sweeney profiles in *The Forgotten Irish*, it was to escape hardship, cruelty and sexual abuse in the industrial schools that they absconded to Britain. This was a traumatising experience for some and some suffered homesickness and, in their inner-city loneliness, alcoholism; theirs can be heartbreaking stories. Thirty-five to 40% of the boys who survived institutions in Ireland decamped to Britain, Sweeney tells us. Many rooted themselves in England. We accompany one of his survivors on his return to Baltimore, Cork after decades away. "I'm patriotic," he says, "I love Ireland. But I'm going back to Birmingham. I'm going home".

Subtending this false notion of chronic exploitation of all the Irish in Britain was the claim of the essential *difference* between the British and the Irish as well as an unjust imbalance between oppressor and oppressed. The cultural difference had to be true and deep if it were to justify the separatist agenda of the early 20th century. That agenda, Foster claims, was subscribed to less by Irish living in England than by those radicals who were actually English such as Gonne, Childers, Aodh de Blácam (Hugh Blackham), Charlotte Despard. We learn from Fitzpatrick that in the later 19th century, "Nationalist organizers struggled hard to involve immigrants in the concerns of Ireland and her politics … Most immigrants avoided all Irish organizations". They were clearly too busy getting on with their lives, though there was later involvement in the Home Rule movement and, as we know from Yeats, an expatriate enthusiasm for Irish drama and literature in Southwark and elsewhere that fed into the incipient cultural revival. But the image that came to prominence was of an Irish population in England in half-voluntary bondage, whose tribulations ("No blacks, no Irish") helped to justify the cause of complete separation of the two countries, culturally as well as politically.

Two sides to the story of the Irish in Britain were indirectly revealed in the Forgotten Irish Campaign that was launched in London in 2007 by President Mary McAleese. It was spearheaded by Peter Sutherland, a businessman and lawyer of Scots ancestry born in Foxrock and who rose to be Attorney General of Ireland, Chairman of Allied Irish Banks and Special UN Representative for International Migration. Queen Elizabeth made him an honorary Knight Commander. He lived in London but at the end returned to Dublin where he died. The campaign was to raise funds and awareness of the elderly Irish in Great Britain who had left Ireland from the 1950s. The campaign manifesto (available online) said they "paved the way for more recent generations of Irish immigrants to Britain – for people like us". So the thousands of successful Irish professionals in Britain were asked to help those working-class predecessors who had not fared so well. Ironically, the Irish in Britain, especially if successful, have been less understandably, sometimes wilfully, forgotten by those Irish still at home, and where a political party that nourishes itself, and starves others, on its anti-Britishness, is sadly popular.

How well the Irish are doing in Great Britain was

revealed by the recent Sewell Commission on Race and Ethnic Disparities which found that the average earnings of the "white Irish" exceeded those of "white British" and that "white Irish unemployment was relatively low". This good news is hardly likely to be trumpeted in *An Phoblacht*. My only reservation about the happy news is in the concept of "white Irish" as an ethnic group. In "Let's Celebrate Irish Success in Britain," a St Patrick's Day 2021 article in *Spiked*, Rakib Ehsan claims that the success of one ethnic group in Britain, the Catholic Irish, is "oft-overlooked" in debates over race and culture. In order laudably to disprove white homogeneity, he suggests ways in which the Irish are culturally different from white British, which differences explain their success. (But that must have sounded too odd to him, so Ehsan tags on the oppression of the Travellers.) In fact, success at the levels I have been referencing (the professions, the arts, the services, the media) is culturally homogeneous; that is why Irish success in Britain is "oft-overlooked" by the British (as well as by Irish nationalists) – the Irish on those levels are invisibly at home in Britain.

In order to achieve even Home Rule, it was, of course, necessary to promote difference between Ireland and Britain, not similarity or shared experience, and this is understandable. After all, one inescapable difference was in the fact that the citizens of one country did not unanimously accept rule by the other country, to put it mildly. But whereas Home Rule would have allowed the Irish in Britain to maintain without reproof their British Isles existence, the republican campaign that climaxed in the Easter rebellion necessarily called that existence into question. After 1922, many Irish in Britain must have felt cut adrift. Those in Ireland who wished to join their compatriots across the water, or were judged to be too British in behaviour or belief, were now West Britons or shoneens and the insult was extended to those Irish in Britain who drew attention to themselves. Were Shaw and Wilde even Irish writers, really? When I was an undergraduate in the 1960s in Belfast, the answer was still No. The Irish in Britain became an unspoken-of population, unless they were McAlpine's fusiliers or equivalent "victims". Unspoken of, and unspeaking, by and large. The Provisional IRA war of the 1970s and 1980s was conducted in England not on behalf of, but despite, the majority of the Irish who lived there.

Yet if we recruit Ferriter's experience, along with the facts of present-day Irish in Britain, the idea of deep separation is patently absurd. But what is the best cultural and policy-form by which the reality of the British–Irish connection can be expressed? No extant policy, political initiative, or major cultural organisation supplies the need. It is a hard question because we are dealing with a network, a web, not alas (or yet), a potential coherent lobby in Britain either of the Irish-born or the British-born Irish; nor is there advocacy back in Ireland. But answers are necessary if we are finally to lay the by-now sorry and reiterative quarrel to rest.

Three

A recurring figure in Ferriter's essay is Kevin Maher whom the scholar would visit in London where Maher lived, and for a time in Camden like many Irish. They shared "a deep-rooted republicanism with a fascination with the activities of the House of Windsor". Ferriter was best man when

Maher married a Kensington woman from a Tory family. As it happens, I got my information about the actress Niamh Algar chiefly from an interview with her in the London *Times* of 29 February, 2020 by Kevin Maher. Maher is from Dublin but left for London in 1994 when he was 22 to find success as a journalist. He did so, for he is now film critic of the *Times* and has worked as a researcher for Channel 4's *Film Night*. Two novels of his have been published by a London house. He lives in Hertfordshire. His kids, he says, are half Irish/half English "so I'm really suspicious of nationalism" – in other words, of any attempt to impose an Ireland-Britain binary; he is one of the few Irish in England apparently willing to question on the record, even indirectly, the *raison d'être* of Irish republicanism.

In turn, I got my information about Maher chiefly from an April 2013 interview with him in the *Spectator* (a mouthpiece for England par excellence, one might think) by J.P. O'Malley, a resourceful freelance journalist from Dublin who left for London in 2009 and has also written for *The Economist* and *The Daily Beast*. Despite the English outlets for his journalism, O'Malley does not appear to share Maher's suspicion of nationalism and regards life in London as responsible for silencing the Irish national narrative; writing about the Irish in London has given him a greater sense of himself as Irish, he says. ("Culture can provide home away from home for Irish in London", *Irish Times*, 14 November, 2014.) But none of this negates the fact of O'Malley's living in the capital of England which in the arts and publishing (and other fields) is also the capital of Ireland. One can feel, or adopt, the identity of an expatriate in England while daily living the life of a resident, inside or outside the loose company of tens of thousands of one's compatriots. It's a different way of being Irish in Britain. Yet another way, made possible by shuttle flights and encouraged in the beginning, no doubt, by the UK's EU membership, is to be part of what airport staff call "the Monday-morning mob" of Irish commuter-migrant professionals whose work week is spent in a British city and whose weekends are back in Ireland (www.irishpost. com, 7 March, 2014).

And how you live as Irish in Britain is now up to you, as the experience of the actress Siobhán McSweeney of *Derry Girls* suggests. After she graduated from University College Cork, she told the *Sunday Times* (Dublin) of 3 May, 2020, she enrolled in the Central School of Speech and Drama in London in 2001. What is crucial to remember is how natural those footsteps are that lead from Ireland to Britain. When she moved from Brockley to Kilburn ("County Kilburn, they call it, because there are so many Irish there"), having come from Celtic Tiger Ireland, "I wasn't that keen on bacon and cabbage; and I didn't have the immigrant mindset, because, in my head, I wasn't one: I was just over in London. The idea I had moved from home hadn't occurred to me". She did not regard herself, obviously, as "white Irish". She was just a migrant, not an immigrant from another land. The accidental geography once she was in a certain London neighbourhood meant she *chose* to embrace the ideas of diaspora, enclave and home away from home, where if you are a professional you describe yourself as "based in London" or "currently living in London" (a formula to disguise a commitment to life in England) rather than "living and making my livelihood and career in London", which you are. Now, she says, "I'm a fully paid–up member of the immigrant community: I break down and weep in the supermarket at the sight of Tayto crisps and Kimberley and Mikado biscuits." But with her wit, self-awareness, talent and success, McSweeney is unlikely to join the old forgotten Irish. There is role-playing here, surely, for she is clearly a NIPPLE, a new Irish professional person living in England.

There are of course other high-profile Irish journalists and commentators living and working in England besides Maher and O'Malley, including Mary Kenny from Dublin; John Naughton from Mayo (also a research fellow at the University of Cambridge); Melanie McDonagh from Wicklow (happily writing for both the *Spectator* and the *Catholic Herald*); Gerard O'Donovan from Cork (*Daily Telegraph*); Laura Perrins, a law graduate from UCD and co-editor of *Conservative Woman*; and John O'Ceallaigh ("luxury travel journalist" who is "based in London", according to his website). Besides being a journalist, Kevin Maher is a novelist, only one of the many Irish writers living in England, including Ruth Dudley Edwards, Jean Casey, Edna O'Brien, Gerard O'Donovan (the same), Caroline O'Donoghue, Declan Ryan, Martina Evans, Olivia Kiernan, the late Josephine Hart from Mullingar, who died in 2011 as Lady Saatchi, and their myriad illustrious predecessors since the Revival, including George Moore, Sean O'Casey, AE and W.B. Yeats. Other Irish writers, such as Marian Keyes from Limerick, spent their creatively formative years in London, where Keyes married an Englishman. Niamh Mulvey from Kilkenny spent formative years in London where she worked with distinction in publishing for ten years and will join the ranks of Irish writers in 2022 with a short story collection from Picador; her London agent is Sallyanne Sweeney from

Dublin. Indeed, so many Irish writers are in the Big Smoke that Tony Murray, a first-generation London-Irishman who teaches at the London Metropolitan University, started the Irish Writers in London Summer School in 1996. Murray catches first- and second-generation London-Irish writers in his net, and they could include, of course, John Walsh, Martin McDonagh and Brendan O'Neill (and before them, J.G. Farrell). The multi-talented Helen Mullane lives in Sweden but is from north London and flies the Irish flag when she races dog-sleds, as RTE is delighted to remind us. In an *Oldie* column, Mary Kenny defended Edna O'Brien (born in Co. Clare but a Londoner of long standing) from Irish attack for accepting her Dame of the British Empire honour in 2018, on the grounds that the Irish were active in the Empire, too. Unless you insist that race or ethnicity defines nationality, Dame Edna is as British as I am.

That Southern Irish professionals are punching above their demographic weight is clear when you ponder their number in front of the cameras and behind the microphones of the British Broadcasting Corporation, over and above Graham Norton: the late Dave Allen, Des Lynam OBE and his nephew Joe Lynam, Dara O'Briain, Fergal Keane, the impressive ex-convent schoolgirl Orla Guerin MBE, Al Ryan, Angela Scanlon, Declan Harvey and Donnachadh McCarthy. Caroline Lennon from Wicklow who lives in east London played for years an Irish villager in *The Archers*, a fictional emblem of the English heartland. Sinead Keenan from Dublin (married to an *EastEnders* director) is making her career courtesy of the BBC and ITV. The BBC radio presenter Dermot O'Leary is actually first-generation English, having been born in

Colchester to where his parents migrated from Ireland; he holds dual British and Irish citizenship and is described in his Wikipedia entry as a "British-Irish" presenter; he is "extremely proud" of his Irish roots, and one hopes that he is proud, too, of his English upbringing; Terry Wogan was an early model for O'Leary. A recent book on writers and the BBC reminds us that even after Radio Éireann was established, Irish writers looked instead to the BBC for opportunities.

There must be dozens of Irish away from the cameras and microphones of the BBC, ITV and Channel Four – producing, directing, scripting, research-assisting. Aisling Bea from Kildare, as well as being a stand-up comedian, writes and stars in Channel 4's comedy drama *This Way Up*; her sister Sinéad (O'Sullivan) Kidao is a costume designer who worked on BBC's *The Pursuit of Love*; naturally they both live in London. Hundreds of Irish work like them at the heart of British culture and help it pump the blood of that culture. Donnachadh McCarthy FRSA was born in Ireland and for a while was a ballet dancer there, before joining the Royal Opera Ballet in Covent Garden. He embedded himself in British culture once he arrived in London in 1986. He lives in a Victorian terrace in Camberwell and has been a Southwark councillor and deputy Chair of the Liberal Democrats. He is a prominent agitator on ecological matters whose CV for the last quarter century reflects an entirely English life. So do those of countless Irish teachers and researchers in the British academy, from colleges and redbricks to Oxbridge itself. At the summit are such eminences in the Humanities as professors Roy Foster FRSL, FBA from Waterford (Hertford College, Oxford), Eamonn Duffy

FBA, a "cradle Catholic" (his description) from Dundalk (former President of Magdalene College, Cambridge) and Bernard O'Donoghue FRSL from County Cork (Wadham College, Oxford).

The other disciplines are just as enriched by Irish expertise. Professor Louise Richardson FRSE, a Catholic from Tramore and whose specialty is terrorism, is the Vice-Chancellor of the University of Oxford and therefore arguably the highest ranking academic in the United Kingdom. Professor Adrian Hill FRCP from Dublin is Director of the Jenner Institute at the same university and directed the search for the anti-Covid 19 vaccine. Working under Professor Hill at the Institute is Professor Teresa Lambe from Kilcullen, Co. Kildare. Aoife Abbey, 36, from Dublin is an IC unit doctor at University Hospitals Coventry & Warwickshire for whom we can predict a luminous future not only as a doctor but as a writer, author as she is of *Seven Signs of Life: Stories from an Intensive Care Doctor* (2019); she has an autobiographical piece in the *Times* Magazine of 1 May, 2020 in which her Irishness tellingly goes unmentioned.

A different kind of professional is the current CEO of British Airways, the nation's carrier. Sean Doyle, who was born and reared in Youghal, Cork, follows Willie Walsh from Dublin as CEO (2005–2011). (Not even the sky is the limit for the Irish in the country of the ancient enemy.) Yet another is the London chef and author Richard Corrigan, born and raised in Ballivor, County Meath, multiple winner of the Great British Menu, and a restaurateur who owns Corrigan's Mayfair, Bentley's Sea Grill in Harrods, Daffodil Mulligan in Islington, and for good measure Virginia Park Lodge in County Cavan.

("Richard Corrigan's Irish Feast," *Times* Magazine 7 December, 2019.) He may think London is led by "a load of donkeys" and the UK by "a bunch of monkeys" (see his Wikipedia entry), but there he is, profitably plying his superb trade in London for decades, too well embedded, I would suggest, for his insults to be anti-British rather than the grievances of an exasperated businessman finding his government boneheaded. Just as successful is Fiona Leahy from Tipperary profiled in a recent *Sunday Telegraph*; she is one of the world's most sought-after event designers, running her agency from London and living joyfully with her boyfriend Alex Antonioni amidst the upmarket Victorian and Edwardian houses of Queen's Park and its "best farmers' market in the UK", as she puts it. Then there is Sir Ciarán Devane who was born in Dublin and graduated from UCD. He was CEO of Macmillan Cancer Support before becoming CEO of the British Council while serving as the non-executive director of NHS England; The Irish Minister for Health, Simon Harris, announced in 2018 that Devane is the first Chair of the Irish Health services (IHS); the British knighted him in 2015 for his services to cancer services.

And I haven't even mentioned the Irish presence in sport in Britain, including, obviously, football and horse-racing, both sports in which there is a unified culture, a continuous, intimate and age-old exchange of talent and management skills. (Four of England's Euro 2020 squad are the sons or grandsons of Irish migrants.) In the case of horse-racing, trainer JonJo O'Neill at Jackdaws Castle ("in the heart of the Cotswolds", according to his website) and jockey Rachel Blackmore from Tipperary (there has been talk of a damehood for her) can personify the unity.

The movement of thoroughbred horseflesh blithely occurs outside the rules of the EU, that bureaucracy that has caused such friction between the two countries during Brexit. Horse-racing is such a mutual Anglo-Irish sport and business that not even the EU can drive that border down the Irish Sea, and nobody in Ireland would dream of doing so. During Brexit negotiations, one *Irish Times* headline ran: "Brexit could decimate Ireland's horse racing industry", but of course it won't: bloodstock is thicker than seawater.

All my names are but tips of an iceberg. The critical mass of Irish presence and talent in Britain makes Irish Anglophobia perversely disconnected from Irish lives in England. And self-harming: whether real or affected, public anti-Britishness shrinks the compass of Irish cultural experience and possibility, and certainly its healthy expression. Why aren't the successful Irish in Great Britain speaking out and saying this?

Four

In 2016, there were 277, 200 people born in the UK living in the Republic where there is a notable historical and ongoing infusion in Ireland of British culture, high, low and middlebrow, via television, radio, cinema, the Internet, newspapers and journals. Often it is a cultural mutuality: as I write, *Normal People*, the BBC TV series from the Irish novel, gets rave reviews and is also being shown on RTÉ. Imported British culture is silently welcomed. Until a few decades ago, British culture was officially discouraged and even denounced as a moral and cultural threat. It was perhaps television transmission that raised the boom because it could not be ambushed by the Republic's film censor as movies were. Before television, surreptitiously tracking the everyday doings of the Brits mingled Irish guilt, pleasure and envy. The Ulster poet James Simmons penned a mischievous couplet back in the Seventies: "Why are TV aerials in Dublin so high?/To eavesdrop on England, that's why". But Ireland no longer needs to eavesdrop: all it has to do is declare that Britain and Ireland culturally interpenetrate in ways that add to the gaiety of both nations and to neither country's diminishment.

A weekly reminder of this healthy silent mutuality (healthier were it to be openly acknowledged) is on the Irish newsstands each Sunday. The Dublin edition of the London *Sunday Times* rivals that of the *Irish Times* in Southern circulation – 68,500 for the former to 79,000 for the latter (but only 56,500 for the latter's print edition). The Dublin *Sunday Times* is also sold north of the border in disregard of Northern Ireland's being in the UK and therefore eligible to receive the London or Scotland edition; but then, since the columnists and reporters who write for the Dublin edition are both British and Irish, the border between the Republic and Great Britain is equally ignored. Half of the features of the main section of the latest issue at the time of writing are over the names of *Sunday Times* Irish staff writers, while the other half are written by such well-known British figures as Jeremy Clarkson, Wayne Rooney, Niall Ferguson and Peter Conradi. Half of the newspaper's Culture Magazine is written by such Britons as Bryan Appleyard, Jonathan Dean, Max Hastings and John Arlidge. The colour Magazine looks as if it is simply the untouched London edition with thirteen of the fourteen writers British (the other, European) and a four-page feature on V-E Day. In other words, the targeted readership of the *Sunday Times* (Dublin) is all the Irish of the island with a keen investment of interest in what is happening on both sides of the narrow water.

One of the more enlightened of the campaigners to sever Northern Ireland from the United Kingdom in order to create a constitutionally unified island is Irish High Court Judge Richard Humphreys, author of *Beyond the Border: The Good Friday Agreement and Irish Unity After Brexit* (2018). May I say that in his book he has courteously given me a good deal of elbow room through quotations from my pro-Union articles. Judge Humphreys has written with generosity about unionist sensitivities and believes that a unified Ireland would work only if the British identity of the unionists were sincerely factored in and protected. And that would be helped along, he believes, if Southern Ireland acknowledged the British dimension to its own experience.

But surely Southern Ireland for the sake of its *own* social health and fidelity to history – and to current reality – would want to acknowledge that dimension with or without Northern Ireland, and moreover should have done so years ago? It shouldn't be the price of annexing Northern Ireland. Judge Humphreys' unavoidable implication is that this dimension has been repressed, and I believe it has. There has been a massive disconnect between the story that Irish politicians and historians tell of the relationship between England and Ireland (usually told in purely political terms and without Scotland and Wales) and the untold truth of cultural history and social reality. The well-intentioned remarks during certain ceremonial occasions about kinship between the two peoples fall comically short of the daily experiences of Irish people on both sides of the Irish Sea. So three short paragraphs on that dimension in a 280-page book suggests to me that even this generous author's heart is not in it.

The book's idea is left unexamined that in a kind of culture reassignment therapy, the Britishness of unionists can be somehow extracted from the UK and grafted on to a united Ireland and "accommodated" therein, while Ireland gaily enjoys its unfettered access to the UK via the media and the Common Travel Area, quietly and officially ignores its own striking British dimension, and asserts instead its ethnic uniqueness. How rich is this? The primacy of Irish ethnic identity – which the campaign for a united Ireland is predicated on – is fine if you wish to ignore the multiculturalism of which Ireland is otherwise seemingly proud, the daily shared experiences that lie below, in and around ethnicity. Ireland has come a long way since a time when commemorating the Great War or welcoming the British Queen would have been unthinkable. Old moulds are being broken. However, there's a marathon distance to go yet, but it requires changes of principle and policy less than it does recognition of the incontrovertible reality of those current and generations-old mutualities that are enacted daily. The Taoiseach Michèal Martin has called for a "re-set" of the UK-EU relationship. It would answer him better to call for a re-set of the UK-Ireland relationship and to do so by making his government's Shared Island Unit the Shared *Islands* Unit.

Five
But are all these Irish in Britain, living, working, sometimes becoming household names, any different from the one million Canadians who live in the United States, where

Jim Carrey, Pamela Anderson, Mike Myers, Dan Aykroyd, Malcolm Gladwell, Matthew Perry, William Shatner, Steven Pinker – all Canadian-born – have found fame? No one, after all, is suggesting in Canada's case that because citizens of a smaller English-speaking country gravitate to the neighbouring English-speaking powerhouse to pursue their career that there are any heavy, much less political implications.

But the North American situation is bereft of the ironies that attend the Irish in Britain. And the ironies speak hitherto unspoken volumes. The million Canadians in the United States are 1/38th of the Canadian population; in 2001, one in every six persons born in Ireland lived in Great Britain. This suggests that the term "migrant" is more accurate than "emigrant" when labelling those who cross the water. Britain is an extension of Ireland – even in some sense a colony of the Irish mind. Why does this provoke embarrassment instead of pride back in Ireland? Isn't there national denial at work?

Nor over the decades of Canadian emigration to the U.S. was there anything comparable between the Canadian view of the U.S. that preceded that emigration and Irish emigrants' preconceptions of Great Britain. In *The Forgotten Irish*, Bernard Canavan remarks on the bitter irony in the banishment of boys to Britain – priests in the institutions, he says, would allocate boys to London neighbourhoods: you to Kilburn, you to Cricklewood, you to Camden, and so on). They were being banished to what was regarded as the godless enemy of Ireland! This was surely arrant hypocrisy, or perhaps cognitive dissonance, since Anglophobia was trumped by the brute facts of Irish work-boots stepping on to British soil. By contrast, educated Irish emigrants simply crossed the Irish Sea without compunction; they weren't deportees and knew better than the Catholic church's nonsense about godlessness and eternal enmity. But unfortunately they have chosen not to speak up.

Furthermore, Canadian emigration to the U.S. involves no political complexity in so far as Canada has no designs on any part of the United States; there is no unfinished constitutional business, no paramilitary campaigns against the U.S. inside its borders. And yet – the Irish keep going to Britain. And they are not turned back at the border; indeed the Common Travel Area means they are treated like returning Britons. This proves that there is a stratum of mutual cultural identity, beneath (or above) the political, a stratum that is thick enough to permit the Irish of all classes to live unmolested in Britain and there flourish (or not) by their own lights. (Though there were, of course, anti-Irish backlashes after bombings, as with the infamous Birmingham bomb, that Sweeney's documentary recalls.)

Nor is there back in Canada a major political party whose primary purpose is to demonise the United States and seek endless redress and concessions from it. And yet tens of thousands of Irish people defy Sinn Féin when they choose to live in Britain, but do not announce their defiance.

Six

Why the silence from both sides of the Irish Sea about Irish relocation to Britain, a silence that encourages the British themselves to keep mum about it? Diarmaid Ferriter writes that the silence was still in force when he left school in 1989, a year in which 70,600 Irish people crossed the water. It is still in force in Britain, and Tony Murray in his 7 April, 2014 *Irish Times* article, "The Irish in London in Fact and Fiction", asks: "So, why had Irish writers been so reluctant to represent their own and their compatriots' experiences of migration to London? Why the reticence? Especially given that they were the oldest and, for a long time, the biggest migrant group in the city? Was it shame, indifference, or plain Irish contrariness?" One answer might lie in Ferriter's reminder of how when Richard Mulcahy, Fine Gael leader, dared in 1946 to describe the attractions of Britain to Irish citizens, he was accused by Fianna Fáil of being a recruiting sergeant for a foreign country; the topic was to be regarded as nationally *infra dig* and buried; to discuss it was unpatriotic. (Presumably the patriotism card was to distract from an embarrassment that has still not been addressed.) That code of silence must persevere in vestigial form among the immigrants in Britain themselves, for I read very little from the successful or contented Irish who are established in Britain about their *being* successful or contented. Or if they do talk, they don't seem to be widely reported. That is why the lonely candour of Mary Kenny, Ruth Dudley Edwards, Brendan O'Neill, Conor McGinn MP, Kevin Maher and Tony Murray is refreshing and potentially emancipating.

Could it be also that the story of victimhood, a plank of the Sinn Féin platform, is the captivating Irish narrative (in both senses) woven around the complementary strand that Ferriter calls "a single, heroic nationalist narrative of Irish history"? Is to discuss the empirical fact of Irish contentment or success in Britain to be regarded as denying or subverting that double-stranded republican narrative? Is that narrative obligatory, even imperative, and risky to disown? Think of the trolling Dara Ó Briain gets from the Irish Twitterati even without his adverting to any narrative but simply for being happy and thriving in Britain. "It's always West Brit Season for Irish celebrities working in the United Kingdom," writes Donald Clarke in a 12 January, 2019 *Irish Times* article: "All kinds of things can get you called a West Brit these days". Ó Briain has responded wittily to his begrudgers: "By definition, I'm not a West Brit, because I actually live in Britain. I mean, get your insults straight, please". How, then, might the deplorable insult be accurately phrased to identify a highly cultivated man born in Ireland, who speaks fluent Irish, supports the GAA, and who is no doubt patriotic, yet who lives and makes his glittering career in Great Britain? A man, moreover, who is, I wager, more comfortable in his own skin than his detractors.

Yet even O'Briain seems to me to be defensive. One must be sensitive to the baggage involved. First-generation Londoner Sean O'Donovan attended the 2014 Irish Writers in London Summer School and wrote about it in the *Irish Times* of 2 June, 2015. It is a touching exercise in the equivocal. On the one hand, he writes of the London Irish living "abroad" which strikes an odd geographic note. He writes of the "homeless Irish heart" of what he calls the "second-generation Irish". He writes of the London-Irish not wishing to integrate, unlike young Afro-Caribbeans, but instead waging "a fierce battle not to be called British"; he was brought up as an FBI, "Foreign Born Irish with an English accent". He was christened Michael but his mother had him call himself Seán to others to sound more Irish – her choice of separateness over integration. On the other hand, he says, seemingly with cheerful realism and embryonic pride (the cheer and pride are in his rhythm and rhyme): "We grew up in Holloway, not Galway; played on the fields of Peckham Rye, not the fields of Athenry. The education, the environment, the TV and radio we experienced were all different". And he has a fond memory of the 2006 Summer School when one student in the pub afterwards expressed his Irish patriotism yet "was also very emotionally attached to the English football team who were playing Portugal in the World Cup. It was going badly and he was not happy... Tony Murray got everyone in that Irish bar in the heart of Holloway to cheer England on for perhaps the first time".

The tiny addendum that England lost on a penalty shoot-out is the joke one uses to cover up one's tears. For there is heartache involved. At the core of O'Donovan's article is the question trying to answer itself: "Is it now possible to remain very proud of being Irish but also begin to acknowledge that growing up in England may possibly have had a positive influence on our lives?" This is a step in a journey towards wholeness, it seems to me. There must be many Irish in Britain who love their lives in Britain; if so, it is a love that dare not speak its name. Literally: O'Donovan's "second-generation Irish" should actually read "first-generation English". In her Wikipedia entry, the comedian and actor Roisin Conaty is referred to as "Irish-English"; her parents met in London, having separately moved to England, and Conaty was born in Camden. On some sites she is referred to as British and I suspect that she is not offended. Daily life in childhood was in Camden, holidays were in Kerry; the difference as she recalls it was between bustling town and remote countryside, not between nationalities or cultures.

If I can risk impertinence, I suspect that Murray's defensiveness reflects the weight of a narrative that proscribes the words and epithets "English" and "British". Proscription prevents self-discovery and liberation from an impersonal and partisan Story (a story of unbridgeable difference and mutual hostility) that is far past its sell-by date. The *Daily Telegraph* economics columnist, Liam Halligan, is first-generation English from an Irish Catholic family. His defence in the 20 April, 2019 *Spectator* ("It's not anti-Irish to criticise Leo Varadkar") of his criticism of the Taoiseach for damaging Anglo-Irish relations by his attitude to Brexit, is a remarkable piece of writing. It may have economics at its heart, but it is also heartfelt. The Taoiseach's anti-English approach pained Halligan. "As someone who physically embodies the binding blood and cultural ties between Britain and Ireland, I'm regularly attacked in the Irish media for having voted to leave". He was supposed to revert to ethnic type and oppose Brexit on the simple grounds of anti-Britishness, not reflect his English upbringing, education, livelihood, and professional economic assessment of the UK's decision to leave the EU. "The fragility of relations between Britain and Ireland is hard-wired into me," Halligan writes. "Having grown up 'London-Irish' in the 1970s and 1980s, all I ever wanted was for the two countries that define my ethnicity to get on". O'Donovan's and Halligan's stories, yet to be fully told, are in their own way as moving as the stories of banished industrial schoolboys.

The proscription applies even more stringently to Irish emigrants in Britain and is aimed at preventing those emigrants from becoming British. The TV presenter Laura Whitmore found out that while the Irish can have successful lives in a tolerant Britain, they must still obey the dictates of the Irish Story. That Story installs the British armed forces as devils incarnate, and so when Whitmore appeared in a British Army podcast, interviewing a female soldier about body issues in a male-dominated occupation, she was tarred and feathered by Irish commentators in the social media for what amounts to treason against Irishness. Her crime was apparently made worse because she followed the interview with a tribute to John Hume who had just died and whose legacy, Whitmore's critics implied, could not permit fraternising with the enemy as Whitmore had just done. ("Laura Whitmore defends decision to appear in British Army podcast after backlash," *Evening Standard*, 6 August, 2020.) This century-old attempt to control the Diaspora is echoed by the Chinese Communist Party's attempt to do likewise in the West and which we rightly deplore. Except, of course, cultural reality and demography suggest that the middle-class and professional-class Irish in Britain are not a Diaspora at all, but simply compatriots across the water.

Having just published his third novel, and making his living by talking, Graham Norton, one might think, should be able to articulate the position of the successful Irish in England and set the matter to rights. But he wool-gathers and his language deteriorates when in *The Guardian* of 26 September, 2020 he is asked by Alex Clark: "What about the UK, his home for decades now?" His answer seems like displacement activity: "There's a lot of charity shops," he says of English small towns, "I know that. We're raising a lot of money for cancer. But see, that's an odd thing I'll do, where I'll say 'we're' raising a lot of money. And, and so I have *that* thing, because I've lived there since 1984; my career is there, my friends are there, I pay tax there, I vote there. And I work for the British Broadcasting Corporation." Graham, just answer the question. Instead, he retreats into pretending that in living inside a non-ethnic tribal bubble in England he isn't really living there. "So there is a sense where that's my tribe. Certainly I found a tribe that I can be part of in that country. And so, I've said this before, but it is that thing where I'm in London, I get on the plane, and I'm going home to Ireland. But when I leave here in September, I'm going home to London. And I think you can do that. I don't think we have to be policed that strictly." So who *are* these police? All clarity is evaded as he dances round "that thing" he daren't identify. He cannot simply say: "well, I am as English now as I'm Irish, living as I am the full British life, and that's perfectly understandable and indeed a rather marvellous privilege". That he was speaking from lockdown back in Cork would, of course, have triggered the self-policing more forcefully.

Why does all this matter, and matter to me? When I say that I believe it healthier for Ireland and the Irish to acknowledge and embrace the Irishness of Britain and the Britishness of Ireland, I am being simultaneously self-serving and altruistic. Altruistic because I have a stake in the welfare of Ireland having spent a lifetime in Irish Studies, having lived and loved over the years in Dublin, which I like better than I do Belfast, but cannot see what purpose is served by sequestering (or even denying outright) a huge portion of Irish historical and present reality and the energy and potential for individual and collective fulfilment involved therein. Brexit, alas, and now the coronavirus, have been exploited by some to reverse in the unspoken name of Little Ireland the amicable potential by the crying up of the differences between the islands. Yet just think of Irish-British relations in the most human, individual and family forms (lives entwined), think of all those living Irish (and dead generations of Irish) in Britain, and the differences shrink to very little.

If I am self-serving, it is because as a Northern Irishman who regards himself as both Irish and irrevocably British, I am offended by the hypocrisy of a political campaign to rescind my Britishness while the Republic of Ireland represses its own British dimension, at home and over the water. Let the Republic do its psychic work and unionists will do theirs, which involves accepting their Irish differences from the mainland British. I suspect, in fact, that many Southern Irish would be relieved by acknowledging, even celebrating, Britain and Ireland's intimate relations. But the Irish are held to ransom by state and Sinn Féin republicanism. A national superego forbids such acknowledgement, much less celebration. But historical and current reality should not be the captive of a political position. Fianna Fáil Senator Mark Daly wants to convene a New Ireland Forum 2 in order to dispel unionist fears of the inevitable united Ireland, fears that would hardly be allayed by the nationalist emblems with which his Senate office is awash, according to a recent profile. I suggest he convene instead, in what I regard as a prior task in every sense, a New Ireland Forum 2 to explore the intimate mutual relations between Ireland and Britain, relations which are no threat to Irish patriotism but are the proper starting-point for a search for final peace on these islands. Such a frank audit, with no one afraid of betraying shoneenism, would liberate energies and dynamics heretofore under taboo and embargo. Think of the diversity of occupation, career and talent that could form the panels and interviewees of such a forum!

Seven

We have to accept, though, that recent cultural developments have supervened to qualify the hope for candour about Irish-British relations. Brendan O'Neill, the editor of *Spiked*, has written about this in one of the most provocative pieces I have yet read on the Irish in Britain: "Bad Immigrants" (28 September 2018). Since he lives in England I assume he could provide case-studies to illustrate his claims. In any event, as a stimulating contrarian, he is refreshingly devoid of defensiveness, guilt, embarrassment, shame, or equivocation when writing as a first-generation Englishman.

During what he calls the second Irish exodus in the second half of the twentieth century (the first was the era of Sweeney's subjects), O'Neill's parents left "the unforgiving boglands of the west of Ireland as teenagers in 1968 and arrived in a Swinging London that perplexed them as much as it thrilled them". Even at that time, Irish immigrants on certain rungs of the social ladder could be regarded as bad immigrants for not fitting in, while being reminded one way or the other that they could never fit in because they were disliked. Yet O'Neill's parents surmounted all obstacles and never pleaded the poor mouth; they were simply newcomers who wished to succeed. The Irish migrants of the third wave arrived from the 1980s during an economically bleak period in the Republic, and many of them were different from their predecessors in being highly educated: by 1989, 30% of college graduates left Ireland. These formed the early NIPPLE cohort. Many flourished just as tensions between Ireland and Britain because of the Troubles were easing. "And yet here is the curious thing," writes O'Neill, "the new promise of accelerated assimilation, the removal of such blocks to assimilation as anti-Catholicism and fear of Irish republicanism, did not lead to a waning of Irish identity, but to the opposite – it coincided with an explosion of new and ever-more self-conscious and separatist expressions of Irish identitarianism in Britain". Something widespread is at work, including identity politics and the philosophy of multiculturalism. This, says O'Neill, has actively discouraged the Irish, and all the other hyphenated identities in Britain, from integrating in the way, and to the extent, that O'Neill's parents did.

O'Neill sees the active encouragement of difference, the cultivation and institutionalisation of diversity, the discouragement of integration – all at the expense of social cohesion, even coherence – as deplorable, leading to the emergence of "coexisting lifestyles – that is, of communal distinction". Western European societies "have abandoned the social project of assimilation" (itself now a taboo word) and have created the spectre "of socially sanctioned separateness" where immigrants are encouraged to think of themselves as victimised and hostile to their host nation. In the Irish case, O'Neill alleges, the new sense of separatism has taken on vivid expressions of Irish nationalism as the Irish in Britain have self-racialised during "the new Irish identitarianism" – being anti-British; Gaelicising their names and their children's names; assuming by historical proxy the status of victim, when they themselves are anything but.

O'Neill's article was a response to a hostile piece

in the *Guardian* that accused him of being a bad Irish immigrant because, unlike the bad immigrants of the past who wouldn't integrate, O'Neill *wishes* to integrate and "wants to feel part of [my host nation], in a real, grown-up way". The subtitle of his article is "I am Irish but I want to be British – is that bad?" So not only is the former encouragement by the host country to assimilate held to be right-wing, but the immigrants' voluntary *wish* to assimilate and embrace the values of their adopted home is just as bad, according to those who are not in any shape or form victims, such as *Guardian* columnists.

If O'Neill is correct about the younger Irish professionals in Britain, then a call for the Irish in Britain to acknowledge the Britishness of their lives, and the Irish in the Republic to acknowledge the British dimension of their own Irish lives, might fall on deaf ears on both sides of the Irish Sea. Nationalism is stronger in the Republic than it has been for decades and has reinforced the northern republican push for a united Ireland. If only those in the Republic could see that the momentous and oddly unremarked Common Travel Area (allowing free movement to and fro between two countries with a history of tension) remains an incipient centrifugal force for expansion, a possible blueprint and inspiration for a structural expression of British-Irish relations. An ideal polity would reflect intimate Irish–British relations. Anyway, deaf ears will not alter one whit the incontrovertible and potent reality of the Irish in Britain and cultural Britain among the Irish. There is no cultural and very little social rationale for the political campaign to separate Northern Ireland (with its huge component of Britishness) from the British Isles in order to create a larger Republic of Ireland. For that Republic will be (as far as the eye can see) in many ways culturally indistinct from the rest of the United Kingdom; distinct by assertion but in fact part of the same supranational cultural and social entity that is the British Isles. In 1941, George Orwell commended to his diary the German journalist Sebastian Haffner's description of the Republic as a "sham-independent country". (This was decades before Ireland willingly accepted the authority of Brussels over its economy and foreign policy, two criteria of sovereignty.) Orwell's diary was kept amid the tensions of the Second World War, hence perhaps his bitter responsiveness to what he thought was an accurate phrase alleging a national self-deception.

In the New York St Patrick's Day parade in 2019 Sinn Féin's Mary Lou McDonald helped hold up a large banner reading ENGLAND GET OUT OF IRELAND. It would be laughable if it weren't such a grim assault by an arthritic ideology on social reality.

Endnotes

1 An earlier version of this chapter appeared in the *Dublin Review of Books*.

The Road to and from Partition

Brian Barton

One

The partition of Ireland has been perceived as being the product of British imperialism. It has been alleged that Westminster politicians manufactured and fomented opposition to Irish self-government in Ulster, so ultimately enabling Britain to preserve its toe-hold in the northeast. Others have projected it as having been contrived by the region's semi-feudal aristocracy and commercial elite, who cynically exploited the prejudices and credulity of the tenantry and urban labour force to advance their own narrow class interests. Neither of these perspectives bears critical examination.

The Easter Rising and its repercussions during the seven turbulent years which followed largely determined the context for the genesis of Northern Ireland. It helped ensure that when in mid-June 1921 the leaders of the Unionist Party sought to establish a functioning government in Belfast they were confronted by problems which stretched their resources to the limit. Those planning rebellion at Easter gave little thought to the opposition to Irish independence in the northeast. Their priority was to proceed with the insurrection, and they regarded the Ulster question as an issue best dealt with later. They had, however, no doubt that the Irish nation was geographically, politically and culturally indivisible from the island of Ireland, and dismissed any notion that a majority in one region of the country had as much right to remain in the British state as they themselves had to secede from it. They characterized their political opponents as having been manipulated or duped into supporting Crown, Empire and Union, and assumed that they would eventually recognize their true Irish identity.

The Easter Rising helped radicalise, define and sanctify the goal of Irish nationalism as being a thirty-two county, independent republic, Gaelic in culture and Catholic in ethos. It also regenerated and legitimized the physical-force tradition as the means to attain it, and provided the precedent and inspiration for a violent, elitist minority to strike to achieve its vision of Ireland's future on which it would brook no compromise. In Pearse's words, "the national demand of Ireland is fixed and determined ... we have not the right to alter it." Connolly stated: "the British government has no right in Ireland ... and never can have."[1] After the insurrection Sinn Féin displaced the Irish Parliamentary Party and, at its *Ard Fheis* (October 1917), committed itself to using "every means available" to achieve an "independent Irish republic."[2] De Valera, its president, described this objective as "a monument to the brave men [of 1916]".[3]

During the December 1918 election, Sinn Féin offered voters the "path to national salvation" – a united Irish republic. De Valera asserted that it would complete this "holy task", so that the "Irish race" would be "permitted to build up the great nation which God intended it to be."[4] The Ulster question was projected as being due to the British presence in Ireland. It was blandly asserted that once independence was achieved the problem would resolve itself, but not by applying any principle of unionist consent. Arthur Griffith asserted that Unionists "must make up their minds to throw in their lot with the Irish nation [and, if not]… the Irish nation must deal with them." Likewise de Valera described the Protestants in the northeast as "planters", "an alien garrison", and stated: "Ulster must be coerced if she stood in the way."[5]

Sinn Féin was victorious in all but three of the constituencies in Leinster, Munster and Connacht, and it regarded this success as a mandate for an Irish republic. Discounting the result in Ulster, de Valera declaimed: "no people on earth ever agreed so overwhelmingly on a great issue."[6] On 21 January, 1919 the Party's successful candidates assembled as the First Dáil, and declared the establishment of a republic, claiming authority over the whole island. As with the Rising, the outbreak of the Anglo-Irish War was due to the "action of a small and unrepresentative minority."[7] Over the next two years, initially sporadic acts of violence escalated into a brutal pattern of terror, counter-terror and reprisal. In these unpromising circumstances Britain attempted a solution to the Irish question: the Government of Ireland Act (December 1920). Ireland was to be partitioned and two states established (six-county "Northern Ireland" and twenty-six county "Southern Ireland"), each with home rule powers. It was too little and too late for Irish nationalists, a dead letter outside the northeast, and brought no abatement in the conflict.

Eventually, the Anglo-Irish truce was agreed (11 July, 1921) and, after protracted negotiations, Sinn Féin and the British government signed the Anglo-Irish Treaty

(6 December, 1921). It fell short of the republic proclaimed in 1916 and reaffirmed by the Dáil, but it did provide for a substantially greater level of self-government than the 1920 Act.

The Treaty was divisive because it failed to provide for an independent republic but preserved the link with the Crown through an oath of allegiance. Nationalist leaders persisted in attributing partition to Britain's duplicity, inherent colonialism and nefarious influence. Lloyd George summarized Griffith's view as "Ulster would come in if we [Britain] let her alone", whilst de Valera asserted that "the difficulty is not the Ulster question. As far as we are concerned this is a fight between Ireland and England" (Lynch, *Revolutionary Ireland*, pp. 103–4). Neither they nor their supporters were willing or able to acknowledge the fact that it was the unionists in Ulster rather than politicians in Britain who were the real obstacle to them securing a thirty-two county Irish republic.

Ulster Unionism had emerged in the 1880s in opposition to the first home rule bill which would have established an all-Ireland parliament in Dublin. By 1900 it had become a strong, disciplined, cohesive movement, with a broad social base and was the most significant counter-revolutionary force in Irish political life. It faced its gravest challenge in 1912 when the Liberal administration introduced the third Home Rule bill, which seemed destined to pass through parliament. Initially its leaders organized protest rallies and demonstrations which illustrated the scale of their support. On "Covenant Day" (28 September, 1912) over 470,000 signatories of the Ulster Covenant swore that they were willing to use "all means … to defeat the present conspiracy to set up a Home Rule parliament in Ireland."[8] But their opposition was ignored, and the measure continued to progress through Westminster. A striking feature of northern unionism during these years was how the impulse towards greater militancy consistently came from the movement's rank and file. In 1912 they sought not just rhetoric but full-blooded armed resistance. RIC Special Branch reported that, by February, there were 12,000 loyalists drilling at 100 separate locations. This initiative forced its allegedly manipulative upper class leaders to become less cautious. On 13 December, they responded by setting up the Ulster Volunteer Force (UVF) and, fifteen months later when subjected to further grassroots pressure, they purchased 140 tons of rifles from Germany to arm it. By the summer of 1914, 90,000 men had enlisted in the UVF.

Unionism had grown naturally and spontaneously out of the soil of Ulster politics, but the effectiveness of its campaign was enhanced by having the sympathy and backing of vital elements in the British establishment. These included the Conservative Party, King George V, and the officer class within the army. By mid-1913 the Unionist leadership had become reconciled to the inevitability of Home Rule, and was arguing for a solution based on partition. Gradually the principle that special provision should be made for the northeast was becoming firmly established at Westminster. Thus, when the Home Rule bill was placed on the statute book (on 18 September, 1914), its operation was suspended until after the war had ended and Herbert Asquith, the Prime Minister, stated unequivocally that the coercion of Ulster was "absolutely unthinkable" (Buckland, p. 104). He indicated that he would introduce an amending bill before the Act was put into effect.

During the war the political position of northern Unionists became stronger. At Westminster, Asquith's ineffective leadership led to a coalition government being formed under Lloyd George in December 1916. He was dependent on Conservative Party support and its capacity to help its unionist allies increased with its powers. By then, however, it was doing so out of a sense of obligation – to honour past pledges – rather than current conviction; it no longer needed Ulster as a "patriotic issue which might help [it]... back into office." Earlier that year, unionists had viewed the Easter Rising "quite complacently, even gleefully" (Buckland, p. 105). In common with their erstwhile supporters in Britain they regarded it as a "stab in the back", struck when the nation was in grave peril. They could cite it as evidence of the perfidiousness of Irish nationalists, and contrast it with their own loyalty. In negotiations held after the insurrection, the terms Britain offered Carson were that Ireland would be granted home rule, but that the six northeastern counties would be excluded. The talks collapsed because the Irish Parliamentary Party insisted that this arrangement should last for no more than three to six years. Nonetheless, for the first time both sides had reached agreement over the area to be partitioned and on terms which foreshadowed those of the Government of Ireland Act. Historians agree that weeks later unionists attained a "new credibility within British political life" (Bew, p. 382) as a consequence of the collective sacrifice made by the 36th (Ulster) Division at the Battle of the Somme (1–2 July, 1916), It has been claimed that thereafter "no British government would ever force [them] ... to accept Dublin rule" (Buckland, p. 104).

The Government of Ireland Act (December 1920)

reflected the broad consensus on the Irish question that had gradually emerged amongst politicians in Britain. Lloyd George considered that in partitioning Ireland and making provision for the establishment of parliaments in Belfast and Dublin, he was honouring past imperial commitments to unionists. He also believed that the arrangement would assuage northern nationalists who, he assumed, would resent direct rule from London more than being governed by their fellow-countrymen. Moreover, he wished to avoid giving any impression that Britain was ruling the northern minority against its will, or was actively supporting unionists in their refusal to unite with the south. In addition, the Act would enable Westminster to disengage from Irish affairs, while protecting its vital interests. Though Unionist MPs abstained from voting on the bill, they accepted it as the most favourable they were likely to be offered. Its provisions recognized the reality of the political divisions in Ireland and embedded in it was the principle of unionist consent to unity. Moreover it would provide them with greater security than continued direct rule from Westminster. They distrusted the Labour Party, which in the 1918 election had demanded self-determination for "all subject peoples within the British Commonwealth" (Lynch, *Partition of Ireland*, p. 41), and were aware that the Conservatives had lost much of their earlier enthusiasm for the unionist cause. To ensure that the incipient institutions were more amenable to Unionist Party control, its MPs amended the measure in parliament, reducing the partitioned area from the nine counties it proposed to six, and ensuring that the senate precisely reflected the relative strength of the political parties in the lower house.

The Act came into operation on 3 May, 1921, and elections for the fifty-two seats in the new House of Commons in Belfast were held on 24 May. All forty Unionist candidates were successful, winning a 67% share of the poll. Sir James Craig, who had succeeded Sir Edward Carson as Party leader in January, 1921, became the state's first premier. In his speech at the opening of the Northern Ireland parliament (22 June), King George V implored Irishmen to "stretch out the hand of forbearance and conciliation, to forgive and forget".[9] It was followed by the Anglo-Irish truce (11 July) and the end of the Anglo-Irish war. There seemed grounds for optimism. In his public statements Craig stated that he would "look to the people as a whole" and be "absolutely fair"[10], and he appealed for cooperation and friendship with Southern Ireland. Guided by Westminster it seemed possible that his intentions and aspirations would be realized. He assumed that Britain regarded the new institutions as being sacrosanct, as he did.

Two

It soon became evident that this was not to be the case. When the 1920 Act was being passed, Lloyd George's hope was that the two incipient Irish states would remain closely bound to Britain and would eventually unite. Thus, under its terms, additional "reserved" powers were to be transferred to them if their institutions merged. A Council of Ireland was to be formed to discuss matters of common concern "with a view to the eventual establishment of a parliament for the whole of Ireland" and it also envisaged the appointment of a Lord Lieutenant to represent the Crown throughout all thirty-two counties.[11] The measure was therefore "slanted towards Irish unity" (Follis, p. 186). For more perceptive unionists, the content of George V's speech on 22 June, 1921 might have provided grounds for concern. In it he referred repeatedly to the "six counties" rather than "Northern Ireland"; this calculated ambiguity in itself might have seemed to imply a lack of commitment in Britain to the new state. Also, his powerful appeal for reconciliation in Ireland was a clear indication that ending the Anglo-Irish War and reaching agreement with Sinn Féin were his government's priority; in Westminster's pursuit of this, Northern Ireland's institutions were regarded as dispensable.

Northern Ireland's first two years were formative. Craig's inexperienced ministers had found it difficult to reach an accommodation with John Redmond's constitutionalist Parliamentary Party. They were now confronted by Sinn Féin with its uncompromising nationalist objectives, and militant republican elements. They had dismissed the terms of the Government of Ireland Act and, as a consequence, the Council of Ireland was stillborn. They regarded partition as unnatural, reversible and due to Britain's nefarious influence; they did not accept the legitimacy of unionist opposition to unity; they refused to recognise the Belfast parliament and increasingly focused on destabilizing and overthrowing the northern state.

The feelings of optimism and expectation shared by unionists in May and June 1921 had been replaced by a deepening sense of betrayal, disillusionment and vulnerability. After the Anglo-Irish truce in July 1921, they feared that the IRA would launch a full-scale campaign in the north. They also deeply distrusted the Westminster government, which was then entering into negotiations with Sinn Féin. During these, even Conservative members of Lloyd George's delegation urged Craig to accept the sovereignty of an all-Ireland parliament in order to secure a settlement and for the sake of the Empire. Meanwhile, so as not to prejudice their outcome, British ministers refused to transfer any of the powers provided for in the 1920 Act to the Belfast parliament. Thus, until 22 November, 1921, the Northern Ireland cabinet was impotent, "a glorified pressure group" (Follis, pp. 55–6); tensions rose, there were recurring outbreaks of rioting in Belfast, and membership of Protestant paramilitary organizations soared, reaching 21,000 by October.

Political uncertainty and economic recession fomented traditional sectarian tensions. But the decisive factor was the deterioration in north-south relations. Craig's government had sought cooperation with the Dublin leadership. On 23 June, 1921 the Belfast parliament had elected thirteen MPs to serve on the Council of Ireland and, with reference to it, he told the House: "the only way they [Sinn Féin] can ever hope to secure Ulster is by winning her, by starting upon a path such as we have begun to tread, the end of which is happiness, prosperity and peace throughout the length and breadth of the land.'[12] This path was not taken. Michael Collins was recognized by the British government as spokesperson for northern nationalists, and also by the latter themselves. He employed a range of strategies with the intention of undermining the northern state: he impeded the transfer of civil servants and government records from Dublin to Belfast; he launched a propaganda campaign alleging that northern Catholics were being brutally repressed and encouraged them not to acknowledge or cooperate with the Belfast parliament. He also covertly sponsored and orchestrated an IRA campaign which gathered pace from January 1922, aimed at causing such mayhem and instability in the northern state as to make it ungovernable.

Given the unreliable nature of the support it was receiving from Westminster, the Northern Ireland government responded by expanding the security forces under its control and by extending its emergency powers. Its objective was to be in a position to cope independently of London with any internal threat or disorder short of southern invasion. Its three priorities were: "the safety of Ulster", "to maintain the confidence of our people" and "to bring the British government with us". It was vital to retain Westminster's sympathy and goodwill as it remained the irreplaceable source of funds, of troops if required and ultimately of power.[13] Craig also recognized that Northern Ireland could not single-handedly survive a "campaign of atrocity" with the south and feared Westminster might "wash their hands of the whole affair". He therefore rejected calls for the imposition of martial law as he considered that in England this would suggest that one side was as bad as the other. In early 1922, however, the number of Special Constables was increased, and on 7 April, 1922 the Civil Authorities (Special Powers) Act (Northern Ireland) became law. This was less far-reaching than its predecessor, the Restoration of Order in Ireland Act, 1920, but nevertheless empowered the Ministry of Home Affairs "to take all such steps… as may be necessary for preserving the peace and maintaining order".[14]

In London these initiatives were regarded with unease, especially the expansion of the Special Constabulary. But no alternative policy was open to Craig. The twenty or so battalions of troops then based in the province had been relegated to a minor peacekeeping role. Lloyd George hesitated to deploy them in Belfast or on the border, fearing that this might result in Collins refusing to implement the treaty, and that it could lead to a renewal of the Anglo-Irish war. Moreover he wished to avoid giving any impression that partition was being militarily imposed.

The level of violence in the six counties peaked during May-June 1922. By then, the two Irish states were "to all intents and purposes openly at war" (Follis, p. 93). On 14 April anti-Treaty forces had seized the Four Courts in Dublin and, as a result, civil conflict in the south seemed imminent. Desperate to avoid this outcome, Collins launched a "shared crusade" (Lynch, *Northern IRA*, p. 126) aimed at crushing Northern Ireland; the eradication of partition was the one issue on which all republicans were agreed. An "Army of the North" was formed, pro- and anti-Treaty IRA units combining with the northern divisions in an all-out offensive to achieve Irish unity. In May, over 600 violent incidents were recorded in the six counties.

Law and order was, however, gradually restored, in large part due to the security measures taken by the Northern Ireland government. The outbreak of civil war in southern Ireland in June also helped. After it had begun, Collins ordered that IRA members "'cease all operations in the six counties' and that 'no troops from the 26 counties... should be permitted to invade'" the area (Lynch, *Northern IRA*, pp. 187, 189). After his assassination on 22 August his successor, W.T. Cosgrave, abandoned his policy of destabilizing Northern Ireland; his priority was the implementation of the treaty. Largely as a consequence of these developments the northern IRA's campaign disintegrated.

The Free State came into existence on 6 December, 1922, and next day the Belfast parliament opted out of its jurisdiction. While Westminster retained sovereignty over Northern Ireland, it continued to be an unreliable partner. Norman Brooke, when Britain's cabinet secretary, stated that during the inter-war years "all political parties" were "able to take the line over partition that there is nothing they would like better than to see a united Ireland".[15] The British government was, in David Harkness' phrase, "often careless of [Northern Ireland's] ... condition" (Follis, p. 182). As a result of the Treasury's niggardliness, during the 1920s and 1930s, Northern Ireland's social services lagged far behind those elsewhere in the United Kingdom, and for most of this period roughly one-quarter of its workforce was unemployed. It took the Second World War to transform the attitude of British ministers towards the region.

The role of the British government in dividing Ireland has been much misunderstood by nationalists who depict the division as a callous imposition. In fact, partition was not the product of self-interested politicians at Westminster. Nor, for that matter, was it the product of unscrupulous class manipulation by Ulster business leaders and landed aristocrats. Rather, it was the institutional recognition of deep-rooted political, cultural and religious divisions in Ireland. These were acknowledged by an unlikely source in a letter to the *Freeman's Journal* (19 July, 1916), once Ireland's leading daily nationalist newspaper. It was submitted by the Rev. M. O'Flanaghan, CC, then secretary of Sinn Féin. He wrote: "Geography has worked hard to make one nation of Ireland. History has worked against it. The island of Ireland, and the national unity of Ireland, simply do not coincide... The test of separate identity is the wish of the people... The unionists of Ulster have never given their love and allegiance to Ireland. They love the hills of Antrim and Down in the same way that we love the plains of Roscommon, but the centre of their patriotic enthusiasm is London ... as ours is Dublin. We claim the right to decide what is our nation. We refuse that same right to Orangemen ... Are we going ... to compel the Orangemen of Antrim and Down to love us by force?"

Endnotes

1 Ruth Dudley Edwards, *The Seven: The Lives and Legacies of the Founding Fathers of the Irish Republic* (London: Oneworld, 2017), pp. 371, 367.

2 Joseph M. Curran, *The Birth of the Irish Free State* (Alabama: University of Alabama, 1980), pp. 17–18.

3 Fearghal McGarry, *The Rising: Ireland, Easter 1916* (Oxford: Oxford University Press, 2010), p. 286.

4 Robert Lynch, *The Partition of Ireland, 1918–1925* (Cambridge: Cambridge University Press, 2019), pp. 41, 46.

5 Griffith and de Valera quoted in Robert Lynch, *Revolutionary Ireland, 1912–25* (London: Bloomsbury, 2015), p. 58.

6 John Bowman, *De Valera and the Ulster Question, 1917–1973* (Oxford: Clarendon Press, 1982), p. 40.

7 Paul Bew, *Ireland and the Politics of Enmity, 1798–2006* (Oxford: Oxford University Press, 2007), p. 395.

8 Patrick Buckland, *Irish Unionism: Ulster Unionism and the Origins of Northern Ireland* (Dublin: Gill and Macmillan, 1973), pp. 55–56.

9 Bryan A. Follis, *A State under Siege: The Establishment of Northern Ireland, 1920–25* (Oxford: Clarendon Press, 1995), p. 50.

10 *Belfast Telegraph*, 24 December 1920; 23 June 1921, *Hansard NI (Commons) i*, cols. 36–37.

11 Michael Laffan, *Judging W.T. Cosgrave* (Dublin: Royal Irish Academy, 2014), p. 198.

12 Speech by Craig, 29 November 1921, *Official Report of Debates, Commons, vol. I,* col. 297.

13 Brian Barton, "Northern Ireland, 1920–25" in *A New History of Ireland VII*, edited by J.R. Hill (Oxford: Oxford University Press, 2003), p. 172.

14 Robert Lynch, *The Northern IRA and the Early Years of Partition, 1920–1922* (Dublin: Irish Academic Press, 2006), p. 223.

15 Quoted in Brian Barton, "Relations between Westminster and Stormont during the Attlee Premiership," in *Irish Political Studies*, vol. 7 (1992), p. 12.

Ulster Unionism and Irish Nationalism

Patrick J. Roche and Brian Barton

Ulster unionism emerged in the 1880s in opposition to the first Home Rule bill, which would have established an all-Ireland parliament in Dublin.[1] By 1900 it had become a strong, united mass movement with a broad social base. It faced its gravest challenge in 1912 when Herbert Asquith's Liberal administration introduced a further measure (the third Home Rule bill) granting all thirty-two counties self-government; this seemed certain to pass through Westminster as the House of Lords had lost its power of veto the previous year. Initially unionist leaders reacted by organizing protest rallies and demonstrations, including Covenant Day (28 September 1912). But the prime minister ignored their opposition and, meanwhile, his legislation continued to make steady, un-amended progress through Westminster. In December 1912, unionist leaders responded by recruiting a paramilitary force, the Ulster Volunteer Force, and proceeded to arm it (Larne gun-running, 24–5 March 1914). The impact of their campaign was enhanced by having the sympathy and backing of the Conservative Party and of other elements within the British establishment. These included King George V, and also the officer class within the British army (illustrated by the Curragh Mutiny, 20 March 1914).

Gradually the principle that special provision should be made for Ulster became firmly established at Westminster. By mid-1913 both Ulster unionists and Conservatives had become reconciled to the inevitability of Home Rule, and were arguing for a solution based on partition. But, in mid-1914, an all-party conference of British and Irish leaders held at Buckingham Palace (21–24 July 1914) ended in failure, unable to reach agreement on the area to be excluded. Civil war seemed inevitable. That this outcome was avoided was due to the outbreak of the First World War, after which the unionist leader Sir Edward Carson and the nationalist leader John Redmond agreed to support Britain's war effort. On 18 September 1914 the Home Rule bill was placed on the statute book but its operation was suspended until the end of hostilities. At the time Asquith stated unequivocally that the coercion of Ulster was "absolutely unthinkable", and that he would introduce an amending bill before the Act was put into effect.

During the First World War the political position of Ulster unionists became stronger. In common with influential opinion in Britain, they regarded the Easter Rising (24–29 April 1916) as an act of treachery and treason in contrast with their own loyalty and fidelity. Months later they could, with justification, assert that they had demonstrated their probity and constancy. In 1914 the War Office had formed the 36th (Ulster) Division specifically to encourage UVF members to enlist in the armed forces. On 1–2 July, the first two days of the Battle of the Somme, the division sustained 5,500 casualties. Historians agree that as a consequence of their collective sacrifice, unionists attained a new credibility within British political life.

Though unionist MPs abstained from voting as the bill passed through the Commons, they considered that it was the most favourable they were likely to be offered. After all, its provisions recognized the reality of the bitter divisions in Ireland, they were based on the principle of unionist consent to unity, and they would provide them with greater security than direct rule from Westminster.

Northern unionists had never sought self-governing institutions or the establishment of a parliament in Belfast modelled on Westminster. They have never claimed to be a separate nation. From the outset they supported the Union for a variety of rational and valid reasons. They felt an instinctive loyalty towards Britain, the nation into which they and their ancestors had been born and which, in their view, embodied civil and political liberty. They valued the security of belonging to its Protestant majority. They shared an acute sense of being different from Ireland's nationalist population not only in religion, but in ethnic origins, culture and political aspirations. They feared that home rule would result in "Rome rule", a state in which the Catholic Church would exercise pervasive political and social influence, and they would experience religious discrimination and exclusion from public life. They were also convinced that the region's rapid economic growth was dependent on continued access to Britain's markets, raw materials, capital, skilled labour, and entrepreneurs; early twentieth-century Belfast was the most rapidly growing city in the British Isles. Unionists accepted the 1920 Government of Ireland Act because it recognized the distinctive entity of the northeast, and their democratic right to remain within the Union.

Irish nationalists have never understood the nature of unionism. Despite the North's distinctive characteristics, they claim that the Irish "nation" is indivisible from the island of Ireland, the "national territory", and are/were unwilling to concede that a majority in one region has as much right to remain in the British state as they had to separate from it. They have held various, often incompatible, viewpoints regarding unionism. To some, the area they disparagingly described as the "black north" long before partition, was like a creeping disease, alien, Anglicized, materialistic, corrupting and degraded. During 1912–14 unionists were widely dismissed as "bluffers" who, despite their rhetoric, would eventually recognize the futility of opposing Irish independence. They were also depicted as having been duped into supporting the Union by conservatives in Britain, or the local commercial elite and aristocracy, and it was assumed that they would eventually recognize their true Irish identity. Both these presumptions still prevail. Conversely, before the Great War, unionists were projected as being a "splendid example" for Irish nationalism because they had "led the way" in opposing Westminster legislation. Irish nationalists have never been either willing or able to recognize the integrity and validity of the unionist commitment to the Union and the consequent strength of unionist opposition to Irish unity. This ideological blindness on their part lies at the root of their long-term focus on the persuasive role of English or at times United States politicians and, on the part of republicans, their commitment to the ultimate legitimacy of the persuasion that comes through the "barrel of a gun" which underpinned the three decades of IRA/Sinn Féin terrorism post-1969.

During the 1918–23 period Sinn Féin was the dominant nationalist party. Entirely lacking a coherent policy towards the North, it projected the Ulster question and partition as being due to the British presence in Ireland, its duplicity and colonialism, and Arthur Griffith argued during the Treaty negotiations that "if England would stand aside, there would be no difficulty". It rejected the principle of unionist consent to unity; Éamon de Valera stated that "Ulster must be coerced if she stood in the way".[2] It regarded the creation of the Northern Ireland state as being unnatural and reversible, refused to engage with the Government of Ireland Act (the Council of Ireland was therefore stillborn), was unwilling to recognize the Belfast parliament, increasingly focused its energies on the north and deployed every means available to destabilize and overthrow it. A vital additional motivation for Michael Collins' intervention in the north was his determination to arrest the deepening split in the south over the treaty by diverting attention to the perceived iniquity of partition.

Collins adopted various strategies to undermine the Northern Ireland government, including non-cooperation and propaganda, and encouraging the northern minority not to recognize or cooperate with its institutions. Above all, in early 1922, he covertly sponsored and orchestrated an IRA campaign aimed at making Northern Ireland ungovernable. Sinn Féin's negative and belligerent attitude largely dictated the Catholic minority's level of engagement with the newly formed state. Its members increasingly supported the IRA's campaign, 1921–2, adopted a strategy of passive resistance and civil disobedience towards Craig's government, and of abstentionism by their elected representatives; public bodies which they controlled pledged allegiance to Dail Eireann. The failure of northern nationalists to recognize Northern Ireland, 1921–22 "robbed them of any say in the future shape of its institutions or political culture", writes Robert Lynch in *The Northern IRA* (2006), p. 210, reinforced their feelings of alienation, and reaffirmed the unionist sense of being under siege. Ulster unionists undoubtedly had a siege mentality but there were also besiegers.

Ulster unionist opposition to inclusion in an all-Ireland state was fully vindicated by the policies adopted by the Dublin government. From the outset W.T. Cosgrave, President of the Irish Free State's Executive Council strove to bring about the "Gaelicization … of our whole culture"; Irish was declared to be the national language of the Free State in its 1922 constitution. De Valera said repeatedly that its "restoration" was a "more urgent national issue than partition"; he was convinced that "Irish nationality would wither if [its] … revival failed". The southern leaders also set about constructing a confessional Catholic state. Cosgrave's government and its successors farmed out core civil responsibilities to the Church, particularly in health and education. It was a policy which its current Taoiseach has had good reason deeply to regret. In his 1937 constitution, de Valera endowed the Catholic Church with a "special position" (Article 44), though fully aware that this would hinder Irish unity. Moreover, Catholic moral values were all-pervasive: divorce was not permitted, birth control outlawed, literature advocating contraception banned, and films and books censored. In the words of Michael Laffan (*Judging W.T. Cosgrave*, 2014) this rendered "independent Ireland an object of international ridicule for the next forty years". A number of its other policies were equally anathema to unionists; it precipitated a trade war with Britain, 1932–38, and it adopted a position of neutrality during the Second World War.

Furthermore, between 1919–23, Protestants in the South were subjected to intimidation, vicious attacks, sectarian murder (as in the Bandon Valley, April 1922) and the burning of big houses. All of this resulted in an accelerating exodus of up to 48,000 Protestants between 1911 and 1926. Those who opted to remain post-independence had to endure further violent outrages in 1935: legislation intended to create a theocratic state; the *Ne Temere* decree which applied the Church's canon law to mixed marriages, and the compulsory learning of Irish throughout the school system. They were enclosed within a society dominated by a nationalist understanding of history, and in which there was an identification of being authentically Irish with being Catholic. Arguably, despite the recent modernization of the state, a residual latent Anglophobia has remained, and was evidenced by the stance taken over Brexit by the Varadkar-led, Fine Gael government in 2019.

Despite pursuing these policies, the South continued to assert its unabated claim to jurisdiction over the six counties; this was enshrined in Articles 2 and 3 of its 1937 constitution. It has continued to regard partition as reversible, generally encouraged the northern minority not to cooperate with the Northern state, and persisted in adhering to "the deeply flawed dogma … that Unionists could be coerced into unity". De Valera considered that in time unity was inevitable and favoured a policy of non-cooperation with Northern Ireland. According to John Bowman in *De Valera and the Ulster Question* (1982), de Valera's "fixed view" was that the partition problem could only be solved in the "larger general play of English interest" (pp. 302–3); he hoped that the Westminster government would commit itself to the unification of Ireland, a perspective sustained by his successors up to the Good Friday Agreement. Robert Lynch in *The Northern IRA* (2006) claims that southern politicians have consistently failed to "confront the realities of partition" or recognize and accept the depth and intensity of the sense of British identity shared by unionists. They have blamed Britain for their continuing failure to achieve unity, rather than work constructively to resolve the widening gulf between north and south.

Northern Ireland pioneered devolution in the UK, though this has never properly been acknowledged in accounts of Britain's constitutional and political development. Its image has been tarnished by northern nationalist allegations of discrimination. These were politically significant because they were widely accepted internationally, so that the cause of violence post-1969 was attributed solely to unionist sectarianism. But this entirely ignores the sectarian outlook and inflexibility of many Catholic leaders and politicians, a legacy of their negative view of the state from the outset: their abstention from the regional parliament until 1925, their unblinking focus on the constitutional issue until the 1960s, and the extreme views expressed by those with influence within the northern minority such as Cardinal Joseph MacRory (1861–1945), Archbishop of Armagh. Their persistent demand for Irish unity has generated and nourished a culture of grievance, a MOPE mentality.[3] It is noteworthy that investigations into devolution written before the "Troubles" are more measured and favourable than those produced after they began. A negative view of the northern state was facilitated by the intellectual inability of unionists to counter effectively nationalist aspersions and by the highly pejorative treatment unionism has historically received. The result was that a broad consensus emerged in London and Dublin that majority-based government was not appropriate for Northern Ireland, and this helped determine the nature of the mandatory, power-sharing institutions required by the 1998 Belfast Agreement.

This negative image of the Northern Ireland state is in large part a distortion of reality. All of the citizens in the region benefited from being in the Union, as unionists always claimed they would, and allegations of discrimination have been grossly exaggerated. For example, post-1921, James Craig, first Prime Minister of Northern Ireland, maintained the same social security provision and welfare payments as in Britain; this was an objective only made feasible because of the financial settlements reached with London. Craig justified these arrangements by arguing that the north had a legitimate claim to its share of the UK's pool of resources because its citizens paid the same taxes at the same rates as elsewhere. His policy also affirmed the region's place in the Union, bound it more closely to the UK and avoided any risk of disaffecting his working class supporters. His government was practising what unionists had long argued regarding the advantages of British citizenship – that UK rights and privileges would apply equitably to all. This "step by step" approach is not open to charges of discrimination as the benefits claimed were available equally to all.

With regard to education, minority allegations of discrimination are weakened by the unconstructive role played by the Catholic Church, notably its refusal to engage in the creation of a new educational system and its uncompromising insistence that it should run its own schools. Despite this, Catholic schools were treated generously – to the extent that education was never adopted as a civil rights issue. Again, in relation to public housing allocation, exhaustive analysis of the relevant statistical data indicates that, contrary to the claims routinely made, "Catholics were over-represented, not under-represented, in social housing at the end of the unionist regime in 1971" (see Gudgin in this volume). The Housing Trust built almost 50,000 dwellings between 1945 and 1971, and was scrupulously impartial. Likewise, the twin basis of allegations of anti-Catholic discrimination regarding employment have been effectively undermined: firstly, the suggestion that a persistent high Catholic/Protestant unemployment ratio is "proof" of discrimination and, secondly, the assertion made in the New Ireland Forum Report (1984) that regional patterns of Catholic/Protestant employment indicate Catholics were "deprived of the means of social and economic development". It is certainly arguable that unionists failed to "take what opportunities they had to bring the nationalists into the political system and to reform the outmoded system of local government". But, whatever the level of discrimination that existed in Northern Ireland, to quote the autobiography of Patrick Shea, *Voices and the Sound of Drums* (1981), it provided "no moral justification for violence or the threat of violence for political ends in Ireland". (The IRA campaign, 1969–

94, caused 3,518 deaths; 59% of them were inflicted by republicans, and fewer than 15% resulted in criminal convictions).

But these considerations have not restrained the leadership and fellow travellers of the republican movement from their pursuit of, in effect, a total re-writing of the history of the conflict. This has a dual objective: the exoneration of the IRA and the focusing of blame on the security forces and the British state. It has been aimed at the glorification of republican violence and at obscuring the fact that IRA terrorism was both a political and military failure. It failed to achieve its stated objective, to secure an all-Ireland "democratic and socialist republic", and it was also militarily defeated. The moral culpability of the leadership and the activists in the IRA, whose members conducted their thirty-year campaign with callous brutality, must not be buried in oblivion in a distorted, airbrushed historical narrative. To do so would amount to a factual and moral perversion of history, and the effacing from history of the suffering of thousands of innocent victims of republican terrorism.

Endnotes

1 The chapter is a summary perspective on Patrick J. Roche and
  Brian Barton (eds), *The Northern Ireland Question: Perspectives on
  Nationalism and Unionism* (Tunbridge Wells: Wordzworth, 2020).

2 Both quotes can be found in Robert Lynch, *Revolutionary Ireland,
  1912–25* (London: Bloomsbury, 2015), p.58.

3 Most Oppressed People Ever, an acronym coined by the Irish
  economic historian, Liam Kennedy.

The British State
and Ulster Unionism:
Case-Studies in Betrayal

William Beattie Smith

Introduction

Lord Trimble – who negotiated the 1998 Belfast Agreement on behalf of unionism – says that the British government betrayed him by signing up for the Northern Ireland Protocol, changing Northern Ireland's constitutional status without consent.

Unionists' experience of British betrayal is as old as unionism, and its history could fill volumes. So I have picked out for analysis two policy decisions taken at a critical period in Northern Ireland's recent history to explore whether Britain failed in its duties as a responsible national government, or whether unionists' expectations were unrealistic.

Unionists tend to assume that their loyalty to the Union should be reciprocated with equal conviction. But it never has been. Randolph Churchill penned the battle cry "Ulster will fight and Ulster will be right", but his son Winston served in the government which legislated for two Home Rule parliaments and a Council of Ireland "with a view to the eventual establishment of a Parliament of the whole of Ireland".

Britain and Ireland agreed on partition by international treaty in December 1921. It was a compromise which Irish unionists reluctantly accepted for the sake of peace. They sacrificed their stake in 26 counties in return for control over six of the nine counties of Ulster. Here they consolidated the new administration (Stormont) and developed a distinctive party political system, separate from Britain's.

There was no longer a dispute requiring British intervention, and London developed the convention that it should not interfere in devolved matters. Dublin went on to declare full sovereignty as the Republic of Ireland, and to claim the entire island as its national territory —a claim baseless in international law.

The Unionist government used the "special powers" inherited from the British to protect its border and prevent insurrection, creating the Ulster Special Constabulary to reinforce the regular police when necessary. It successfully suppressed violent IRA cross-border campaigns in the 1920s and again in the 1950s. It had no desire to take territory from the south, and its people shared equally in the benefits of the UK welfare state.

Five decades of stability ended in 1968. Over the following five years, and in response to demands from nationalist Ireland, Britain stripped Stormont of control over security and then suspended the devolved government altogether, replacing it with the colonial system of direct rule.

The British enjoyed sovereignty, powerful security forces, superior material resources, and international influence: so why did they sacrifice the long-established devolved government with so little resistance? Were they actively trying to push Northern Ireland into the Republic, or focused on higher priorities in the national interest?

The transfer of security

Harold Wilson, Labour prime minister from October 1964 to June 1970, made no secret of his sympathy for the Irish nationalist position. He wrote an open letter of support to the organisers of the "civil rights" campaign in 1964 and called for a dialogue with Dublin on Ireland's future. In 1966 he even suggested that Northern Ireland's MPs should be removed from Westminster and their functions transferred to a north/south parliamentary committee.

Wilson had two political motives. His constituency (Huyton in Liverpool) had a high proportion of Irish voters; and he resented the fact that the twelve Unionist MPs at Westminster voted with the Conservatives on issues which did not concern Northern Ireland. In January 1967, he threatened Unionist leader Terence O'Neill that unless the Unionists stopped interfering in Britain's affairs, his backbenchers would insist on interfering in Stormont's.

The Unionists did not stop, and Westminster did intervene. In response to a breakdown in policing during prolonged intercommunal rioting in August 1969, Wilson sent 6,000 soldiers to restore order. This gave him a locus from which to undermine Stormont. He personally drafted the Downing Street Declaration (ostensibly issued jointly with Stormont) setting out the new dispensation. On top of the reforms in local government and housing demanded by the campaigners, he stripped Stormont of its security powers, transferring control over operations to the British General Officer Commanding.

The responsible minister, Home Secretary Jim Callaghan, commissioned the Hunt Report which provided a fig leaf for disarming the Royal Ulster Constabulary and disbanding the USC, which Wilson described as the Unionists' "private army". Stormont's future now depended on British soldiers operating under the political direction of an unfriendly national government. Wilson also assigned officials to Belfast (UK Representative or UKREP) to oversee the reform process. As recorded in the diaries of his cabinet colleague, Barbara Castle, Wilson depicted Britain's role not as upholding Northern Ireland's constitutional status but as holding the ring between two fighting factions: "...we were not going to underwrite a reactionary government.... We must keep firmly in the middle of the road" (*The Castle Diaries 1964–1970*, 1984, p.700).

Did Wilson have options? Yes. In August 1969, Northern Ireland's prime minister, James Chichester-Clark, had asked Callaghan for police or army reinforcements. British police forces and unions were reluctant to go, so Callaghan took the easier option of sending soldiers. Home Office doctrine agreed with Stormont that the role of the military should be to act in aid of the civil authority to merely reinforce the police. Wilson's colleagues warned him that breaching this principle by taking control over security policies would undermine Chichester-Clark, provoke unionist "hardliners", and encourage republican dissidents. Callaghan himself tried to constrain Wilson, and as recorded in the diaries of fellow minister Richard Crossman, defence secretary Denis Healey complained about the prime minister's "crazy desire to go out there and take things over" (*Diaries of a Cabinet Minister*, 1977, p. 478). But Wilson overruled them.

Did Wilson act under pressure from his backbenchers? Yes and no. By June 1965, sixty Labour MPs had come together as the Campaign for Democracy in Ulster, mirroring a civic organisation rooted in Irish immigrant communities across England. The CDU gained momentum after the general election of March 1966, when Gerry Fitt joined them as republican socialist MP for Belfast West. Together they recognised the potential for combining street theatre with parliamentary tactics. When the protests first turned to violence in October 1968, CDU MPs positioned themselves in the front row, up against the police lines. Fitt's biographer, Michael Murphy, records republican activist Bernadette Devlin saying, "Gerry stuck his head under a police baton" (*Gerry Fitt – Political Chameleon*, 1977, p. 120). The CDU prepared a report for Wilson, asserting that the police had attacked unarmed demonstrators without provocation, and pressed him to take control of the RUC. Helped by sympathetic media coverage, the CDU had placed Northern Ireland on the national political agenda. The backbench pressure was real, but Wilson helped to create it and then used it to overturn the *laissez-faire* doctrine of the Home Office and Stormont.

If Wilson and his most influential ministers all favoured Irish unification, why did they not pursue it more proactively? Because it was a long-term goal and they recognised that it would be counter-productive to say so in public. But in September 1969 Wilson commissioned a confidential report from officials on removing obstacles to Irish unification. According to papers in the UK National Archives, the British Ambassador in Dublin reported on a conversation with the Taoiseach (Jack Lynch), who conceded that the Republic would be "quite incapable" of taking over the north for the foreseeable future: the necessary preparations could take up to 15 years. (CAB 130/422, *Interview with Taoiseach*, 17 September 1969).

Internment

My second example of betrayal was by the Conservative and Unionist government of Ted Heath. Disorder morphed from street protest towards armed insurgency during 1970 as two IRA factions (Provisionals and Officials) emerged, each capable of sustaining a concerted campaign of terrorist violence. Britain's priority shifted from reform to coercion, a military-led approach to security which began with curfews and mass house searches in republican neighbourhoods, moved through the internment of suspected republican activists in August 1971, and culminated in the "Bloody Sunday" killings.

The Conservatives replaced Labour in July 1970. Ted Heath became Prime Minister, Reginald Maudling Home Secretary. Responding to a request from Chichester-Clark, Maudling agreed to soften the public impression that "the army sat above the devolved government". For a few months it appeared to unionists as if the tide had turned and that the British government was now serious about tackling its republican enemies. But tensions persisted: unionists complained that the Army was too soft, permitting the IRA to operate with impunity from "no-go areas". Sandwiched between pressure from "hardliners" in his own party to take tougher measures and UK ministers who refused to agree, Chichester-Clark resigned. Brian Faulkner – more energetic and competent – replaced him.

As IRA attacks worsened in 1971, the Unionist Party fragmented. In attempting to reduce popular support for "hardliners" (Ian Paisley, William Craig), London let the army apply coercive measures derived from its experience in colonial counterinsurgencies. This enraged the nationalist communities on the receiving end and reinforced the republican narrative of British oppression. In 1969, British soldiers had been welcomed as saviours; now they were shot.

London decided to support Faulkner as the last available Unionist leader that they could work with: if he too were replaced by a "hardliner", they would have no choice but to introduce direct rule. They recognised that this would be an unenviable challenge: as US political scientist Richard Rose put it: "As things stand, governing Northern Ireland is an insoluble problem for anyone who can think only of government by a fully legitimate regime. But it is also insoluble for those who like to think of governing a fully coercive regime. Anyone seeking to govern Ulster must accept the limitation that he governs without consensus" (*Governing without Consensus,* 1971, p. 395).

In response to an upsurge in IRA violence in July 1971, Faulkner asked Heath for permission to introduce internment as the only "tough" measure still untried, arguing that no reform initiative could succeed while such a high level of IRA violence persisted. Heath agreed on the understanding that Faulkner would shoulder the political responsibility. In the event, the internment operation ("Demetrius") was poorly co-ordinated and carelessly implemented. Many dangerous criminals fled across the border, and many of those caught were merely political activists. In four days, 23 people were killed, and there were over 100 explosions. Republican areas erupted in protest and IRA recruitment soared. According to records in the UK National Archives, John Hume of the SDLP travelled to London for an urgent meeting with Maudling at which he demanded that Stormont should be replaced by a new system of government, "in which Nationalists shared power as of right... This was the only credible way to reduce support for the IRA." (CAB 164/879, 13 August 1971). Otherwise, the SDLP would initiate a campaign of civil disobedience and set up its own rival "alternative assembly".

Direct rule

Heath finally introduced direct rule in March 1972. The decision was taken only after a comprehensive policy review, lengthy debates and a series of contingent events. Senior policymakers argued against it to the end. Why did he do it?

In August 1971, Taoiseach Lynch had publicly castigated the British government for introducing internment. Heath had replied with a curt telegram telling him that it was unacceptable for Dublin to interfere in the UK's internal affairs. Faulkner was initially delighted, but the British ambassador in Dublin persuaded Heath that humiliating Lynch would make it harder for the Irish to cooperate in tackling the IRA – if Lynch fell from power, his successor (Charles Haughey) would be worse.

The negative consequences of internment persuaded Heath to make Northern Ireland a personal priority. He invited Lynch to two weekend meetings at his country house, Chequers, in September. Lynch asked him to work towards unification as the only sustainable long-term solution: meantime (as Hume was arguing) power at Stormont should be shared between unionists and nationalists. As a first step, full control over security should be returned to Westminster. Heath replied that 50/50 power-sharing would be unfair to the unionist majority, but agreed that nationalists should have "full and fair participation in government" until such time as a majority of the electorate might favour unification. (For a fuller account of these historic meetings see my *The British State and the Northern Ireland Crisis*, 2011, pp. 211–3).

These meetings for the first time gave Dublin direct input into British policymaking at the highest level. Heath instructed the Cabinet Office to undertake a fundamental policy review, drawing in senior officials from the FCO and Ministry of Defence (MoD). The review group recommended a radical political initiative, inviting Heath to choose between three broad options: repartition, coalition government, and joint sovereignty. Heath opted for coalition government and asked his officials to work up ideas based on experience in "other divided societies" (such as Lebanon).

In November, after discussions with Irish ministers, Wilson – now leader of the opposition – announced his own plan for a coalition government leading by stages to unification. This ended the bipartisan consensus at Westminster. Dublin rejoiced: Unionists would now have to accept that a future Labour government would introduce powersharing. This pincer attack by Wilson and Lynch increased the pressure on Heath to announce his own initiative. On 25 November, he offered the SDLP a conciliatory gesture, telling the Commons, "if at some future date the majority of the people of Northern Ireland want unification, and express that desire in the appropriate constitutional manner, I do not believe any British government would stand in the way".

This officially declared at the highest level that Britain's role was to not to stand up for the Union but to mediate between two equally valid (albeit to him incomprehensible) traditions.

On 10 January 1972, Cabinet Secretary Burke Trend summarised progress with Heath's policy review. Officials had agreed on the outline of an incremental initiative, to be introduced after the IRA had been defeated. Stormont would retain control over security because otherwise Faulkner's government would collapse. Their analysis of divided societies had indicated "a promising approach": the nationalist minority would have "a reasonable share in representation not only in parliament but in the government". There would be stronger legal safeguards against discrimination.

Maudling then threw a heavy spanner into the works, with contrary proposals dated 18 January. These recommended that responsibility for security *should* be transferred to Westminster and a package of radical political reforms *imposed*. If necessary, there should be an interim period of direct rule to break with the past. Whereas Trend's paper was consistent with traditional Home Office doctrine (and probably would have been acceptable to Faulkner), Maudling's reflected the views of diplomats, army commanders and intelligence officials (which would not).

Maudling's new stance reflected advice given by one of Faulkner's officials. Ken Bloomfield visited Howard Smith (UKREP) on 17 December 1971. According to Smith's record of the meeting in the UK National Archives, Bloomfield told him that "Faulkner's hopes that when (or if) violence was put down the Catholics would come round to cooperation were quite unrealistic": Westminster should impose a coalition government, and this should be done on a basis which would be acceptable to Dublin. (DEFE 24/201, 18 December 1971.) Smith advised Trend that Bloomfield's views should be seriously considered in light of his knowledge, ability and experience: Trend passed this to Heath with the comment, "Bloomfield discounts all-party talks and seems now convinced that only an imposed settlement will meet the needs of the situation" (Smith, *The British State*, 2011, p. 228).

When the cabinet discussed Maudling's paper on 21 January, one minister argued that they should seize the opportunity for a political initiative before the Protestants "reverted to an unyielding attitude against what they would regard as a beaten minority". The clear implications of this are that the military approach to security was at last yielding results, and that some ministers wanted to reform Stormont irrespective of the initiative's impact on the IRA. Ministers were still debating what to do when events intervened. On 30 January, British paratroops shot thirteen people dead at an anti-internment demonstration in Londonderry ("Bloody Sunday"). Nationalist Ireland mobilised in outrage and a crowd set fire to the British embassy in Dublin. The IRA planted bombs at Aldershot and in Whitehall. Additionally, on 23 February the Northern Ireland High Court issued a ruling which indicated that the army had been acting outside the law in many of its operations in Northern Ireland, including internment. This ruling highlighted how the Conservatives had allowed political control over security to drift to Faulkner and commanders on the ground. Maudling responded by rushing a bill through Westminster retrospectively empowering Stormont to confer emergency powers on the army. To do this quickly he had to secure Wilson's cooperation: in return, Wilson demanded prompt publication of the government's proposals for a political initiative.

Immediately after Bloody Sunday, Heath circulated a memo to the Cabinet which declared "we cannot continue as at present". This built on Maudling's package, providing for coalition government and the full transfer of Stormont's security responsibilities – including control over policing and the criminal justice system, which had hitherto been devolved matters, even after Wilson's reforms. If Faulkner demurred, he should be allowed to resign: direct rule was now reframed as a positive step to allow for "a period of purgation" in which to repair "Catholic alienation". It took Heath seven weeks to push his colleagues into full acceptance of these proposals. Meantime he instructed officials to prepare draft legislation and contingency plans for direct rule.

Unaware of these developments, Faulkner sent London proposals for further reforms including constraining Stormont's powers of internment; stronger safeguards against discrimination; more places for the SDLP on parliamentary committees; a reconstruction programme for nationalist neighbourhoods; and a north/south intergovernmental council. He was constrained by what his party colleagues would accept while IRA violence continued, but later in his memoirs, *Memoirs of a Statesman* (1978), he indicated that he could have offered more if pressed.

At cabinet, Maudling dismissed Faulkner's offer as too little too late, since it would not give the SDLP a "fair share" in government. The Home Secretary argued that the UK government therefore had to take more radical action, which would require an interim period of direct rule. There would be a border poll which would "put the problem of the Border into cold storage" and "in the new climate of generosity thus created", moderate leaders would make coalition government work. It had succeeded in other divided societies: why not Northern Ireland?

Defence minister Lord Carrington endorsed Maudling's proposals, claiming that they would weaken popular support for the IRA. But the Lord Chancellor, Lord Hailsham, objected that the package would alienate the majority without winning over the minority, and would encourage IRA violence. If it failed, London would be stuck with direct rule indefinitely. The meeting concluded by agreeing to the security transfer and border poll, but not direct rule or coalition government. Further meetings failed to achieve unanimity.

Losing patience, Heath finally offered to sound Faulkner out about the proposed security transfer, summoning him to London on 22 March. He did not invite Faulkner to present his reform proposals or to negotiate, but bluntly (and misleadingly) told him that the cabinet had agreed on a package including the security transfer and coalition government. If Faulkner had consented to this, witnesses to the meeting agree that Heath would simply have added further demands until the Unionist leader had no alternative but to resign.

Heath's betrayal of Faulkner was both political and personal. According to the memoir by Faulkner's Private

Secretary, Robert Ramsay, even as his officials were drawing up contingency plans for direct rule, Heath had told Faulkner: "we are in this together and we'll support you all the way, however long it takes" (*Ringside Seats*, 2009, p. 101). In his own memoirs, Faulkner describes his reaction to Heath's ultimatum: "I was shaken and horrified, and felt completely betrayed" (p.152). The British Army had been responsible for the ill-treatment of internees and for Bloody Sunday, and the Unionist government was sacrificed to atone for its mistakes.

Heath told the final cabinet meeting on 23 March, at which Maudling's package was agreed, that Faulkner had been "uncomprehending" and "intransigent". Foreign Secretary Douglas-Home assured the prime minister that Dublin "would endorse an interim period of direct rule as a means to advance coalition government". The PM clinched the argument by appealing to ministers' collective ego: "it would be politically intolerable for the government to retreat so far from the requirements which the prime minister had indicated to Mr Faulkner that it would be clear that they had no greater freedom of political initiative than the Northern Ireland government were prepared to allow them".

Assessment

We have examined two high-level policy shifts which finished off the Westminster doctrine of maximum devolution to a majoritarian government. The new doctrine, untested in any country, replaced it with an experimental paradigm whose components included the aspiration to reconcile incompatible demands over national sovereignty: a coalition government which must include secessionists;

a pathway towards a single unitary state; and a "guarantee" for nationalists provided by input from a hostile foreign government. Underpinning this concept was the ill-founded hope that it would be possible to defang republican violence, first by bringing the SDLP into government, and later by rewarding the IRA for shifting from a strategy of "armed struggle" to political campaigning, with generous rewards for mere compliance with the law.

This doctrine was originally branded "powersharing with an Irish dimension", but for Dublin and the SDLP the powersharing component was merely transitory: their strategy was always intended to lead irreversibly to unification. Originally formulated as the Sunningdale Agreement of 1973, which a majority of unionists opposed, it resurfaced in the Anglo-Irish Agreement of 1985, which formalised Dublin's input to policy in return for (unfulfilled) promises of cooperation in tackling the IRA, and in the Belfast Agreement of 1998, which remains the basis of British policy despite its obvious failings.

After almost fifty years of strenuous effort and road testing, the powersharing doctrine has failed to provide Northern Ireland with good governance, stability, or improved community relations. Political attitudes are even more polarised than in the 1960s, and partition is still the core issue in party politics. The two tangible achievements of British policy have been to destroy the Ulster Unionist Party and to reduce the constitutional status of unionists from a secure majority in Northern Ireland to an insecure minority in Ireland and the UK: hardly the best approach to curing them of their "siege mentality".

Betrayal?

In light of this assessment, Unionists' allegations of betrayal seem hard to refute. But was it ever reasonable to expect London to rank their security higher than national priorities such as membership of the European Economic Community; Britain's "special relationship" with the USA; Anglo-Irish relations; the lives of British soldiers; or the costs of prosecuting an unwinnable counterinsurgency campaign? Doesn't the British state have an obligation to take decisions in the interests of the whole nation, of which Ulster unionists comprise less than 2%?

Clearly the answer is yes. But an ethical state has superordinate duties which transcend individual policy issues and the interests of discrete groups. These duties include protecting national sovereignty; guarding national borders; honouring constitutional laws and conventions; securing the rule of law; and guaranteeing equal citizenship for all. Above all, a state which is authentically committed to human rights and the values of equality, justice, freedom and democracy must neither encourage nor reward politically motivated violence or threats of violence.

In its dealings with Northern Ireland since 1969, the British state has demonstrably failed to discharge these basic duties. It has not treated Northern Ireland as it would any other region of the United Kingdom (imagine the army tackling riots in Brixton) but instead like a disruptive colony requiring either to be coerced into submission or "handed back" to the natives. Conservative and Labour ministers alike undermined and deceived their partners in government at Stormont, blaming them for London's own mistakes. By wavering between toughness and appeasement, they appeared now cruel and now soft, harvesting the worst of both approaches. They overturned the long-established constitutional relationship between Britain and Northern Ireland in response not to reasoned argument or the democratically expressed will of the people, but to violence and the exploitation of violence by aggressive nationalism and its apologists.

Unionists contrast the performance of the British state with that of the Republic, which has consistently asserted its constitutional aspiration to sovereignty over the whole island and ruthlessly exploited opportunities to advance that aspiration through diplomacy and bad faith.

Driven by hostility towards his political opponents, Wilson misrepresented the nature of the conflict and the appropriate role of the national government, and destroyed the very institutions which could have prevented the downward spiral into thirty years of violence.

Heath's Conservatives were initially more sympathetic. But their priority was to minimise British entanglement, rather than sustain the Union. They hoped (on a weak evidential basis) that this could be achieved by bringing nationalist representatives into the devolved administration, and they introduced colonial rule rather than work with a duly elected but "hardline" unionist leader. Heath failed to assert British sovereignty in his dealings with Dublin. He undermined established constitutional norms – and good democratic practice – by excluding Stormont from his 1971 policy review. His betrayal of Faulkner was both systemic and personal.

Unreasonable expectations?
Of course, some unionist politicians made unreasonable

demands. If they seriously expected to shelter behind British guns while failing to address the legitimate grievances of their nationalist fellow-citizens, they were destined for disappointment. A national government has duties towards all its citizens, including secessionists. Wilson was right to insist on full and prompt reforms to remedy such legitimate grievances as may have existed over local government and public housing in the 1960s. (Graham Gudgin's chapter in this volume quantifies the real nature and extent of these grievances.) Heath was wrong to permit the army to apply the military security approach to policing in nationalist neighbourhoods from June 1970, which was both unethical and counter-productive.

However, the misuse of the army in a policing role was a direct consequence of Wilson's evisceration of civil policing. It was London, not Stormont, which deployed the army to impose a rough semblance of order, a task for which it was wholly unfit. It was British soldiers and security officials who mistreated internees. And it was British ministers, not Faulkner, who authorised the use of paratroops on Bloody Sunday. The Commander of Land Forces, Major-General Robert Ford, wrote to the General Officer Commanding, Harry Tuzo, in advance, arguing that the army had been failing in its duty to maintain order in Londonderry city centre: "I am coming to the conclusion that the minimum force necessary to achieve a restoration of law and order is to shoot selected ring leaders amongst the Derry Young Hooligans after clear warnings have been issued" (Peter Taylor, *Brits: the War against the IRA,* 2002, p. 88). In contrast, RUC chief superintendent Frank Lagan (a Catholic) had asked the army to allow the protest to take place without any military intervention. (For a fuller account of Bloody Sunday and its impact on British policy see Smith, *The British State,* 2011, pp. 178–183, 231).

Ambivalence

Our analysis has focused on two prime ministers at the apex of the machinery of state. In reality, decisions emerged from discussion and negotiations among multiple actors with diverse interests at lower levels, particularly in the two Whitehall departments which joined the policy-making process in 1969: the FCO and MoD. The more fully these two were engaged, the less likely policymaking was to favour the traditional and sensible laissez-faire doctrine of the Home Office.

British diplomats were concerned to maintain good relations with Dublin and did not care for the status quo in Belfast. British ambassadors in Dublin routinely advised the Taoiseach on tactics to take in negotiating with British ministers. Ambassador John Peck's memoirs described the suspension of Stormont as "one of the most courageous and honest political acts of the century" (*Dublin from Downing Street*, 1978, p. 145). In Belfast, UKREP, staffed by diplomats on secondment from FCO, fed material to the SDLP, advising Hume not to negotiate with Faulkner, but to hold out for a better deal under direct rule (Barry White, *John Hume*, 1984, p. 112). British diplomats made no attempt to persuade Dublin to crack down on IRA cross-border activity, advising their own ministers that this would be counter-productive; nor did they try to persuade Lynch to at least acquiesce in internment. They had many tools of influence at their disposal, but chose not to use them.

Defence chiefs and army commanders likewise advised

ministers both to take control over security away from Stormont (it was bad enough having to serve one set of politicians) and after internment (which they had opposed) to introduce direct rule. They maintained that security decisions should not be distorted by political considerations, and that having a single hierarchical structure would improve coordination between national and local intelligence services.

Conclusion

Between 1969 and 1972, London effectively ditched Northern Ireland's 1920 constitution; shattered Northern Ireland's governing party; granted Dublin formal input into its policies on Northern Ireland; made it a condition of any future devolution that nationalists should be fully included in governing the jurisdiction which they aspired to extinguish; and imposed the colonial system of direct rule, whereby Northern Ireland was governed by ministers and officials from "the mainland" for over 30 years.

In 1998 they went further: the Belfast Agreement shepherded unrepentant terrorists into government even without laying down their weapons, secretly gave many an effective amnesty, and provided by international treaty for the irreversible dissolution of Northern Ireland, and hence of Ulster unionism itself. Each of these actions was a surrender to violence and threats of violence rooted in the reactionary ideology of nineteenth-century ethnic nationalism and marinated in the blood cult of the 1916 Easter Rising, a tragedy and illusion which the Irish Republic continues to embrace as its foundation myth.

The British state has been ambivalent and inconsistent in defending the Union, depicting itself as mediator rather than sovereign power. Individual prime ministers (although not all – Margaret Thatcher is a notable exception), and Whitehall departments have planned to detach Northern Ireland from the UK by stealth in order to avoid a violent reaction from Unionism.

If this does not constitute betrayal, what does? The offence is the greater insofar as the same people in private assurances to Unionist leaders and in public statements have declared their unswerving support for the Union, and have even maintained that such concessions as they have offered to nationalism have strengthened the Union in the long term.

None of this is to belittle the enormous sacrifices – in blood, risk, gold and international goodwill – that Britain has made in solidarity with the people of Northern Ireland. Nor is it to suggest that Northern Ireland would be better off outside the Union. Rather, my argument is that the UK would better serve its own national interests by standing firm against terrorism and the threat of terrorism, offering no concessions to criminal violence, and no encouragement to its enemies.

How should the current British government proceed? Its stated policy is that it values the Union and seeks to protect the Belfast Agreement. Yet it also says that the EU Protocol must be implemented. Since the Protocol undermines both the Union and the Agreement, both statements cannot be true.

Boris Johnson's first priority should be to ditch the Protocol. Or at least – to save diplomatic faces all round – to soften and qualify the terms of its implementation so as to restore the integrity of the UK internal market, the equal constitutional status of Northern Ireland, and the equal rights of its citizens, as requested by all pro–Union parties.

Second, with the UK out of the EU, more attention urgently needs to be paid to "the totality of relationships between these islands". Never mind the fantasy of Irish unification: the immediate agenda is to improve relationships between the UK and Ireland in the new context where the UK is (or should be) entirely outside the EU and Ireland (for the present) is still a member. The implementation of the Belfast Agreement needs rebalancing, with a much greater emphasis on the east/west dimension.

Third, it should align itself with the efforts of reasonable Ulster Unionists to correct the mischievous rewriting of history by aggressive Irish nationalists attempting to present their continuing assault on Northern Ireland as if it were a just claim to an essential human right.

Historical Injustices

Edgar Haslett

Introduction

Irish nationalist propaganda has had remarkable success in persuading many people that it presents a special case of injustice and so is worthy of special sympathy and support. The image of a small friendly nation still suffering post-traumatic stress after centuries of ill-treatment by its more powerful neighbour has been accepted uncritically by many people abroad who should know better, and supported by others for political gain.

That the people and government in Britain should swallow the nationalist propaganda defies any simple explanation. We have Prime Ministers who seem prepared to accede to every demand from the Irish Republic for the dilution of sovereignty within this part of the United Kingdom. We have a British public which, tired of a problem that won't go away, is anxious to distance itself from the grim realities of terrorism. Overall, too, and obstructing rational thought, hangs the feeling that the propaganda holds some truth and that there is the need to make amends. As a result, policy in Northern Ireland seems to be a public demonstration of contrition as the prerequisite for forgiveness. In the circumstances, it is worth considering to what extent, if any, the United Kingdom is in debt to the Irish.

One

An essential feature of the propaganda is its implication that all the old wrongs are as relevant today as ever they were; that the discrimination of the Penal Laws in the 18th century has to be added to the discrimination of the Stormont era, that nationalist claims have to be applied in retrospect to the centuries before nationalism was invented.

It is a good trick but it was running into serious difficulties of belief and indifference until the "Civil Rights" movement provided the hard-core nationalism of Fianna Fáil, Sinn Féin, instant parties like the People's Democracy and the SDLP with the opportunity to resurrect the old ghosts of injustice, partition and discrimination. For more than twenty [fifty] years now this nationalist front has mounted a campaign to convince the world that the Irish problem is a unique case of unparalleled oppression. Its continuous self-pity diverts attention from the critical findings of modern historians and avoids any obligation to appeal to objective analysis in the perspective either of history or of current trends. Injustice and oppression are comprehensively documented, but it is time that they were perceived and understood in their historical context. Their value as justification for action today can then be better assessed.

"Historical injustices" is a phrase much favoured by Dublin politicians. There is a comforting generality about it, fortified by its undertones of moral indignation. Sometimes it is translated as 800 years of English misrule, but the period from the Tudor conquest till the present day provides ample material from which some basic but seldom heard qualifications of the accusation may be gathered. This was a period of fierce conflict amongst the European states, a continuous battle for power by the acquisition of wealth and territory. At first the conflict was largely confined to Europe, but it quickly spread round the world as exploration opened up fields of opportunity beyond the adventurers' wildest dreams. The conquest of land, the forcible subjection of people and the pillaging of their cultures led to every form of oppression and injustice – all made more bitter and ruthless by religious and racial intolerance, by the hatred between Protestant and Catholic powers and by the contempt of all Christians for the "heathens" abroad.

Within this wider concept of history rather than in the usual narrow approach are injustice and oppression in Ireland more properly considered. They then cease to be unique as they are put in place amongst barbaric contemporary events elsewhere. The point must be illustrated, but so vast is the catalogue of wrongs that only a random and inadequate dip into its pages is feasible here.

For example, by the year 1600 there had already occurred in France the St. Bartholomew's Day massacre of the Protestant Huguenots, while Spain, in the cause of Christianity and commerce, had wiped out the whole Inca nation by ruthless genocide. The bloodshed in 17th-century Ireland, whether from the Irish during the rebellion of 1641 or from Cromwell's army, as it exacted revenge at Drogheda and Wexford, has to be measured against far greater destruction and suffering during the Thirty Years War. In that bitter struggle the farmlands and towns of central Europe were put to fire and the sword on a scale which Ireland never knew.

Oppression after conquest is another historic injustice

which knows no boundaries of time or place. In the 18th and 19th centuries the lot of the Irish peasantry was unenviable, but oppression, poverty and hunger abounded elsewhere. In England itself, the land of the oppressor, the lives of children and adults in the mines and factories and of the village labourers in the fields were little more than survival contests. Further afield, the peasants of France and Russia had nothing to learn about oppression from the Irish and the thought occurs that as the emigrant ships made their way across the Atlantic in the 19th century, they were sailing waters recently and reluctantly surrendered by slave traders. History is a chronicle of injustices and there is no power against which charges cannot be brought. The Irish themselves are not without fault. Celtic tribalism was always aggressive and, in modern times, the Irish have shown no moral reluctance in assisting the subjection of North American Indians, the Aborigines of Australia and the Maoris of New Zealand, not to speak of Africans, Indians and Chinese amongst numerous other victims.

It is not the purpose of this essay to rewrite history. The hardships suffered by the Irish under English rule were very real but, by admission, they are historic injustices and their place is in the history books as lessons to be learned from the past. They have little value in today's political debate. If all the states of Europe were to bring their historical injustices into current political bargaining as the Irish have done, the chaos would be complete . Just imagine the lists of ancient grievances between France and Spain, France and Germany, Belgium and Holland, Austria and Italy, Germany and Poland. The European Union would dissolve overnight. No one should encourage this historic line of argument. It obscures the issues of the present day by encouraging self-pity and anger about the past and replaces the problems of the living with the problems of the long dead. The end result is the continuation of injustice. Learning from history means moving on from history and never was such a step more necessary. We now see daily on television atrocities far worse than anything in the past but always linked to earlier quarrels .

For this reason, the significance of the European Union as an attempt to call a halt to centuries of conflict may prove greater than its significance as an attempt to construct a common market. Its policy is simple and clear: the acceptance of things as they now are, the renunciation of border claims and the creation of a Europe where minority groups can feel secure in their own cultures. Only the Republic of Ireland amongst its European partners refuses to reconcile itself to the policy and pursues a campaign to acquire territory from a neighbouring state. In doing so, it is guilty of a modern injustice and must bear a major share of responsibility for the suffering of the past twenty-five years.

Not unusually, John Hume applies his own peculiar logic to the situation. He has, for some time now, been telling us that we are living in the era of post nationalism, and yet the only solution he offers to our political problem is the establishment of an Irish nationalist state throughout the whole island. Fine words, too, were heard at his recent party conference. As a result of the ceasefire [1994], but apparently for no better reason, he declared, "the time has come to leave the past behind us, to draw a line over it and let history judge it". He does not say exactly what is to be left behind but, in the spirit of his post-nationalism era and of the European Union he so admires, the obvious choice should surely be the nationalist claims to Northern Ireland. If Germany and Poland can accept the course of the rivers Oder and Neisse as their border and thereby also accept that many thousands of Germans and Poles will be on the wrong side of it, there should be no reluctance by the Republic to endorse the line of its border with the United Kingdom. Hume, of course, is a prisoner of his own dogma that Ireland is an island and must, therefore, be the territory of only one nation state. Post-nationalist thinking is to be enthusiastically welcomed in his brave new world – everywhere except in Ireland.

Two

Partition and the discrimination of the Stormont era are the injustices of the more recent past around which Irish political thought rotates and, like the earlier wrongs, require an objective and comparative review. At the end of the Great War in 1918, a major attempt to stabilize Europe by re-shaping it was undertaken. A redrawing of boundaries by the partitioning of territory on the basis of national self-determination radically altered the political map and redefined the association of people with where they lived. Thus, Germany lost Alsace-Lorraine to France and some eastern provinces to Poland: the Austro-Hungarian Empire was divided up into its component parts and Czechoslovakia, Austria and Hungary emerged as independent states while Yugoslavia and Rumania were considerably enlarged. Russia, for her part, gained territory from Germany but ceded independence to Finland, Estonia, Latvia and Lithuania. All these and other territorial alterations were made in the interests of peace, to give independence to racial groups who sought it and so to remove the causes of conflict. But it was an impossible mission. The peoples of Europe were too interspersed to permit of any clear-cut separations and hence of any definitive boundaries. Throughout the continent and indeed the world, borders take all sorts of shapes, from straight lines to tortuous irregularity and, in terms national identity, are always imprecise.

The partitioning of the United Kingdom in 1920 was not a direct part of the post-war settlement but it was carried out on the same basis of national self-determination and embodied all the same problems. A boundary was agreed which was far from perfect and left many stranded on the wrong side. Nevertheless, the great majority of Irish nationalists were given their freedom, a major part of the island and the right to choose their own form of government. The separation of some of them on the United Kingdom side of the border is only a minor example of a widespread problem and it is ridiculous that they should attract such a disproportionate and ill-considered amount of international pity. Surprise and impatience at the persistence of Irish territorial claims and sympathy should mark the European reaction. In 1975, the Republic of Ireland signed the Helsinki Agreement and so agreed not to make territorial claims against the other signatory states or to interfere in their internal affairs. That the United Kingdom does not publicly denounce the continued breach of this Agreement but seems instead to aid and abet it provides grounds for the gravest suspicion about the objectives of its Northern Ireland policy.

When all the relevant factors are considered and reliable province-wide statistics are used instead of selective examples, the nationalist complaints about discrimination are found to be further instruments of propaganda rather than objective statements of fact. The details of the exaggerated and misleading claims have been set down in official documents such as the Cameron Report and challenged in findings such as those of the 1971 census. They have also been the subject of a number of published articles, pamphlets and books. It is not the intention here to pursue them nor to consider the extent to which nationalist refusal to co-operate and willingness to engage in subversive activities have been responsible for their proclaimed condition of second-class citizenship. Instead, and in keeping with the general theme of this article, its aim is to remind people that discrimination on the grounds of race, religion, political belief and many other prejudices has been and still remains, sadly, a common feature of political life. The French government discriminates against its Algerian citizens, the German against its immigrant workers. In Italy, the people of Lombardy have little time for their compatriots in the south, and in Belgium, Walloons and Flemings have relationships marked by bias and partiality. Deeply ingrained discrimination against those of West Indian, Indian and Pakistan origin is still a major social disease in England and the record of the Irish Republic requires a mention.

In its years as an independent state the Republic has discriminated against Protestants, against those who did not speak Irish and fiercely against those who did not subscribe to a moral code prescribed by a theocracy and enforced by a militant, illiberal clericalism. To believe in family planning, divorce or abortion was to invite a sort of civic excommunication, and to admit to such belief was to ensure an end to public career prospects. To that has to be added the censorship of books, plays and pictures, so there can be little surprise that the best of Irish artistic talent was exercised from outside the Republic. It is ironic that nationalists north of the border, free from these restrictions, are now pitied as the only victims of discrimination in Ireland.

In analysing the validity of the "historic injustices" factor in today's relationships between the United Kingdom and the Republic, one other item must be introduced. It is reasonable to ask whether there is anything to enter on the credit side to balance all the real and imagined suffering which the Irish have had to bear. The answer is that no separatist movement was ever granted independence on better terms than was the Irish Free State. It was given a credit card in the form of dual citizenship, a concession which allowed it to retain many of the economic and political advantages of being in the Union without detracting from its independence. Since 1920, the United Kingdom has provided a readily available market for Irish skills be they those of the labourer or the consultant physician. The pressure of rising population and unemployment has thus been removed from the Dublin government and the responsibility for providing employment or welfare benefits quietly passed to Westminster. It is difficult to overestimate the value of this facility but it is said that the chief export of the Republic this century has been people, and most of them have gone no further than the United Kingdom.

The movement still goes on, rising and falling with the economic health of the Republic but always maintaining a steady outflow of Irish nationalists, who appear to find no difficulty in living under British rule. Nearly one million Irish people who were born in Ireland now live in the United Kingdom; that is one million first generation immigrants to be added to the several million descendants of earlier settlers. It is hard to understand why the complete integration of Northern Ireland into the United Kingdom is not seen as the obvious way to accommodate Irish nationalism here on the same basis as that which applies in Britain.

There would be much to gain and chiefly by the Irish themselves. Within Britain the names and often the accents reveal the penetration of Anglo-Irish citizens into every aspect of life. They are found at the executive level in trade unionism and in company management, in all the major professions and in political involvement at local and central government levels. And they form a substantial part of the ordinary work force upon which the economic and social fabric of the country depends. Without this British outlet it is very possible that the Republic would by now have collapsed through lack of resources to, cope with its problems. Even today, dependence on the British connection is finding new lines of profitable one-way traffic. British taxpayers pay for the higher education of increasing numbers of young people from the Republic and training of others for careers such as nursing. They have also accepted responsibility in homes north of the border for the residential care of elderly citizens from south of the border. Now would be an appropriate time for someone to query the future of these and other bargains should Ireland become united and left to fend for itself.

Three
Space and time have limited the detailed treatment which

the argument of this essay deserves but enough has been said to cast doubt on the force of traditional nationalist claims. Intentional or not, the plea to "historic injustices" has become a sob story designed to win sympathy where none is justified and has had an unwarranted influence on British policy. We are far down the line of appeasement but it is not too late to reassess the position.

The Republic wants to eat its cake and still have it but it should be warned that subsidised independence is not forever. A British declaration of intent to withdraw dual citizenship and its attendant benefits in the event of unification would transform the situation and cause panic throughout the nationalist camp. This is not a silly suggestion: what is silly is optimism that the Westminster government would ever have the courage to adopt such a policy or the will to carry it out.

For reasons never explained except in jabberwocky language about reconciliation and peace, present policy is justified by acceptance of the injustice theme and there is nobody willing to declare that the emperor has no clothes. It is a policy which amounts to a public apology for the political aberration which created and maintained Northern Ireland, a policy through which Northern Ireland is to be sacrificed in expiation of the perceived sins of the fathers.

There is an alternative and more honorable policy to deal with the latest manifestation of the Irish problem. Full recognition and acceptance of the border as it stands, and a policy of non-interference, offer the best chance of creating conditions in which the healthy growth of good neighbourliness and co-operation can be firmly rooted. Once the political implications of cross-border enterprise have been removed, its scope will be greatly increased. By way of reference, it should be noted that the Netherlands and Belgium's Flanders region have agreed to dredge the River Scheldt to give greater access to Antwerp from the North Sea, but neither party sees any need for inter-state management boards.

As with economic matters, so too with cultural aspects of life. Rightly or wrongly, the public display of nationalist culture is often seen as evidence of a separatist, subversive element in the state. With acceptance of Northern Ireland as an undisputed part of the United Kingdom, the threat would be removed and nationalist culture would become an enriching ingredient for everyone in a multi-cultural society. There never has been any impediment put in the way of the practice and enjoyment of Irish culture. If it were not exploited in pursuit of republicans' wider political agenda it could become a source of pleasure for all of us and an important factor in building understanding between Northern Ireland and the Republic. (1995)

Discrimination in Housing

Graham Gudgin

Accusations of discrimination by Unionist politicians and officials against Catholics played an important role in Northern Irish politics in the years leading up to the outbreak of the Troubles in 1968.[1] After the Belfast Agreement of 1998, the issue largely disappeared, although objective conditions changed little. Once nationalists were in a power-sharing government there was little political mileage to be gained from campaigning on the issue. Its disappearance – other than to remind audiences why the civil rights movement was justified, and that Unionists could not be trusted – indicated that it had always been used for propaganda purposes. The salient issue was Irish unity: even minor instances of discrimination were used to argue that Northern Ireland was a failed political entity.

Among neutral observers, accusations of discrimination formed the backbone of antagonism towards unionism. Although unionists had minimal power from 1972 to 1998, the accusations were regularly repeated during this period. There were essentially four areas in which discrimination was alleged: housing, employment, gerrymandering and the abuse of emergency powers.

This paper will address discrimination in housing. Its burden is that discrimination was never as important in social and economic terms as it was made out to be: it was, however, enormously important in political terms, because nationalists used it to persuade the world that they had been hugely disadvantaged.

Unionists remained strangely inert in face of accusations which they must have known were greatly exaggerated. Part of the problem was the anti-intellectual nature of political unionism: even when it controlled the civil service machine, the Unionist Party put little effort into gathering and analysing data or arguing their case. For example, they failed to make any submission to the 1968 Cameron Commission on the causes of the disturbances in Northern Ireland. Fifty years later the surviving politicians from that time remain unable to explain this lapse. Typical of unionist feebleness in this respect was the view, cited in Henry Patterson and Eric Kaufmann's *Unionism and Orangeism in Northern Ireland since 1945* (2007) of Westminster MP Martin Smyth, that Protestants were constrained from responding to republican allegations of discrimination by "decent Ulster decency".

Public opinion in Britain had little understanding of nationalistic territorial disputes and was easily convinced that discrimination was the cause of the disorder. It was easier to view Northern Ireland through the lens of sectarianism manifesting as discrimination.

The allegations permitted nationalists to argue that Protestants could not be trusted to form a government even if they gained a clear majority of votes in democratic elections. This assertion underpinned the talks leading to the Belfast Agreement (1998) and resulted in a form of power sharing which admitted former terrorists to the executive. The terms of the Agreement provide an apparent justification for the view that all previous forms of regional government in Northern Ireland were unacceptable.

A belief in the importance of past discrimination is not the only factor underpinning the policy of power sharing. The need to end IRA violence and accommodate a large permanent minority led to a search for unconventional political arrangements. However, the form of these arrangements was heavily coloured by nationalists' depiction of themselves as victims and unionists as oppressors. The British and Irish governments broadly accepted this account. The outcome might otherwise have been very different: the Spanish authorities have not chosen power sharing as their solution to comparable conflicts inside their country.

Little changed in the two decades after the suspension of the Unionist parliament in March 1972. Discrete problems with discrimination had been addressed through a radical restructuring of local government, initiated by the Unionist government before the disorder had begun. While protesters were correct to complain about earlier abuses, the civil rights movement used them as a stick with which to beat unionism.

Historians' accounts

In any other society, the reaction to localised problems of discrimination in housing would be to reform housing allocation in the offending councils. In Northern Ireland, the issue initiated 30 years of violent conflict. This over-reaction has been granted an undeserved legitimacy by its treatment in academic and journalistic coverage of the period. Michael Farrell's self-consciously partisan account in *Northern Ireland: The Orange State* (1976), for instance, highlights only one area (Fermanagh), confuses housing shortage with misallocation, and fails to mention any of the established instances of nationalist discrimination against Protestants.

Most histories of the Unionist Stormont period (1921–72) tell the story of the civil rights protests and the descent into violence from which Northern Ireland is yet to fully recover. The nationalist narrative and its ceaseless repetition have created an uncritical connection in many people's minds between discrimination and the Troubles. This narrative is almost axiomatic across the nationalist community in Ireland and amongst its supporters elsewhere. Republican violence is widely depicted as a justified reaction against the unfair and oppressive behaviour of the Unionist government. This view is increasingly common, too, in younger middle-class unionist circles, where a sense of shame shapes political attitudes.

One result of the years of largely undefended allegations is that Northern Ireland's Protestants are frequently described in terms usually reserved for the world's least savoury political cultures. Consider the following from Bowyer Bell, professor of history at Columbia University, author of *The Irish Troubles: a Generation of Violence* (1993): "Many Protestants, who were mostly plain, often poor children of their own history, were also prejudiced practically from birth, decent folk but fearful of the alien. The system began by teaching toddlers differences, superiority and privilege. Thus, most were bigots, some simple and gentle, others nasty and if need be brutal."

To the celebrated Irish historian, J. J. Lee, in *Ireland: 1912–1985* (1989), northern Protestants have a "herrenvolk" mentality. Political scientists Brendan O'Leary and John

McGarry in *The Politics of Antagonism: Understanding Northern Ireland* (2016) take a similar view, stating that "the UUP could rely on ingrained ethnic prejudices to sustain discrimination". Even the *New Ireland Forum Report* (1984), an official publication of the government of Ireland, asserts that Catholics were "deprived of the means of social and economic development".

Historians from a unionist background have tended to downplay the issue rather than presenting evidence which exists, and which would refute the allegations. Patterson and Kaufman give it only seven glancing references in *Unionism and Orangeism in Northern Ireland*. Patterson's *Ireland Since 1939* (2006) and Paul Bew's *The Politics of Enmity* (2007) have some limited discussion of discrimination in housing. Both focus on politics rather than the underlying social and economic factors.

Jonathan Bardon's *History of Ulster* (1992) has many useful anecdotes about discrimination but makes no attempt to provide a comprehensive assessment of discrimination in housing or employment. He focuses on individual cases in Dungannon but gives the impression without supporting evidence that this was an example of a much wider malaise. He tends to overstate and over-generalise the problem. This stems no doubt from a general frustration with the Unionist regime and its failure to bring Catholics into its party or government. Effective one-party states are not uncommon across Europe and Japan, and it is perhaps with hindsight that the Unionist regime's failure seems so stark, but most commentators agree that more could have been done. This is, however, different from discrimination in housing, where much was in fact done to achieve fairness. In criticising local authorities' reluctance to provide houses for new Catholic tenants, Bardon gives no figures for the social housing provided by the state-funded and scrupulously fair Housing Trust. Once the Trust's contribution is taken into account, Catholic families were in fact over-represented in social housing, at virtually all income levels.

Discrimination in housing?

Accusations of discrimination in housing were among the most important criticisms of the Stormont regime. This is not only because of the intrinsic importance of housing but because the civil rights movement emerged from complaints about housing allocation.

There has been much exaggeration. Professor Tom Wilson stated in *Ulster: Conflict and Consent* (1989): "The charge of discrimination directed against unionist policy has been repeated so often and with such total assurance that its validity now appears to be widely accepted without evidence, as though it had been fully substantiated as to have made any further presentation of the evidence no longer necessary."

Allegations of discrimination in housing have a long history in Northern Ireland, but they first came to more than local prominence in the civil rights campaign initiated in 1964. It began with a protest against the misallocation of housing by Dungannon rural district council. The campaign was initiated by two local doctors, the McCluskeys, and advanced by Austin Currie and others. (Currie later became a minister in the 1974 power-sharing executive and an Irish TD.) They organised squatting in two council houses by two Catholic families. One was evicted and the house allocated to a Protestant, who was also secretary to a local unionist councillor. As Currie said, "if we had waited a thousand years, we would not have got a better example", indicating that this was an unusually stark case. It was widely reported internationally and came to symbolise the abuse of civil rights by Unionist authorities.

It attracted widespread sympathy because it followed on from years of similar allegations at local level. These largely concerned small towns in Dungannon and Fermanagh. Figures from the McCluskeys' and similar reports are repeated in most histories of the Troubles. These instances are usually taken uncritically as examples of discrimination in Northern Ireland as a whole, but figures for the rest of Northern Ireland are not included: Belfast is almost never mentioned. The intensity of the accusations has grown over the years and become all-embracing.

The picture painted is widely believed, including by many Protestants. It is, however, untrue, as can be seen from the 1971 census. In that year there were 148,000 local authority dwellings in Northern Ireland, of which between 45,000 and 55,000 were occupied by Catholic families (depending on what is assumed about the religion of those who declined to state one). We can see immediately that the idea that there were few houses for Catholics is completely wrong. In fact, Catholics had a disproportionately large share of local authority housing. They comprised 26.1% of households but occupied 30.7% of local authority households. Some 40% of Catholic families were in local authority houses compared with just over 30% of Protestants.

We might ask how it can be so widely believed that unionist authorities built few houses for Catholics, when the statistics show that, in fact, they provided proportionately more for Catholics than Protestants. The first thing to say is that even with these figures, unionist authorities may not have been responding fully and fairly to the needs of Catholics. There are three obvious ways to measure needs: relative to income, family size, and existing housing conditions. By luck there is good evidence on these issues. A major survey was undertaken in 1968 by an American professor, Richard Rose. This was published in his authoritative book on Northern Ireland, *Governing Without Consensus: An Irish Perspective* (1971). The survey covered a wide range of political and social issues and provides an invaluable benchmark of conditions and attitudes in the years immediately before the Troubles.

Rose's survey included a section on housing conditions. He discovered what was later confirmed by the census, that Catholics had a disproportionately large share of local authority houses. Their advantage was very marked in Belfast, which had a Unionist council (19% of Catholics in local authority houses compared with 9% of Protestants), and in areas with nationalist councils (39% of Catholics compared with 15% of Protestants). Elsewhere, Catholics and Protestants got an equal share of local authority houses. Professor Rose's conclusion was that there was: "…no evidence of systematic discrimination against Catholics. The greatest bias appears to favour Catholics in areas controlled by Catholic councillors".

Rose revealed that Catholics did not get more local authority houses only because they were poorer: at any given level of income, they fared better than Protestants. The reason for this advantage is probably their larger family size – in most housing allocation systems in the UK larger families receive priority – a practice formalised by the Northern Ireland Housing Executive from its inception in 1971.

The thorny issue of differences between Catholics and Protestants in family size is important in understanding the housing issue. How can housing be allocated on a fair basis when one community has consistently higher birth rates than the other? One book describes the difficulties in an open way: Maurice Hayes's autobiographical *Minority Verdict* (1995). Hayes was town clerk in Downpatrick, Co. Down working to a nationalist council. The council tried to introduce a fair points-based allocation system in the 1960s. This favoured larger families, so Catholics got most houses. To avoid this over-representation, the council introduced two separate lists, one for Catholics and one for Protestants. This in turn had the undesirable consequence that single Protestants were allocated houses while large Catholic families remained on the waiting list. This, too, was viewed as unacceptable, so the council reverted to its earlier points system. Similar problems may have been responsible for a disproportion in the allocation of council houses in Newry in 1963, where all but twenty-two of the 765 houses were allocated to Catholics.

Here we have a conundrum. When a unionist council in Dungannon gave a house to a single Protestant in preference to a Catholic family, the result was the civil rights movement leading to international condemnation and on to the Troubles. When a nationalist council did the same, for the best of motives, it attracted no national or international attention whatsoever, then or since. Despite the fact that Catholics did better in local authority housing, unionist councils as a whole became tarred with the brush of discrimination. Although the clearest evidence was of nationalist councils discriminating against Protestants, nationalists attracted little opprobrium.

Much of the argument over housing took place between 1964 and 1969, when the Northern Ireland Housing Executive was announced. Few reliable figures on the allocation of housing across Northern Ireland between Catholics and Protestants were available until Rose's book was published in 1971 and the 1971 census results were published in 1975. By then nationalists had won the argument.

Even so, we might reasonably ask why the facts have not subsequently been corrected or at least acknowledged by historians of the Northern Ireland problem? One answer is that, in general, political historians rarely examine statistical sources. They see their task as reporting significant events such as the origins of the civil rights movement and repeat what contemporary activists said about them. Because the accusations of discrimination in housing were not countered at the time, some historians were content to report contemporary opinion. Historians might also argue that what people thought at the time was a more important influence on events than what was true.

It may be correct that some Catholic families in Dungannon were not able to get social housing to the extent that would have been the case under an objective points system giving priority to low incomes and family size. However, this is a long way from the impression given by most historians that it was difficult for any Catholics in Dungannon to gain access to social housing. Perhaps the best summary of the housing issue was made by Charles Brett, the first chairman of the Northern Ireland Housing

Executive: "It is my view that the majority of councils did not consciously or deliberately engage in any kind of discrimination; but a minority did so and thereby discredited the whole" (*Housing in a Divided Community*, 1986).

Many councils, including Belfast, had a blameless record in housing: according to the senior civil servant responsible for the reform programme, John Oliver, most "struggled manfully to maintain standards and to do the right thing".[2] Even the Cameron Commission in commenting on the four councils most affected by disturbances concluded that houses were allocated in rough proportion to numbers of Catholics and Protestants.

Almost all allegations of discrimination in housing ceased when the Northern Ireland Housing Executive was set up in 1972 to take responsibility from local authorities and the Housing Trust. It should be said that the Unionist government's delay in responding to the indefensible behaviour of a few councils west of the Bann was inexcusable and contributed to its downfall. Local control of housing is always open to abuse in one-party administrations, and it is only the unusual circumstances of Northern Ireland west of the Bann which made the problem so much worse than in similar one-party situations in Scotland, South Wales or Northeast England.

It was, however, typical of political unionism to ignore the need for institutional change. Whereas Ulster conservatism contributes much to aspects of social stability in Northern Ireland, unionist conservatism in delaying the reform of badly performing institutions was the Achilles' heel of a government faced with daunting problems. Oliver, a permanent secretary during this period, concedes, "our failure to deal with those attitudes and practices was one of our most serious failures overall, for while the practical effect was limited, their psychological and political effect was great".

Catholics were over-represented, not under-represented, in social housing at the end of the unionist regime in 1971. The evidence is that this over-representation reflected the fact that they had on average larger families. As the difference in family size has declined, the degree of Catholic over-representation has diminished.

The degree of opprobrium heaped on the unionist regime was unwarranted. That a few small local authorities tried to house Catholic tenants where unionist electoral advantage was served was wrong, but it did not lead to Catholics receiving fewer houses.

The lesson unionists should have drawn from the complaints is that they had a reputation for discrimination which they had done little to dispel. When accusations were made of discrimination, outsiders found them easy to believe. The evidence of Professor Rose was ignored after the fall of the Unionist regime, and few seemed interested in analysing the data. Nationalists had won the political battle and unionists made no effort to counter their accusations. The UK government was more interested in pressing through institutional reforms for perceived problems in order to counter nationalist disaffection and republican violence: whether the problems were real was a secondary concern.

Conclusion
Having reviewed the statistical evidence, it is difficult to disagree with the conclusion of John Oliver, that "the so-

called grievances and complaints that have been publicised all over the world have been hugely exaggerated." Oliver notes that the grievances began before the Unionist government had made any decisions and continued long after its demise. In his view the faults, mistakes and shortcomings of the regime were used by nationalists to denigrate the state and pull it down. This is not to deny the abuse of local powers by some local authorities, mainly in border areas, for electoral advantage.

The Cameron Commission had some sympathy for the position in which Unionists found themselves: "It is in a sense understandable that, given the political history of Northern Ireland, in certain areas in particular, local unionist groups should seek to preserve themselves in power by ensuring that local authority housing is developed and allocated in ways which will not disturb their electoral supremacy." In reference to the disturbances which we now know led to thirty years of violence he added, "It is however natural that most Catholics should feel that the basis of administration in such areas is radically unfair"

With the benefit of hindsight, it seems likely that Cameron underestimated the extent to which civil rights protests would mutate into more direct nationalist ambitions. His hope that the reforms announced by the government would constitute an important step towards "eliminating causes of division and sectarian strife ... helping to unite the people of Northern Ireland" now looks naive. Thirty years of violence followed his report.

It is possible to agree with Oliver that nationalists made a blunder in not throwing in their lot with the state before 1945. Their decision not to put their aspiration for Irish unity on ice made the emergence of the Troubles more likely. We might note that Irish nationalism has never pressed for a more practical solution to the problem of identity (such as a repartition taking majority Catholic border areas into the Republic). The pressure has always been for a full territorial transfer including all areas in which Protestants are in a majority.

At the same time, Oliver is surely correct in his assessment that the unionists' failure was greater, since they let slip opportunities to bring nationalists into the political system. The history of the 1950s and 1960s contains many examples of a hard line being taken when greater generosity would surely have paid dividends. Both unionists and nationalists were trapped by history and crippled by an unnecessary constitutional uncertainty (all of which remain with us), but the quality of their struggle against these difficulties left much to be desired.

Finally, it is easy to agree with Patrick Shea's conclusion in his autobiography, *Voices and the Sound of Drums* (1981) after a lifetime as a Catholic in the Northern Ireland civil service: "I am totally convinced that whatever may be said about the righting of past wrongs or the maintenance of inherited power and privilege, there has been no moral justification for violence or threat of violence for political ends in Ireland at any time in the present century."

Endnotes

1 This is an abridged version of Dr. Gudgin's "Discrimination in Housing and Employment in Northern Ireland" in *The Northern Ireland Question: Perspectives on Nationalism and Unionism,* eds. Patrick J. Roche and Brian Barton (Tunbridge Wells: Wordzworth, 2020). The original version includes eleven tables and charts and 82 endnote citations.

2 John A. Oliver, "The Stormont Administration" in *The Northern Ireland Question: Myth and Reality* (Aldershot: Avebury, 1991), p. 92.

Challenges

The Idea of the Union

The Idea of the Union

Arthur Aughey

One

Unionism has been noted for its inarticulateness. This has little to do with the rhetorical skills of unionist politicians. It has to do with the ability of unionists to convey to others in an intelligible, defensible and coherent manner what they believe. Unionist may speak cogently unto unionist but, as Bairner has observed, "problems grow when unionists try to explain to others how they want to live".[1] Because unionist politicians have failed in the past to explain to others or even give their politics a second thought, it has been quite easy for opponents to fix upon unionism the label of an ideology of sectarian supremacism or to dismiss it as nothing but the flotsam and jetsam of Britain's imperial past.

In other words, it is commonly held that unionism embodies no idea which is worth taking seriously. It is nothing other than a set of prejudices which pose an obstacle to political progress in Ireland (the line which has been assiduously peddled by nationalists, constitutional and militant). Or it is the self-justification of an exclusive sect of bigots, a primitive local cult given to rituals of a quite barbaric nature (an understanding prevalent in much of British public life). Once these notions have taken root (and there is no doubt that they have taken root) they tend to become self-reinforcing. They are established as unexamined truths from which all explanation and understanding must naturally flow.

If unionism is a much misunderstood political doctrine then unionist politicians must carry most of the burden of culpability. Indeed, it is quite remarkable how they have come to take it for granted that they are the guardians of a faith which has been universally travestied, denigrated and abused. Like flat-earthers they have responded not with a rational and considered response but with a self-righteousness founded on an inner truth, the evident justice of their cause. This may be magnificent but it is not politics. It stresses even more the anachronistic tone of unionist discourse and its apparent inability to strike a harmony with contemporary political values.

This was not always so. The question of the Union was one which for two decades either side of the turn of [the last] century concentrated the mind of the entire British establishment and encapsulated the preoccupations of an empire. It brought forth a vast literature on the value of the Union as a political idea. Like conservatives in 1789, unionists in both Great Britain and Ireland had been "alarmed into reflection". They were forced to make intelligible that which hitherto had been instinctive and natural.

Of course, history never repeats itself. It only stutters, as French radicals would say. Unionism can never recapture the imagination of British politics as it did in the years before the First World War simply because the conditions conducive to that achievement no longer exist. This should not be a cause for lament, for nostalgic wistfulness. Nor does it mean that Ulster unionism ought to fade away or to climb into the waste-bin of history as Irish nationalists and British policy-makers have been encouraging it to do. It means that it is vital for unionism to think seriously about its own tradition and to draw upon the ideological resources which it contains, resources which might enable it to effectively engage those currently deep-seated prejudices which are ranged against it. An ideology shows its character by adapting to what Santayana called the "fertile principles of life".

The Anglo-Irish Agreement (1985) ought once again to have alarmed unionists into reflection. For the Anglo-Irish Agreement has sprung from contentious assumptions about nation, state, identity and religion in Ireland found in the collective mind of Westminster and Whitehall. Unless these assumptions are adequately addressed and shaken, and unless unionists can formulate an articulate case to contest them, then the game is well and truly up. It is the argument of this essay that unionism is a rational and defensible idea; indeed, that its underlying principles are more appropriate to modern conditions than the romantic nostalgia of Irish nationalism.

Two

But why should unionism be in this defensive position in the first place and why has it neglected the battle of ideas?

A significant part of the answer lies in the establishment of devolved government in Northern Ireland. It is not too fine a distinction to argue that the outcome of the Home Rule debate was not a victory for unionism at all and only a partial victory for Ulster unionists. A partial victory only – for unionists had both won and lost. They had been able to prevent their absorption into a narrow and authoritarian Catholic, nationalist state. What they had not been able to assert convincingly, and what they had been unable to make the British government in London fully acknowledge, was their full and unequivocal membership of the United Kingdom. After 1920 unionists were cast back upon their own resources. They depended on their capacities and strength of political will alone to ensure that Northern Ireland remained a part of the Union. What ensued was a dialectic of stubborn self-righteousness within Northern Ireland between unionist and nationalist. It was sponsored on the one hand by a British government equivocal about the integrity of its own state, thereby encouraging unionist intolerance founded on insecurity; and an Irish government hypocritically and irresponsibly playing the irredentist card, thereby encouraging Catholic alienation from the state and helping to provoke those very features of the Stormont regime which it smugly condemned.

Unionism as a political idea responded by turning in upon itself. It became totally absorbed in the practice of devolved government and in the maintenance of the security of the province. This was understandable. But in doing so unionist politicians began to confuse the politics of Stormont with the idea of unionism. They simply neglected the business of how to formulate unionist principles in a manner understandable to those outside the so-called unionist family. To worry about principle and about the wider philosophical intelligibility of what one stands for was the problem only of those who were excluded from power (like nationalists in Ulster, for instance). Under the old Stormont regime unionism was more concerned with the solid bulk of things, the substantial inner life of the state, its institutions, offices, laws, administration and prerequisites.

No one has ever doubted the capacity of unionist politicians to mobilise support and to keep their electoral bloc together. No one has ever denied the potency of the good cry of "no surrender" or "not an inch" or "this we will maintain". But it has been all too exclusive and self-indulgent and has generally lacked a deep or ideologically sensitive reflection upon the character of the unionist tradition. This was to prove its great weakness when the Lloyd George settlement collapsed. After the abolition of Stormont in 1972 unionism could not rely on the same certainties which it had celebrated heretofore. The new dispensation ought to have encouraged a fundamental reconsideration of unionist beliefs and an intelligent restatement of the unionist case.

Three

One of the expressions which emerged into common currency in the 1970s as the ultimate legitimate claim of unionism was the notion of the "right to self-determination". And in the aftermath of the Anglo-Irish Agreement no speech by a unionist politician seems to be complete without some reference to this inalienable right. However, there has been little or no attempt to explore exactly what is meant by this term. The unfortunate truth is that, with few exceptions, unionists do not care to move beyond the shadows of the parochial cave to try to attain the clarity of theoretical argument.

By failing to do so they tend to leave themselves open to misinterpretation and misunderstanding, for it is easy to convict the claim to self-determination of special pleading.

That usually takes the following form. Whenever unionists oppose some constitutional initiative, like the Anglo-Irish Agreement, in the name of the right to self-determination, those with little knowledge of Ulster affairs will respond: "There you have it. Unionists keep on asserting what good and loyal citizens they are, are keen to wave the Union Jack and prostrate themselves before the feet of the Royal Family. Yet whenever the government of the United Kingdom does something which they do not like out they come with all this talk of self-determination. Well, I am afraid, they cannot have it both ways. It is contradictory for unionists to claim to be good citizens while eluding the obligations of citizenship with this escape-hatch of self-determination". The thrust of this understanding is that unionist politics is all about trying to have your political cake and eating it.

In his book *Queens' Rebels* (1978), David Miller begins with a unionist conundrum and develops a persuasive solution to it. He argues that "few aspects of the contemporary Ulster problem are more perplexing to British and other outside observers than the conditional character of the loyalty professed by those known as loyalists". He resolves this perplexity by an interpretation of unionism which puts it squarely within "a venerable theory of political obligation – that of the social contract thinkers" of the 17th century, in particular "the peculiar Scottish variant of contractarian thought and practice, covenanting".

What does Miller's thesis say about unionism? First, unionist "loyalty" is the neat coincidence of self-interest and constitutional principle. Unionists are never loyal to mere governments but to those constitutional requirements necessary to maintain and secure the supremacy of the Protestant way of life. Therefore unionism is rather uncomfortable in the real world of politics with all its compromises and imperfections, for it seeks refuge in ideal absolutes – absolutes like the Williamite settlement, the coronation oath or the will of the majority. Secondly, this explains why unionism is at one and the same time absolutely loyal and utterly rebellious. It is absolutely loyal to the symbols of the union because they are invested with the purposes of Ulster Protestants. It is utterly rebellious because it will take to the streets with an anarchic fervour if there is any suggestion that those ascribed purposes will be "compromised".

In this light, unionism is a political contradiction and stands condemned as essentially self-serving and particular. The notion of self-determination is simply the rephrasing of the theme of conditional loyalty, of covenanting thought, and this is "anomalous in our own day". Unionism is a contemporary irrelevance because the theory of political obligation which it embodies is redundant. The development of the modern state since the 17th century has superseded it. Unionist conditional loyalty, the covenanting spirit of self-determination, remains as a curious fossil within the solid mass of the British polity.

However, Miller's thesis, which has become part of the received wisdom of the media, is founded on a number of questionable assumptions. First, it assumes a progressive view of politics in which the problems of Hobbes, Locke or even Knox have been solved and remain of mere antiquarian interest. Now, the idea of a contract between sovereign and subject may be ambiguous and perhaps may not help us much to understand the politics of welfare or budget management. But in the sphere of constitutional arrangements it does seem remarkably fresh and apt. Not just to unionists but to successive secretaries of state at the Northern Ireland Office who, from William Whitelaw onwards, have been reminding unionist politicians that United Kingdom rights carry with them corresponding duties. That is the language of contract if nothing else. The major issue of Ulster politics is not to make unionists recognise that there are obligations which attend their membership of the United Kingdom. The central problem since 1972 has been that the conditions and obligations which British governments have wanted to impose on unionists have seemed an intolerable qualification of their ultimate constitutional right to remain part of the United Kingdom.

Moreover, Miller's argument does not differentiate the meanings of loyalty. It if had done so it would have come to a very different conclusion. For instance, the authority of the institutions of the British state does not lie in an appeal to the nation. There is no such thing as the British nation. There are only British citizens who happen to be English, Scottish, Welsh, Irish and some who would be none of these. Loyalty in United Kingdom terms must mean something else than loyalty to the "nation" of which Miller makes a political fetish.

We get closer to what it means when we consider the proposition that it involves loyalty to the idea of the Union. The idea of the Union is the willing community of citizens united not by creed, colour or ethnicity but by a recognition of the authority of the Union. Its relevant concept is citizenship and not nation. In contemporary circumstances, citizenship is a democratic ideal which embraces different nations, different religious, different colours as equal citizens under the authority of a single state.

The notion of the Crown is as close as one can get to a working theory of the British state. At this point it may be said that unionism, despite its archaic and curious formulations, does express the wisdom of both these aspects of modern British politics. The Solemn Covenant of 1912 speaks of "the cherished position of equal citizenship in the United Kingdom" from which unionists had no wish at all to secede in the name of "self-determination."

The Anglo-Irish Agreement has revived the cry of equal citizenship as the touchstone of unionism. Irish republicans, on the other hand, did not and do not subscribe to the pluralism of equal citizenship for that conflicts with the distinctiveness of the nation one and indivisible. Unionism too has celebrated loyalty to the crown and distinguished this from loyalty to the actions of particular governments. This is no peculiar self-indulgence at all. It is an understandable and rational distinction and underlies the practice of modern political life. Thus Ulster unionism, far from being a historical curiosity, expresses self-consciously the operative values of the British state.

According to Bikhu Parekh, to suggest that the state should be based "on the unity of nationhood in the hope of returning to a state of primitive simplicity is to understand neither its nature nor its wider context". The modern state "is a self-sufficient institution based on the rational unity of its authority".[2] As such it can allow for diversity and liberty and social experimentation, the very insight which led Hegel to distinguish between state and civil society, to define the affairs of state in terms of right and not race.

That is the notion of the state to which intelligent unionism subscribes. It was the notion from which the present Republic of Ireland seceded in order to construct a state on the principles of national and religious exclusiveness. And it is a very strange situation in which the political intelligentsia in Great Britain seemed disposed to ignore the rationality of the Union as a guarantee of both religious diversity and political right in Northern Ireland and to subscribe to the ultimate authority of the idea of a united Ireland. For the authority of that idea is a reactionary one and deeply imbued with the spirit of racism. However, Ulster unionists have to deal not only with the crypto-racism of Irish nationalism. They have also to deal with the crypto-racism of the British political establishment which has sought to exclude them from full membership of the United Kingdom. No wonder, then, that the theory of the state adequate to the defence of the rights of racial minorities in Britain, and so effectively advanced by thinkers like Parekh, should find favour with Ulster unionists today. For that theory is really the idea of the Union.

Therefore, it is an issue of profound constitutional significance when the government appears to put the integrity of the Union at stake, for instance by directly involving the government of the Republic of Ireland in the administration of Northern Ireland without the consent of the majority in the province. Unionists hold that in this case the government is not acting within its sovereign power for it is not within the gift of governments to alter unilaterally the conditions of the Union, simply because the Union is not fully theirs to do so. The Union belongs to its citizens, not to the denizens of Whitehall.

It is not Ulster unionists who are conditionally loyal to the British state but British governments themselves that have only been conditionally loyal to the idea of the Union, that have been reluctant to live up to the duties and responsibilities implied by the expression "a sovereign state". Miller himself recognises this though he cannot understand its significance. Westminster "was unwilling to give meaningful assurances of a determination to make the United Kingdom the state in Northern Ireland". In this light, conditional loyalty to the government of the day is quite rational. It is essentially a response to a crisis of will on the part of the sovereign.

There is more to the idea of the Union, unionists believe, than merely being subject to the sovereignty of parliament. It means something more than a meekly grateful people bowing before the wise injunctions of an elected leviathan. That is another muddle assiduously cultivated by those who like to exercise power but find it inconvenient to acknowledge such difficulties as limits, justice and right. Sovereignty is not unconditional authority. Sovereignty is the whole body of a political association at one in the acknowledgement of the legitimate conditions of rule. British policy in Ulster has often seemed a repudiation of the spirit of United Kingdom sovereignty, a reluctant exercise of authority which has helped foster the conditions of instability.

Unionist resistance to "constitutional initiatives" such as the Anglo-Irish Agreement is founded on the basis of holding the government to the principles which it, in other circumstances, professes to espouse. Thus, the crisis of "conditionality" from which Northern Ireland suffers is not the conditional loyalty of Ulster unionists. Instead

Northern Ireland suffers from an ambiguity at the very heart of British rule. British governments have systematically acknowledged that Northern Ireland is an integral part of the United Kingdom and equally systematically failed to act on that principle. Such ambiguity has fuelled nationalist intransigence and unionist bloody-mindedness. In an excellent survey of the territorial dimension in modern British politics, Jim Bulpitt concluded in *Territory and Power in the United Kingdom* (1983) that "whatever the morality of the issue" unionist "fears of a sell-out seem justified" given the experience of the pusillanimity of successive British governments.

Four

How do these preliminary considerations inform an interpretation of the unionist idea of "self-determination" and the nature of our present political and semantic confusions? Traditionally, unionists have been advocates of a form of self-determination which is the opposite of that conventionally understood in political discourse. The principle of self-determination is usually advanced by those groups seeking some form of separate development. The principle of self-determination is most often a claim to fashion a form of political association which differentiates a specific communal identity. The institutions of state are to be employed to establish authoritatively this identity, to define its boundaries and to perpetuate its character.

Historically this form of self-determination was precisely what unionist leaders did not want. They had no desire whatsoever to make Northern Ireland into a distinct and differentiated residuum of the United Kingdom. The accepted wisdom of unionist politics was to ensure that the rights as well as the duties of citizenship were equal throughout the state. In this respect unionists wanted to be the same as, and not different from, all other British citizens. Their concern for self-determination was not one of positive ethnic, religious or national special pleading. Rather it was a negative one: namely, that British citizens ought not be compelled against their will to become part of an Irish state. On the other hand, British governments have had a positive notion of self-determination for Northern Ireland and have wanted to encourage a separate political identity amongst unionists separate from the rest of the UK.

This has been for two related reasons. First, it has been common ground between the political parties in Great Britain to keep Ulster's affairs as far as possible out of the mainstream of British public life. Lloyd George's Government of Ireland Act (1920) was precisely an attempt to conjure, as A.J.P. Taylor has put it, the Irish question out of existence. Devolution of one sort or another, from the Stormont model to power-sharing, has been part of a consistent strategy to achieve this marginalization of Ulster from the affairs of the British state. Second, it was originally hoped that devolved government for Northern Ireland would encourage an eventual coming together of Irish people north and south in amity and concord. Therefore, as Birrell and Murie point out in *Policy and Government in Northern Ireland* (1980), the devolved governmental institutions established in Belfast which have gone down in history as the "Orange state" or the "Stormont system" were not set up "in response to demands within the six north-eastern counties of Ireland for a form of regional government". Unionists had only accepted it, as Sir James

Craig made painfully clear, as "a final settlement and supreme sacrifice in the interests of peace" in Ireland.

It is rare to find politicians reluctant to accept power. Yet unionist leaders had no desire to exercise the responsibilities thrust upon them. In particular unionist leaders had no desire to "dominate" Catholics in the pursuit of loyalist self-determination. As Lord Carson argued in the House of Commons which then, as now, was not prepared to listen, unionists had never asked to govern any Ulster Catholic but were perfectly happy that both Protestants and Catholics should be governed directly from Westminster. The strongest foundation for the good government of Ulster, he argued, was the fact that Westminster was aloof from the religious and racial distinction of its inhabitants. These are hardly the words of a power-hungry supremacist. They are a recognition that, to use Churchill's phrase, the integrity of the quarrel in Ulster could not be solved by confining it to Ulster (by political or military "Ulsterisation") nor by abandoning Ulster unionists to Irish nationalist prejudice (which would appear to be the aim of those who equate the political will of Ulster unionists with the echoes of English imperialism). That quarrel could only be properly addressed within the framework of a modern state which was above the passions of either faction. Despite the impeccable logic of this argument, Westminster forced unionists to accept the "necessary evil" of devolved government and cast them back upon their own resources to decide whether Northern Ireland remained within the union or succumbed to the "natural" eventuality of a united Ireland.

An understanding of the reluctance on the part of unionists to accept the future mapped out for them by Lloyd George and his colleagues is essential to a deeper understanding of the unionist idea of self-determination. Founded on this original premise of what self-determination in Northern Ireland meant for unionism there developed a style of devolved politics which was both rational and necessary. In a memorable phrase, Brendan Clifford has characterised this style as "masterful inactivity". The system imposed on unionists in 1920 was designed to exclude the province from British political life. "For more than forty years the disruptive bias of that system was partially counteracted by the approach of the Unionist Party". This was done by "minimizing political activity in the province". Masterful inactivity was the genius of unionist self-determination. It was designed to prevent "Stormont from becoming a state" – at least from becoming a state which has illusions about being self-determined. So the efficient secret of unionist politics after 1920 was political indolence. It was the avoidance of all those statesmanlike values which have been subsequently lauded; values like constitutional dynamism, imagination and initiative. These may be relevant in an independent state like the Republic of Ireland but quite contradictory in the conditions of willing subordination manifested historically by the practice of devolved government in Northern Ireland.

However, masterful inactivity regarding the powers available to Stormont was only one side of the coin. The other was a considered determination to ensure that Northern Ireland kept fully in step with the standard of public services available in the rest of the United Kingdom. As R.J. Lawrence has argued in *The Government of Northern Ireland* (1965), the concern of the unionist leadership was not political independence but material improvement within the United Kingdom. Parity of public provisions was the material dimension of equal citizenship and it was always a unionist maxim that this should be recognised as a right and not as a charity. This masterful activity meant that Ulster remained in harmony with the substantial achievements and the inherited values of the British state. It did so because, very wisely, unionist "self-determination" operated under a popularly acceptable and politically rational self-denying ordinance. The great exception to this was security. Unionist interest in devolved government really focused on the control of security. Yet even this supreme concern was a rather negative enterprise. It had to do with preventing Republican insurgency and containing political disaffection inflamed by the irredentist claim on Ulster territory made by the Irish state.

Stormont's essential purpose was to hold Ulster for the union and not to lay the foundations for an independent Protestant state (the stuff of nationalist mythology). This was a progressive enough task given the alternative of absorption within a narrow and exclusive Gaelic nation state, the ethos of which owed more to the right-wing authoritarianism of central Europe than to the traditions of western liberal democracy. But this task had to do with self-defence rather than with a grand theory of self-determination.

Five

Now it may be countered that the interpretation so far is a one-sided view and does not do full justice to the character of unionism; that it ignores a deep current of political thought which places more emphasis upon an "Ulster identity" than upon British citizenship; and that this current of thought is indeed separatist, is concerned to attain an explicit form of political self-determination even to the extent of going for independence.

Of course that current does exist and finds expression in a number of popular ways from bar bravado to the waving of Ulster flags. And there is no doubt that it is a legacy of 50 years of unionist government at Stormont. That is a long enough time for some politicians and citizens to confuse the shadow of power with its substance and to invert the purpose of unionism, to confuse government in Belfast as an end in itself rather than as a means to secure the end of maintaining the union of Great Britain and Northern Ireland.

However, an investigation of these attitudes only reveals more clearly the validity of the preceding argument. Unionist response to the Anglo-Irish Agreement provides us with a useful example to test the proposition. Rumination on the idea of independence or other forms of separatism has taken place since Hillsborough and has appealed to political emotionalism. It claims justification by reference to a (rather ill-defined) right to self-determination.

And so, nearly every unionist politician worth his or her salt would argue that the alternative to the Union is not some form of united Ireland – or at least not while there is still a unionist majority in Northern Ireland. The "naturalness" of a united Ireland is usually countered by an argument which proposes the equal naturalness of an independent Ulster. If the Irish can claim to be a nation then the British of Ulster can equally claim that right to "national" self-determination. If unionists are going to be cast out of the union then they have the right to decide under what form of governance they should live. The emotionalism lies not in the justice of the argument itself but in the imagery it conjures up – imagery of the sturdy Ulster folk, their industriousness, cheery character and determination in adversity. "Our wee Ulster" becomes the centre of its own universe, deciding its own fate from the inner resources of the popular will.

But the ground of this reaction is a valid concern with the quality of the Union. The Union is an idea. It is not just whatever temporary set of constitutional arrangements the government of the day sees fit to impose upon a number of its citizens. The idea of the Union embodies rights and values which cannot be bartered away in an agreement with another state without the wiling consent of those to whom the agreement applies. Therefore independence is really a claim for the people of Ulster to be treated as full and equal British citizens and not as serfs or chattel. It is a rather convoluted way in which to make that particular claim but it is so nonetheless.

There is absolutely no evidence that unionists have ever seriously considered declaring some form of Unilateral Declaration of Independence. Nor is there any evidence at all that unionist voters would in 1985 have been prepared to support such an action. The fact that the anti-Agreement campaign has followed the very restrained and limited course that it has done is because unionist leaders have been well aware of the spirit of their support. That support is for the Union and not for full-blooded "self-determination". Thus Peter Robinson who talked of Northern Ireland being on the "window-ledge" of the Union was the same Peter Robinson who argued that unionists should not jump off that window-ledge. He was in favour of taking every "practical step to get back to good order and government". Indeed, he made it very clear that the aim of unionism should remain "the union, the whole union and nothing but the union".

The unionist idea of self-determination is a very tricky term for the unwary or for the superficial commentators (who account for the bulk of what passes for analysis of Ulster unionism). And because of its confusion it would probably be best for unionists themselves to be cautious and restrained in their use of it. It would be advisable if they kept faith with the expression "equal citizenship" appropriate to a doctrine concerned with the integrity of state, which unionism is, rather than self-determination, which is an appropriate response to the abiding concerns of nationalists. Equality of citizenship is a vital principle to articulate and to advance, for only the Union can accommodate the diversity of private and public life to be found in Ulster.

Six

Irish nationalism cannot. Unlike unionism, it is fully exercised by the issue of identity, with degrees of nationhood defined in cultural rather than political terms. It is not concerned with the autonomous principles of the modern state but with the absolute justice of claims made on the basis of ethnic community, "an Irish imagined community" complex, rich and emotional, celebrated in art, language and religion. The Irish Republic embodies this notion of identity in state form and has constructed a political order around those principles.

Before the Anglo-Irish Agreement was signed, the Republican state made some pretence to embrace all the people of the island of Ireland within its exclusive definition of identity. After the Agreement such a claim is either laughable or dishonest. The Agreement establishes the particularity of Irish nationalism as a political ideology. As a political expression it has defined itself as being only concerned with the satisfaction of Catholic demands and interests in Northern Ireland in particular and in Ireland in general. It has been convicted of such exclusiveness by its own authoritative and respectable advocates – the SDLP in Ulster and the vast majority of the political establishment in Dublin. That modern admission of the incorrigible sectarianism of Irish nationalism contradicts flatly all the musings about pluralistic Irelands so prevalent at the time of the New Ireland Forum Report (1984), so common in the moralisations of the leader columns of the *Irish Times.*

Unionists should give at least two cheers for the Anglo-Irish Agreement for revealing that clearly as never before. Sinn Féin and some Fianna Fáil members, to the credit of their own ideological purity and consistency, have refused to acknowledge the legitimacy of the Agreement on a principled basis (unlike those unprincipled advocates of the Agreement in the media, academia and public life who want to have the best of both worlds). But then, no one could ever accuse the IRA or their fellow-travellers of being interested in the unionist "ethos" or of having the slightest regard for liberal sensitivities.

Unionism, on the other hand, cannot be understood in terms of "nationality assumptions". It has little to do with the idea of the nation and everything to do with the idea of the state. Unionism is a very pure political doctrine in the sense that it is concerned almost exclusively with issues of right and citizenship. It has like Irish nationalism its large share of bigots and sectarians and religious fundamentalists.

But to imply that the idea of the Union is subordinate to the "supremacy" of loyalists or that it is just the political superstructure of evangelical Protestantism is to indulge in analytical inversion.

Unionism embraces a political allegiance the nature of which is to allow one to express whatever cultural values or identity one wishes. The idea of the Union, properly speaking, is one which transcends such outdated concepts as nationalism. As Parekh has put it, modern states are "by their very nature composed of different races, religions and cultures, and necessarily multi-national. Nationhood is not at all a practicable ideal for them. Nor is it a desirable ideal, for the glory of the modern state consists in creating a non-natural or non-biological basis of unity and uniting people with nothing in common save the state itself".

The principle of the modern British state fully and democratically applied in Northern Ireland is therefore appropriate to an amelioration of the current crisis for it in no way aspires to attain Parekh's "regressive and inherently impracticable goal of nationhood". That idea of the state which is embedded obscurely but nonetheless deeply within unionism is one which addresses the common problem of equality of rights and citizenship within a just political order. That idea is only obscured by the use of the term "self-determination". It is best illuminated by the unionist claim to the right of equal citizenship within the United Kingdom, a right which can accommodate the differences as well as the common ground between Protestant and Catholic in Ulster. (1995)

Endnotes

1 A. Bairner, "The Battlefield of Ideas: The Legitimacy of Political Violence in Northern Ireland," *European Journal of Political Research* 14 (1986).

2 B. Parekh, "The New Right and the Politics of Nationhood," in G. Cohen (ed.), *The New Right* (1986).

Loyalty Unrequited: Northern Ireland and Great Britain

Owen Polley

A few years ago, during our honeymoon in Cuba, my wife and I spent a few days at a beach resort. The hotel had arranged a meal for its British guests, in the way that these places do, and we found ourselves in conversation with a couple from the home counties. As we chatted, the husband embarked on a rambling monologue about the relative merits of people from the Republic of Ireland, as compared to those from Northern Ireland.

The southern Irish, he told us, are warm, friendly and fun, while the Northern Irish are dour, humourless and aggressive. He finished the lecture by asking, "Which part of Ireland are you from?", as his wife's face reflected the dawning realisation that her dinner companions were two of the cold, grim, hard-eyed breed of Irish.

I doubt he meant to insult us, but many Ulster people will have met fellow Brits, at home or abroad, who were similarly ignorant, naïve or mildly pejorative about our part of the UK. The refused Northern Irish banknote in a shop or taxi, the question about whether we use the euro, the comment that seems to assume we're governed from Dublin rather than London.

We may be shocked by this level of unawareness about a constituent part of the UK, but generally, the people concerned are not much interested in constitutional politics or current affairs in the regions. To unionists in Northern Ireland, though, it can feel like even the most politically engaged sections of the mainland British public are, at best, indifferent to the province's place in the Union and ambivalent about the concerns of Ulster unionism.

Often, it seems that nationalists' claims about the Troubles and the peace process, for example, are accepted more readily on the mainland than unionist views. On the left, outright support for republicanism is not uncommon. While Jeremy Corbyn's sympathies for Sinn Féin were controversial during his leadership of the Labour Party, it is doubtful they were a major factor in his eventual political downfall. The former *Daily Mirror* editor, Roy Greenslade, remained for many years a doyen of the media establishment, though it was widely known that he had written for *An Phoblacht*, the IRA's in-house newspaper.

On the right, the Conservative and Unionist Party often stresses its commitment to Northern Ireland's place in the United Kingdom. During his first prime ministerial visit to the Stormont Assembly, in 2011, David Cameron told MLAs, "I will never be neutral in expressing my support (for the Union)." This form of words, or something like it, has been repeated by Theresa May and Boris Johnson.

Unionists, though, will point out that successive Conservative governments have failed to challenge investigations into the legacy of the Troubles that focus, for the most part, on deaths caused by Britain's armed forces, rather than paramilitary crimes. Meanwhile, three different secretaries of state seemed reluctant to criticise

Sinn Féin while it refused to participate in power-sharing government from January 2017 to January 2020. When Julian Smith eventually allocated blame for the logjam, in 2019, he criticised the Democratic Unionist Party (DUP) rather than the republican party that crashed Stormont and linked its restoration to a lengthy list of demands (*Belfast Telegraph*, 19 December 2019).

The most traumatic recent example of the Conservatives' indifference to Northern Ireland is the Northern Ireland Protocol that sealed a Brexit deal for the United Kingdom. Infamously, while Theresa May was Prime Minister, Boris Johnson attacked her proposed "backstop" arrangement at the DUP's annual conference in 2018, declaring, "No British government could or should" agree to regulatory checks or customs controls between Great Britain and Ulster, a declaration the (Belfast) *News Letter* remembered on 17 October 2019. The Protocol which Mr Johnson signed little more than a year later placed just such an economic border in the Irish Sea, separating Northern Ireland from the rest of the UK's internal market.

That decision, which most unionists see as a betrayal, may well have been a pragmatic manoeuvre on the Prime Minister's behalf intended to make a Withdrawal Agreement with the EU possible. From the Northern Irish perspective, though, it looked like an acceptance of the nationalists' argument that a sea border was necessary because no extra checks or infrastructure could be contemplated at the Irish land frontier. Like Theresa May's "backstop", it prioritised nationalists' desire to protect links with the Republic of Ireland at the expense of unionists' right to see Northern Ireland treated as a full part of the United Kingdom economically and politically.

These events raise some potentially tricky questions. Are unionists right to feel that they do not get a fair hearing from their compatriots in the rest of the UK? Is there really widespread sympathy for or naivety toward the claims of Irish nationalism, at the expense of unionism? And if attitudes to Northern Ireland in Great Britain are often ambivalent and indifferent, why has this happened? Do Northern Irish unionists share any responsibility for being misunderstood by their fellow Britons and how can they communicate their ideas more clearly and compellingly to the rest of the UK?

Troubled history

The idea that unionism is treated unfairly by leaders in Great Britain is not new. Arguably, Northern Ireland's formation and the creation of a home rule parliament was regarded by loyalists as the original betrayal. When Johnson signed his Brexit deal, many unionists who were struggling to come to terms with the Protocol quoted a well-known speech by Lord Carson, delivered after the government brokered the Anglo–Irish Treaty in 1921 and agreed to the formation of the Irish Free State: "What a fool I was. I was only a puppet, and so was Ulster, and so was Ireland, in the political game that was to get the Conservative Party into power".[1]

This quotation has become a cliché, used as often by nationalists who want to imply that Ulster unionists' political bond with Great Britain is inauthentic, as by unionists who feel let down by Tory politicians. But it shows that the tradition of feeling abandoned by English statesmen is a long one in unionism; as is the idea that Northern Irish unionists must look after their own interests, because they cannot rely upon the national parliament.

If the events that created Stormont were viewed originally as a "betrayal", by 1972, when the Northern Ireland Parliament was suspended in favour of direct rule from Westminster, its abandonment was seen as appeasement of the IRA. Edward Heath's government took the decision as the province's security situation degenerated in the aftermath of Bloody Sunday, but unionists felt they had been failed by the Conservative prime minister. For a majority, their negative view of Heath deepened a year later, when the Sunningdale Agreement attempted to replace unionist majority rule with a power-sharing executive. The cross-border Council of Ireland was considered by many unionists, and some nationalists, to be a vehicle designed to bring about an all-Ireland state. When Heath died, the veteran Ulster Unionist Party (UUP) politician, Lord Kilclooney (formerly John Taylor, former deputy leader of the UUP), told the BBC on 18 July, 2005: "His perception of Northern Ireland was one of distaste and he did not look kindly upon Ulster Unionists."

Whether Lord Kilclooney's judgement was accurate or not, it was certainly a comment that could be applied fairly to many other high-profile members of the British establishment. The former chancellor of the exchequer, Ken Clarke, once condemned a Conservative pact with the UUP with the contemptuous observation, "You can always do a deal with an Ulsterman, but it's not the way to run a modern, sophisticated society."[2] Similarly, in a column for *The Times* ('We'll all pay for the EU obsession of the right', 19 November 2019), the celebrated journalist, Sir Max Hastings, boasted that, when he became editor of *The Daily Telegraph*, he insisted, "No further leading articles or columns should enthuse about hanging, the

Pretoria government or the Ulster Unionists." This level of disdain was remarkable, given that it was directed at a group of people who simply wanted to maintain their place in the United Kingdom.

Unionists feel most hurt when they believe that they have been treated with bad faith by politicians who largely support their outlook. Margaret Thatcher's signature of the Anglo-Irish Agreement in 1985 was the most infamous example from recent history, at least until Johnson accepted the Protocol in 2019. Thatcher gained respect and trust from unionists by taking a tough line with IRA hunger strikers. She later ruled out a "unified Ireland", or sharing "joint authority" over Northern Ireland with the Dublin government, in forthright terms (www.rte.ie/archives). But, one year later, the Anglo-Irish Agreement gave the Republic a direct say in the North's affairs in a way that unionists felt resembled joint authority. The Anglo-Irish Intergovernmental Conference that the Agreement established had a "consultative" role, but that did not comfort pro-Union politicians in Ulster, who had been excluded from the negotiations when it was agreed. While Dublin could propose policies for Northern Ireland through the new body, unionists were excluded from decision-making until they accepted a devolved, power-sharing government for the province.

After the Ulster Unionists negotiated the Belfast Agreement in 1998, they argued that it replaced the hated Anglo-Irish arrangements with institutions that prevented Dublin from interfering in Northern Ireland's internal affairs. Within unionism, there is still a hotly contested debate about whether the Good Friday deal benefited the province and the Union, or whether the moral compromises it entailed were unjustified. Some unionists believe that the text of the Agreement, which emphasises the "principle of consent", gives added force to their arguments that Northern Ireland should be treated as an integral part of the UK. If nationalists have repeatedly used the document to make contentious claims, by relying on references to its "spirit" and "context", this is partly because pro-Union politicians have been reluctant to "own" the accord. This way of thinking has led unionists to launch a case challenging the legality of the Northern Ireland Protocol on the basis that it is incompatible with the Agreement.

In contrast, the Loyalist Communities Council (LCC), which claims to represent paramilitary groups like the Ulster Volunteer Force (UVF) and the Ulster Defence Association (UDA), recently withdrew its support for the Agreement, due to its opposition to the Protocol. Other unionists see the Belfast Agreement as one concession to nationalism in an unbroken stream of similar defeats. The Downing Street Declaration of 1993, which is viewed as a key development in the lead-up to the Good Friday negotiation, stated that the British government had no "selfish strategic or economic interest in Northern Ireland."[3] In a letter to the *Irish Times*, the academic Michael J. Donnelly later pointed out that the absence of a comma between 'selfish' and 'strategic' made a significant difference to the meaning of the clause ("A strategically placed comma", 17 December 2008). The snub to unionists may not have been as strong or as deliberate as it is sometimes portrayed, but nevertheless it caused lasting offence to many British people in Northern Ireland.

The merits of the Good Friday Agreement are difficult

to assess, without considering the events that followed its implementation. Many unionists feel they have received little in return for the trauma of freeing unrepentant terrorists. Rather than show contrition for its crimes, the republican movement has collapsed the institutions at Stormont repeatedly, and has made constant demands, while celebrating its bloody past and demonising unionism. The devolved executive, meanwhile, passed few laws while it actually was sitting and failed to tackle the province's persistent problems with economic underachievement, segregated housing and education, outdated public services and inadequate infrastructure.

The actions of the national government since 1998 have contributed to this sense of unease about the Agreement's legacy. We now know, for instance, that Tony Blair's administration devised a secret scheme to provide "letters of comfort" to IRA men who were wanted for terrorist crimes. It was disclosed that, during the same period (2000–2002), sixteen republicans received royal pardons for existing convictions. Against this backdrop, many unionists are persuaded that the Belfast Agreement and the "peace process" are examples of decision makers in Great Britain mollifying Irish nationalists and treating unionists with disdain.

Accepting the nationalist narrative?
At the heart of the Belfast Agreement is an acknowledgement that "the present wish of a majority of people in Northern Ireland, freely exercised and legitimate, is to maintain the Union and, accordingly, that Northern Ireland's status as part of the United Kingdom reflects and relies upon that wish ... it would be wrong to make any

change in the status of Northern Ireland save with the consent of a majority of its people."

This commitment to the "principle of consent" explains why many unionists believe that the Agreement benefits unionism and strengthens its position. It is a coherent argument, but there are signs that, in Great Britain, nationalists' imaginative claims about the document are frequently more influential than unionists' literal citations of the text.

The idea that the Agreement somehow prevented Northern Ireland from leaving the European Union featured early in the Brexit negotiations and was never challenged effectively by the government, even after it was rebuffed by the Supreme Court. These arguments relied upon interpreting the "context" or "spirit" of the 1998 document, though sometimes nationalist politicians went so far as to assert the literal existence of hidden content. The Social Democratic and Labour Party (SDLP) MP Claire Hanna told a conference in southern Ireland that the Agreement included a "fourth unwritten … strand. The European dimension".[4]

In a briefing note for the think tank, Policy Exchange (The Backstop Paralysis: A Way Out, 2019), the historian and crossbench peer, Lord Bew, noted that "The most remarkable aspect of the UK's negotiation to leave the EU is the way in which the British Government has allowed the Irish Government to control the narrative around the Good Friday Agreement unchallenged." His observation was made during the negotiations. After they concluded, Joe Biden's U.S. administration, with its links to the influential Irish American lobby, took to implying that any deviation from the Northern Ireland Protocol was a breach of the 1998 deal.

Nationalism's creative interpretation of the Agreement is not a new problem for unionism. Alongside the concept of "parity of esteem", nationalists have used the deal's provisions on identity to argue that the Republic of Ireland's symbols and institutions should in Northern Ireland enjoy equal status to those of the UK. Most recently, these clauses were cited by an unsuccessful campaign that tried to undermine British citizenship law in the province. A court challenge claimed that conferring British citizenship automatically on people born in Northern Ireland, under the British Nationality Act 1981, was a breach of the Agreement's commitment to protect "the birthright of all the people of Northern Ireland to identify themselves and be accepted as Irish or British, or both, as they may so choose." The Upper Tribunal for immigration and asylum ruled decisively: "If the parties to the multi-party Agreement and the governments of Ireland and the United Kingdom had intended this concept of self-identification … to include a person's ability to reject his or her Irish or British citizenship, it is inconceivable that the provisions would not have dealt with this expressly."

Perhaps unionists could have been more relaxed about this case had the prime minister at the time, Theresa May, not delivered a speech in Belfast, promising that the home secretary would "review these issues urgently". Her secretary of state for Northern Ireland, Julian Smith, told the Northern Ireland Select Committee, "We need change … citizenship is very clear in that document and that Agreement and we will deliver on it."[5] It seemed to many unionists that while the courts were able to spot a misrepresentation of the Good Friday accord by nationalists, the British government was nowhere nearly as dependable, even when Conservative and Unionist ministers were in office. It deepened their suspicions that the Agreement could be used to distance Northern Ireland from norms in the rest of the UK.

Affection in the face of hostility and contempt in the face of loyalty? Many commentators, both in Great Britain and Ireland, have claimed that anti-British sentiment in the Republic increased in frequency and ferocity after the EU referendum in 2016. The Dublin government, particularly Leo Varadkar and Simon Coveney's Fine Gael administration, appeared to foster a confrontational atmosphere. Columnists, even in reasonably staid newspapers like *The Irish Times*, felt free to make sweeping generalisations about British people. Eilis O'Hanlon accused the influential journalist, Fintan O'Toole, who enjoys popularity among liberal British readers as well as a domestic Irish audience, of inspiring "a dangerous new wave of anti-Britishness in Ireland" (28 January 2019: www.reaction.life).

In nationalist youth culture, too, observers detected a growing appetite for casual anti-British slurs and glorifications of republican violence. Some young Irish people took to describing British people routinely as "Tans"; a pejorative reference to irregular units of soldiers, known colloquially as the "Black and Tans", recruited by the Royal Irish Constabulary during the Irish War of Independence. The phrase "Up the 'Ra" (the IRA) reportedly enjoyed a resurgence. In *The Spectator*, the journalist Jenny McCartney wrote about "The chilling rise of IRA TikTok" (6 March 2021). She described a video on the social media platform created by somebody called "thatprovosniper", who filmed himself at a window, dressed in a balaclava, against a caption that read, "watching my British neighbour get into his car in the morning."

You might have expected this atmosphere of Anglophobia to encourage suspicion of Irish nationalism in Great Britain, or even a wave of sympathy for Northern Irish unionism. Some newspapers, magazines and websites certainly published commentary that expressed support for Northern Ireland's place in the Union and rejected political or economic barriers between the province and the mainland. At the same time, a slew of columns and features encouraged the notion that Northern Ireland's absorption by the Republic was imminent or claimed that an Irish Sea border was necessary to protect the "peace process". More significantly, political and institutional push-back against Dublin's sermons was hard to find.

During the Brexit negotiations and the associated debates at Westminster, Irish ministers kept up a running commentary on internal UK politics. The habit extended to the British justice system. When he was Deputy Taoiseach and foreign minister, Simon Coveney publicly challenged the detention of the dissident republican terrorist Tony Taylor, drawing a rebuke even from the Alliance Party, which describes itself as "agnostic" on Northern Ireland's constitutional future (*News Letter*, 10 May 2018). More recently, in an article in the *Guardian* (11 February 2021), the Irish president, Michael D. Higgins, accused Britons of feigning "amnesia" about the legacy of British imperialism, while claiming Irish citizens were engaged in "ethical remembering" of the two islands' shared past.

It is unlikely that any member of the British establishment would feel comfortable writing about the Republic in such a lecturing tone, particularly in a southern Irish newspaper. It is even more improbable that a UK minister would consider involving him or herself publicly in current political debates or court cases taking place in a neighbouring state. Yet none of these slights drew any response from British ministers. Indeed, not a few government MPs, like Simon Hoare, the chairman of the Northern Ireland Select Committee, habitually used social media to share nationalist interventions on Britain, Brexit and Northern Ireland with tacit approval.

Commentators have frequently alleged that there are similar attitudes in other influential British institutions. In his book, *Can We Still Trust the BBC?* (Continuum, 2007), the journalist Robin Aitken wrote, "Within the context of the Northern Ireland conflict it has often been the case that the BBC has presented ... republicans as the good guys whose aims are largely justified; by contrast, unionists are the 'blockers' standing in the way (of)... a just settlement." In an article about recent anti-Protocol violence by loyalists, the former political editor of *The Spectator*, Bruce Anderson, tried to explain why attitudes to nationalism in England often seem more forgiving than attitudes to unionism. "Ulster unionists have always been good at economising on charm," he asserted, whereas "Irish Catholics never make that mistake, though foreigners would be well-advised to remember that charm is not synonymous with truth" (12 April 2021: www.reaction.life). This is a rather broad generalisation, but it highlights stereotypes about Northern Ireland that shape views in Great Britain and offers an insight into the ways that unionism and nationalism are commonly perceived.

Unionist responsibility for the state of relationships with GB

If unionists in Northern Ireland are often viewed negatively or indifferently by fellow Britons, do they share any responsibility for that perception, or are they ignored and misunderstood without good reason? In the *Daily Telegraph* (2 March 2019), the former Conservative MEP Daniel Hannan argued that unionists' loyalty to Great Britain was always deeply conditional. "Don't underestimate the canny, materialistic aspect of unionism," he warned readers, during the parliamentary debates about Theresa May's Brexit "backstop".

Unionist parties in Northern Ireland do not always act in a way that allays these suspicions or quells the notion that they are out of tune with mainstream British politics, values and ideas. The DUP, which has led unionism in Ulster since 2004, played a role in the national EU referendum and signed a "confidence and supply" arrangement with the Conservative Party in support of Theresa May's government, but it has a long history of exceptionalism. The party's founder, Ian Paisley, frequently railed against the perfidy of "the Brits". He once claimed that Ulster Protestants were scared only because "We're in the hands of our English masters and we understand that they are not our friends … they would like to destroy us."[6] In an article for *The Guardian* (12 September 2014), Gerry Adams claimed that Paisley told Martin McGuinness, "We don't need Englishmen to rule us … we can do that ourselves." And at the party's 1991 conference, its future leader, Peter Robinson, delivered a speech expressing the belief "that an independent Ulster is an alternative to a united Ireland or to a mutation between Dublin rule and direct rule" (*News Letter*, 25 August 2018). His remarks showed that the DUP's loyalty to the British state was deeply conditional at that time.

During "confidence and supply" talks with the Conservatives, the party could have sought a full coalition government and genuine influence in national politics. Instead, it claimed it had secured £1 billion of funding for Northern Ireland as the price for its support. Some commentators suggested that this transactional approach eventually made it easier for the Tories to ditch the DUP and accept an Irish Sea border.[7] At the same time, the party supported profound differences between Northern Ireland and Great Britain in law and politics. They included sensitive social issues like same-sex marriage and abortion, but also everyday matters, like libel reform and the devolution of Corporation Tax powers.

This tendency to treat Northern Ireland as a "place apart" from the mainland is not restricted to the DUP. The Ulster Unionist Party, initially sceptical about the creation of a home rule parliament at Stormont in 1921, became deeply attached to its powers. There is a compelling case, though it is frequently overstated, that, rather than focus on creating a modern, integrated part of the UK, they misused these functions, allowing nationalist grievances to fester and deepening opposition to the Union.

After the Northern Ireland Parliament was abolished, "integrationists" in the UUP, who wanted the province to be absorbed fully into national politics, clashed with "devolutionists", who concentrated on restoring Stormont's powers. In more recent years, there were similar tensions in the party after it formed an electoral pact with David Cameron's Conservatives. The Ulster Conservative and Unionists New Force (UCUNF) resulted in some of the most strident pro-Union rhetoric from a national party leader in decades, but failed narrowly to secure Westminster seats, and broke-up amidst accusations and recriminations.

Many unionists argue that they are wary of politicians in Great Britain precisely because they have been let down so frequently in the past. They point out, with justification, that Westminster formed Northern Ireland and gave it a home rule parliament specifically to distance London from the province and relinquish the "Irish problem".

The difficulties in this relationship, though, work both ways. Indifference to Northern Ireland on the British mainland causes unionists to feel detached from national politics. In turn, a lack of support for national parties here encourages government ministers to neglect or disregard the province's interests. Pro-Union people in Northern Ireland are willing to distance themselves from the British mainstream, so it is easier to treat them as something connected to, but different from, the rest of Britain.

Winning friends in Great Britain
While Northern Ireland was once an exception because of its political institutions, devolution in the United Kingdom is now firmly established and relatively popular. Thanks to separatism in Scotland and Wales, neither is it such an oddity that our politics focuses on constitutional issues. In strictly legal terms, the Union is secure until a majority of voters in Northern Ireland decide otherwise, through a border poll. Does it matter, then, if unionists are not viewed sympathetically in Great Britain?

I believe the answer is yes, for two important reasons. Firstly, though the UK is held together by laws and shared institutions, it also relies on a degree of social solidarity between its nations and regions. Northern Ireland's economy is dependent upon sizeable transfers of money from Westminster. At a time when the Union is being challenged on both sides of the Irish Sea, unionists cannot afford to allow their relationships with fellow Britons to deteriorate unchecked.

Secondly, the Protocol is a reminder that Northern Ireland's Britishness can be eroded without consent, as well as attacked directly. Unionists are furious because they believe they have been cut off from Britain's internal market to placate nationalists, who saw potential checks at the Irish land border as a blow to their own national all-island aspirations. Earlier, I highlighted the campaign to change British citizenship law in Northern Ireland. Persistently, nationalists claim that UK symbols or institutions are not appropriate here, or that their equivalents from the Republic of Ireland should be granted equal status.

It is partly for this reason that unionists find themselves constantly making defensive arguments. Many of the things that we oppose are important and should not be ignored, but perhaps we could spend more time telling a positive story about what we actually want. In a column for the *News Letter*, I suggested that one of unionism's key goals should be "to ensure that Northern Ireland plays as full a role as possible in the social, political and economic life of the (British) nation".

If the goals, worries and preoccupations of Northern Irish unionists were understood in that context, in Great Britain, would they be regarded with greater sympathy and command more influence? If they were tested consistently against such a principle, would unionism's campaigns, policies and arguments be stronger, more coherent and less alienating to fellow Britons?

There are good reasons for unionists in Ulster to feel that their loyalty has not been repaid adequately, and that they have been ignored and misunderstood by their compatriots. Equally, pro-Union politicians, commentators and academics have often failed to explain their positions clearly and sympathetically on the mainland. If Northern Irish unionists agree that strong relationships, right across the UK, are critical to maintaining the Union, they have a duty to engage with their counterparts in Great Britain more positively, persuasively and sincerely in the future.

Endnotes

1 House of Lords Debates, 14 December 1921 vol. 48 cc5–56.

2 "General Election 2010: unionist deal could make David Cameron prime minister", *The Daily Telegraph*, 4 May 2010.

3 'Joint Declaration 1993 (Downing Street Declaration)", www.dfa.ie

4 Owen Polley, "Footnoting the Belfast Agreement's invisible annex", *The Critic*, 3 August 2020.

5 "Julian Smith does not rule out amendments to British Nationality Act after DeSouza case is raised," *Derry Journal*, 23 October 2019.

6 Brian John Spencer, "Unionism's anglophobia", brianjohnspencer. blogspot.com, 16 February 2016.

7 See, for example, Henry Hill writing as a Tory unionist in the *News Letter*, 27 December 2019.

The Re-emergence of Devosceptic Unionism

Henry Hill

For two decades, unionists have been playing a game where their only permitted move is "backwards". Every challenge by separatists in any of the devolved territories can only be met by more concessions; the failure of those concessions to satiate the nationalists proves only that the concessions weren't ambitious enough. The result, two decades on from the advent of New Labour's new institutions, is a United Kingdom that feels closer than ever to breaking up – and a growing mutiny amongst unionists disenchanted with devolution.[1]

The re-emergence of devoscepticism is the result of the sustained failure of devolutionary unionism to deliver on the grand promises it made in the 1990s. Nationalism has not been killed "stone dead", and hundreds of new politicians have not produced a better class of public administration. For decades, Northern Ireland has offered unionists on the mainland a grim preview of the damage that legislative devolution does to the UK. Many of the worrying trends we can now see emerging in Scotland and Wales – the polarisation of politics around the constitution, the decline of substantive ideological dispute, and the attendant alienation of the party system from national governance – are long-standing features of Ulster politics.

It should deeply concern all of us who cherish the Province as part of our nation that to so many of our countrymen it crosses their radar only in the context of strife and dysfunction, let alone that it might offer a glimpse at the future for unionism in Scotland and Wales. Rather than acknowledge that there are fundamental flaws at the heart of their project, devolutionary commentators follow its logic to absurd conclusions, and advocate for an increasingly ethereal Union wherein the ambit of the central state is confined to such areas as foreign affairs and defence. Even there, common governance as Britons would give way to "shared rule", or horse-trading between the Home Nations.

A United Kingdom reorganised on such terms would not survive, and would not deserve to. For we would be asking voters to reject the separatists' conclusions whilst accepting their fundamental premise: that Britain is not a legitimate political or national community. It is folly to imagine that such a thing as a "British taxpayer", content to see their money distributed across the UK, would continue to exist if British governance did not. Without the pooling and sharing of decision-making, there can be no long-term consent for the pooling and sharing of cash.

Devoscepticism is thus an urgent and overdue challenge to the orthodoxies that have misruled unionist thinking since the Nineties. It asks essential questions not only about whether or not the tactics of the past two decades have worked or can hope to work, but whether the sort of Union implied by the logic of "devo max" is the one we actually want to be fighting for. What those questions are, and how those posing them are organising in British politics, is the subject of this chapter.

What is devoscepticism?
When Boris Johnson reportedly told a group of Conservative MPs that devolution had been a "disaster", he broke an *omertà* two decades in the making. Even if you agree that the devolution settlements drawn up by New Labour have wrought terrible damage on the United Kingdom (and there are plenty who do, across both the parties of government), in public one is supposed to feign enthusiasm for the "New United Kingdom" that is supposed to be emerging from Westminster's haphazard constitutional retreat from Scotland, Wales, and Northern Ireland.

Before explaining why devosceptic sentiment is on the rise, we should first clarify what exactly devoscepticism is. Much like "euroscepticism", it actually covers a broader range of opinion than it might first appear, ranging from outright abolitionists to those who merely wish to see a greater role for Westminster in national life and believe that a stronger and more assertive central authority is essential to balancing the various centrifugal energies unleashed by devolution. What they have in common is the belief that the orthodoxies that have dominated unionist thinking for the past two decades – essentially offering more and more concessions in the hope that eventually separatist sentiment can be bought off – have failed, and failed not because they have been applied with insufficient imagination or vigour but because the underlying assumptions on which they rest are fundamentally wrong.

The first school of devoscepticism – the "abolitionist"

tendency – is currently confined to minor parties. But just as the UK Independence Party (UKIP) managed to exert huge influence on national politics without winning major representation in Westminster, so might the various Abolish parties (and by the same means, namely exerting pressure on the Conservatives).

In Wales, an openly abolitionist party – the aptly named Abolish the Welsh Assembly Party – has attracted several defectors from what was once the UKIP caucus in the Welsh Parliament and at the time of writing is polling strongly enough to secure representation in its own right at the next Senedd. In Scotland, the unrelated "Abolish Holyrood" has secured the top spot on the regional ballot paper for the upcoming elections, and is pitching to a sizeable minority of unionist voters who remain unreconciled to the Scottish Parliament. In Northern Ireland devolution is much longer established, having been imposed (despite the wise warnings of Sir Edward Carson) as far back as the 1920s, and an "integrationist" party in the tradition of Robert McCartney's UK Unionist Party (UKUP), 1995–2008, has yet to emerge. But the crisis precipitated by the imposition of the Irish Sea border may yet prompt some in pro-Union circles to reconsider the wisdom of a political tradition which has left them with only tenuous links to the parties of government upon whom, as the saga of the Protocol illustrates, Northern Ireland's place in the United Kingdom depends – especially if the next election leaves them facing the prospect of a Sinn Féin First Minister.

Whilst the direct electoral impact of these parties is as yet limited, they can cast long shadows. In Scotland, polling suggests that a majority of Conservative voters would choose to do away with the Scottish Parliament if given the chance. But the concerns of Douglas Ross, leader of the Scottish Conservative Party, must pale when compared to those faced by his colleagues in Wales, where the leadership in Cardiff Bay faces not only a more powerful abolitionist challenge from outside but also a mounting revolt amongst their own grassroots. Several Tory candidates for the Senedd are publicly in favour of doing away with devolution, a number which is likely to increase as a new generation of sceptical activists comes of age and starts seeking office. Already the Party has been forced to abandon its long-held hope of ousting Labour via an arrangement with Plaid Cymru, the Welsh nationalists, a decision whose full implications for the future development of politics in Cardiff – polarisation around the constitutional question, or "Ulsterisation" – seems not yet to have been grasped by many observers.[2]

However, whilst it may secure an electoral beachhead in the Senedd, there is limited appetite for this sort of head-on confrontation at Westminster (at least in public). There is currently no prospect of a British government legislating to abolish the devolved institutions. At the centre a different school of devosceptic thought prevails. Its most signal achievement to date must be the UK Internal Market Act (UKIM), and for want of a more elegant label the UKIM School is as good a name for this branch of devoscepticism as any.

UKIM was a watershed moment in the British constitutional debate. The Government defied both post-1997 constitutional orthodoxy and the furious opposition of the devocrat class, jealously protective of their new post-EU powers, to reassert Westminster's prerogatives. Why?

First and foremost, as the name suggests, UKIM was

meant to protect the integrity of the British internal market. Its architects were motivated in part by the need to reverse the May Government's defeat over what was then Section 11 of the EU Withdrawal Bill, which would have seen powers formerly exercised by the European Union – including a huge range of economic powers – repatriated to Westminster. Those who drafted Section 11 believed this was urgently important because otherwise, a hostile government in Edinburgh or Cardiff could mandate dozens of small changes which would add up to serious disruption. But despite a clear case for it (perhaps best articulated by Daniel Robinson in his 2017 paper for These Islands, "Continuity, Devolution, and the EU Withdrawal Bill"), a House of Commons coalition of Labour, the Nationalists, and some of the Scottish Tories defeated it. UKIM was the fightback.

But it also signalled a much deeper shift in thinking, because the legislation empowered the Government to spend money directly in the devolved territories on policy areas for which their local legislatures are responsible. The hope is that the new spending powers authorised by UKIM will allow ministers to raise the profile of the Government and allow the British state to play a more active and visible role in areas where two decades of conceding "more powers" had left it an increasingly spectral presence. There is already talk in Conservative circles about a UKIM II which would expand the range of areas Westminster could intervene in yet further.

Ministers are keen to stress that this is always *additional* money, and the original budgets of the devolved legislatures are undiminished. This is true as far as it goes, although it represents a shift in power towards Westminster insofar as spending commitments made under UKIM don't generate Barnett Formula consequentials, which would have flowed to the devolved ministries. Nonetheless it does make it much harder for the latter to resist – what ordinary voter is going to object to receiving extra cash?

But the specific challenges posed by Britain's departure from the European Union don't explain the broader rise of devosceptic sentiment, especially amongst younger unionists who have come of age in the era of devolution. That hinges on two distinct but deeply entwined questions about the means and ends of the pro-UK movement. First, will the orthodox devolutionary approach actually save the Union? And second, what do we really mean by "save the Union", anyway?

Devolution in practice: retreat and defeat

In his book *The Question of Scotland: Devolution and After* (2016) Tam Dalyell, the pre-eminent devosceptic of his age, said that the huge danger of devolution to the United Kingdom was "predictable and predicted, foreseeable and foreseen". Yet someone who only started following the debate after the advent of the new institutions would be forgiven for not realising this. Time and again, as harried Westminster politicians have sought to buy off nationalist sentiment with tranche after tranche of constitutional concessions, the debate has proceeded as if the fundamental assumptions on which devolution rests were obviously sound. From the advent of New Labour in 1997 until arguably the passage of the UKIM Act in 2020, this was the hegemonic orthodoxy guiding unionist thinking as successive governments tried, and failed, to stabilise the constitution and stem the rise of the nationalists.

But take a look under the bonnet of many modern apologias for devolution and what one finds is not a conclusion drawn from the evidence, but an article of faith. Tony Blair, in an interview with ITV in April 2021, rested his defence of New Labour's constitutional approach on the following claim: "If the Labour Party hadn't implemented its manifesto commitment to do devolution in 1997, the union would already be in tatters." This is a common devolutionary claim. One of its chief advantages is that, like all historical counterfactuals, it is completely unfalsifiable. Only cling to it and not even the most ferocious onslaught of real-world experience can force one to confront the possibility that devolution not only hasn't worked from a unionist perspective but was doomed to fail. The idea that devolution is good for the Union is thus transformed from a proposition which can be tested against the evidence into an assumption that precedes it. Most of the more outlandish devolutionary proposals being advanced today, such as the idea that the solution to Scottish grievances is an English Parliament, make more sense when understood as the product of reasoning backwards from the pre-ordained conclusion that devolution must work.

Such thinking also spares devolution's defenders from engaging with the substance of the devosceptic case. This is an understandable reflex. A few brave souls, such as Eddie Barnes, have tried to acknowledge that "Michael Forsyth and Tam Dalyell were right" without conceding that such an admission prompts a fundamental rethink of what they were right about.[3] Most of his comrades, however, seem to recognise that this is a fool's errand. But many of Blair's generation seem trapped by the need to vindicate their original support for the idea, and if you must concede that devolution hasn't worked but can't concede that devolution was wrong, the only option really left open is to demand more of it, even if the result is a shallow, mercenary arrangement built on fiscal transfers that is a long way from whatever positive vision for Britain – including the "real cultural ties" the neglect of which Blair laments in his interview – one thought one was delivering in 1990.

The practical case for devoscepticism, on the other hand, is simple: devolution was supposed to "kill nationalism stone dead", and it hasn't. Whilst there were always those for whom it was an end in itself, the whole project was sold to unionists in these terms. George Robertson wasn't freelancing: the Labour manifesto for the 1997 election put it very clearly: "A sovereign Westminster Parliament will devolve power to Scotland and Wales. The Union will be strengthened and the threat of separatism removed". That's not how it has panned out.

Why this should be is no mystery to those prepared to countenance the devosceptic case. Devolution creates a system wherein the political incentives of all the major players, whether they're nominally unionist or separatist, are aligned against the integrity of the Union. The institutions sustain a class of politicians and assorted civic hangers-on (for whom I coined the term "devocrats") who derive salaries, sinecures, and status from them and profit from their aggrandisement. It is thus the invariable habit of devolved politicians to exploit the public's hazy understanding of who is responsible for what to shift the blame for their shortcomings on to Westminster and insist that the remedy is more money and powers for themselves.

This has the same corrosive effect on public attitudes towards the United Kingdom that decades of taking pot shots at "Brussels" had on voters' opinions on the European Union.

It also starts to estrange even unionist politics in a devolved territory from British politics. There is strong pressure for such parties to maximise their short-term electoral prospects by cutting inconvenient ties to national parties that restrict their freedom of manoeuvre. This is most obvious in Northern Ireland, where it has been decades since the Province returned any MPs who might have played a formal role in a British government. But the temptation for unionists to play nationalism locally is evident in Scotland too, where both advocates of Murdo Fraser's plan to split the Conservative Party and spokespeople for George Galloway's vehicle, the Alliance for Unity, have denounced the national parties "cracking the whip in Scotland"[4] and the onerous need to "defend mothership UK policies". Shockingly, having nobody prepared to fight Westminster's corner in a nation's politics does nothing for Westminster's reputation there.

If what it does to the unionists is bad, what it does for the nationalists (both separatist and otherwise) is worse. An increasingly powerful devolution settlement has given them plenty of pulpits, arsenals, and treasuries to turn against the United Kingdom. In Scotland the Scottish National Party (SNP) have taken great pains to excise symbols of the Union, even to the extent of trying to abolish the British Transport Police in the teeth of overwhelming opposition from officers on the ground. Meanwhile both they and the Labour administration in Wales have exploited their control of data collection to repeatedly either opt out of standardised international testing or else make the figures non-comparable on a UK-wide basis. Indeed, Cardiff ministers are so allergic to attempts to compare their performance with England that in 2014 Huw Lewis, then their education minister, accused Michael Gove of "indestructible colonial attitudes" when the latter had the nerve to pen an article for the *Western Mail* contrasting school outcomes on either side of Offa's Dyke. Of course, such aversion to clear and comparable metrics is understandable when the devolved administrations' actual records on key areas such as education and health are examined.

Northern Ireland, of course, is somewhat *sui generis* in that its devolution settlement is mandated by the Belfast Agreement, but Stormont is if anything even worse, combining a visible cycle of crisis and collapse with deeper-seated governance failures of the sort brutally exposed by the Renewable Heat Incentive fiasco, expertly chronicled by Sam McBride in *Burned: The Inside Story of the 'Cash-for-Ash' Scandal* (2019). Robert McCartney may be gone, but it ought to concern unionists more than it seems to that they are currently forced to accept the Union only on such extremely qualified and increasingly dysfunctional terms.

Devolution was supposed to see off the threat of nationalism, deliver better government, and bring power closer to the people. Instead, an avowedly separatist party has held office in Edinburgh for 14 years whilst Labour is standing pro-independence candidates in Cardiff; public administration is rarely improved and often noticeably worse; and both administrations have concentrated power rather than dispersing it. It is little wonder that a growing number of unionists have tired of the experiment.

Devolution in theory: repudiating Britain

But the practical failure of devolution to fulfil its promises to unionists is only part of the answer. Another is that for two decades, the debate on devolution has been framed by its advocates as being exclusively about means, as if the debate were merely about which tactics. Meanwhile what was meant by the supposed common aim of "saving the UK" was left unexamined. When this vital question is again considered, unionism divides.

On the one hand, there are the so-called "utilitarians", who support the UK for the practical benefits it brings to them. At the periphery, this is usually a combination of nationalism and a degree of practical hard-headedness – a programme of maximal fiscal transfers with minimal pooled obligations perhaps best described as the nationalism of the numerate. At the centre, it is often people who value our country's greater clout in foreign affairs, who prize the Armed Forces and the permanent seat on the UN Security Council, but have little invested in maintaining Britain as a unit for domestic government. (A dishonourable mention goes to a generation of largely Labour politicians who tried, by ignoring the West Lothian Question, to protect their role at Westminster even whilst refusing to protect Westminster's role in their constituencies.) This is the coalition that helped to deliver two decades of "devolve and forget".

Arrayed against them are those we might call "existential unionists", but could just as well call "the British": those for whom Britain is their preferred political community and the United Kingdom is their national state. Even a doctrinaire nationalist must concede that, counting those who say they are either "British only" or "More British than" anything else, there are millions of such people. They feel British, are loyal to British institutions, and wish to be governed as such along with the rest of their fellow Britons. Devolution leaves increasingly little space for this.

Once again, Northern Ireland was the canary in the coal mine. The logic of the arguments advanced by the Campaign for Equal Citizenship (begun 1986) may have been forgotten by unionist politicians with comfortable jobs at Stormont, but they are gaining currency on the mainland. There must be more to unionism than merely the existence of the UK, otherwise unionist parties risk ending up as little more than Union Jack-branded local nationalists, and devolved politics acquires the symbolic fury and ideological hollowness of an Old Firm match.

Utilitarian unionists can fairly ask why they should be concerned about the defence of the British nation if they don't feel any loyalty to it themselves. But an underlying sense of nationhood is the essential cement of any long-term political union – especially if it cannot avail itself of near-universal elite buy-in as the EU can. Without it, the core functions upon which the utilitarians base their case are unsustainable. It is folly to imagine, as some "federalists" seem to, that the pooling and sharing of resources on a needs basis (let alone a needs-plus basis, à la Barnett Formula) can endure if government on the basis of a shared identity does not. But under maximal devolution, money is increasingly all that is left of the case for a Union which can do less and less to make a direct difference in people's lives. That's the implication of describing "devo-max" plus full fiscal transfers as "the best of both worlds", as some figures in the multi-party Better Together campaign started to do during the 2014 referendum on Scottish independence.

To build a positive case for the Union that extends beyond money, unionists need to champion a Union that *actually does things*. This doesn't have to entail the outright abolition of the devolved legislatures and a return to the levels of centralisation witnessed under Margaret Thatcher. But it does mean making sure that the British state can act on the issues that matter most to its citizens. For example, there should be limits to the extent to which devolved administrations – especially those in receipt of grants from the centre – can mismanage public services before Westminster steps in to help. Ministers should retake control of the census and mandate the Office for National Statistics to collect comprehensive and comparable statistics for public sector performance across the UK. The Government should take the lead in building cross-border partnerships in areas where it makes most sense for passengers, pupils, or patients, for example by challenging the Welsh Government's stubborn insistence on north-south models that ignore Wales' economic geography.

In fact, such a programme need not be exclusively centralising at all. A hallmark of the devolutionary era has been devocrats putting the squeeze on local government. In Scotland, in particular, local authorities in places such as Aberdeen and the Northern Isles are actively reaching out to Westminster, looking for help to gain a greater measure of independence from the SNP's overweening authority in Edinburgh. This is a rich seam of potential support for the UKIM school of devosceptics. The salient point is that the UK's relationship with Welsh, Scottish, and Northern Irish voters should not be that of an arrangement entered into by their governments. The British Government is their government too. It should be on their side and able to help.

One might suggest that a waning sense of British nationhood is too weak to support the more assertive British state of the sort devosceptics are fighting for. But that is a two-way relationship. It is no coincidence that the British identity has waned after several decades in which the various institutions which lent a British shape to life – latterly Parliament, but before that the various nationalised industries and the other architecture of the post-War settlement – have been dismantled or diminished. The SNP did not wait around for a more separate sense of Scottishness, they used the institutions of the state to shape it. Devoscepticism demands that unionists do the same, whilst there is still time.

Whither Unionism?

From the perspective of the Spring of 2021, it is impossible to tell when exactly, if ever, the next pitched battle for the future of the United Kingdom will be fought. The Government has pledged to refuse the Section 30 order necessary to authorise a second referendum on Scottish independence even if the separatists do secure a Holyrood majority. The Labour administration in Cardiff Bay can be expected to grow even more nationalist if, as expected, it ends up depending on Plaid Cymru to hold office but support for independence still underpolls scrapping the Senedd. And whilst the situation in Northern Ireland is extremely volatile, most polls suggest there is not yet anything like the level of public support for annexation by the Republic that would put pressure on the Secretary of State to grant a border poll.

This means unionism has the political space for a serious rethink, and with the Conservative and Unionist Party's position in the national polls looking secure, it may actually get one. As bipartisan commitment to the post-1998 settlement starts to wane and older ideological differences re-emerge, devolution may yet become another of what Andrew Rawnsley identified in the *Observer* as the "pillars of Blairism" which now lie "broken in the dust" (10 July 2016). It is fashionable to describe the United Kingdom as a union of nations, which of course it is. But its true strength was that it also became *a nation of unions*, and the difference is as between fission and fusion. Unionism is at its strongest when it combines both approaches. Alone, a surly defence of the symbols and prerogatives of the "British community" has no appeal to swing voters whilst a mercenary appeal to fiscal transfers undermines the shared community on which consent for such transfers depends. If devolutionary unionism has forgotten this latter point, it is important that devosceptics not forget the former when trying to balance the scales.

A positive case for Britain must start with a positive idea of what Britain is and could be. Developing this is a challenge that we have neglected for too long. But whatever the answer is, we won't find it by drawing a polite veil across twenty years of retreat and taking a badly-designed and misfiring settlement as our inviolable starting point.

Endnotes

1 Henry Hill, "New polling shows Welsh devoscepticism is no longer a fringe interest". [online] ConservativeHome. (2021) Available at: <https://www.conservativehome.com/thecolumnists/2020/06/henry-hill-new-polling-shows-welsh-devoscepticism-is-no-longer-a-fringe-interest.html> [Accessed 11 June 2020].

2 Henry Hill, "Welsh politics shows how devolution has failed". [online] *The Spectator*. (2021) Available at: <https://www.spectator.co.uk/article/welsh-politics-shows-how-devolution-has-failed> [Accessed 1 March 2021].

3 E. Barnes, "Let's stop the devolution blame game and work on a British way forward". [online] CapX. (2021) Available at: <https://capx.co/lets-stop-the-devolution-blame-game-and-work-on-a-british-way-forward/> [Accessed 29 April 2021]

4 A. Maciver, "Too little too late for Tories?" *The Scotsman* [online] (2013) Available at: <https://www.scotsman.com/news/opinion/columnists/andy-maciver-too-little-too-late-tories-1592115> [Accessed 29 April 2021].

Legacy: when Warfare Turns to Lawfare

Jeffrey Dudgeon

Legacy is as complex as our history. Indeed it *is* our history and likely to be our future politics. Legacy is the remains of history, an inheritance or gift from the past, but in Irish politics it is an encumbrance. The legacy of the Troubles is the sum total of their appalling impact but it has been restricted to the deaths they caused. The history of legacy in the latter sense, particularly since the Belfast Agreement (1998), would require a book in itself. I can deal here only with some political outcomes of the last 25 years and the current state of play in a rapidly evolving game. Given that deaths from 50 years ago are being "excavated", it seems we may have another 50 to go.

Some legacy questions appear unanswerable, given the tortuous path we have followed since 1998. UK governments are trammelled by obligations that they have largely brought upon themselves. British diplomats have failed to challenge Dublin and Strasbourg at the Council of Europe: they seem to prefer the cosy consensus that makes an independent British foreign policy impossible.

Almost amnesty

The Belfast Agreement did away with the Royal Ulster Constabulary (RUC) and released all paramilitary prisoners who had served two years in jail. This was a police force that had suffered 300 deaths (the equivalent in Great Britain terms of 10,000). Otherwise, the Agreement kept away from the past, something many now regret. The prisoner releases constituted a significant element of amnesty, one that did not disturb the European Court of Human Rights (ECHR) despite the degree of impunity involved. It was effectively two-thirds of an amnesty. Later concessions have brought that figure up to 90%. These include the On-the-Run (OTR) letters of comfort for hundreds of IRA volunteers; an "amnesty" (the term used in the legislation) in relation to the use of forensic evidence on decommissioned weapons and the bodies of the disappeared (if discovered); Royal Prerogative of Mercy pardons like that for Gerry Kelly the convicted IRA bomber; prosecution indemnities for witnesses giving evidence at tribunals such as the Bloody Sunday enquiry; and the complete lack of investigations into the colossal number of people involved in the 16,000 bombings and 37,000 shootings of the Troubles which did not involve deaths. For some 50,000 people who were "only" injured there is to be no justice. Given the anticipated paucity of future prosecutions, except for Army veterans, we are close to a full amnesty in all but name.

Few dare to speak that name, or its variants: drawing a line, a statute of limitations, and putting the past behind us, as happened in both parts of Ireland in the 1920s. Ironically, Amnesty International is vigorously opposed to an amnesty, but many of the politicians involved privately admit to wanting one. Influential public figures in

Northern Ireland who have openly supported an amnesty or variant include influential Catholics and nationalists: John Larkin who as Attorney General proposed a stay on prosecutions; former Assistant Chief Constable Peter Sheridan; Dennis Bradley of the Consultative Group on the Past; the Lord Chief Justice Sir Declan Morgan; and the former Director of Public Prosecutions, Barra McGrory. Another notable advocate is Sir Desmond Rea, first chairman of the Northern Ireland Policing Board. None, however, has advanced proposals on how to tackle "lawfare", surely a necessary concomitant policy.

In 2005 Secretary of State Peter Hain introduced the Northern Ireland (Offences) Bill which provided for a "judicially based" amnesty for OTRs and others. He said then it was ECHR, Article 2 compliant. The deal in the Bill had been agreed with Sinn Féin, but when it transpired that it might apply to members of the security forces it foundered. The OTRs had to await another, secret operation put together by Tony Blair and Gerry Adams, involving 156 "letters of comfort" notifying IRA members that they were not wanted by the police for questioning. After the existence of these letters emerged during the trial of John Downey in February 2014 (for the 1982 Hyde Park bombing), the Police Service of Northern Ireland (PSNI) revealed that 100 of those who received letters were in fact suspects in 300 murder cases. The Commons' Northern Ireland Affairs Committee (NIAC) investigated the scheme and concluded that it had "distorted the process of justice".

Police investigations
In September 2005, following critical judgments at

Strasbourg, the Committee of Ministers endorsed a proposal for a Historic Enquiries Team (HET) made by the Chief Constable of the PSNI, Sir Hugh Orde. HET was to investigate 3,269 unsolved murders committed between 1968 and 1998. It had three objectives: to work with families of those who had been killed; to ensure that cases were conducted to modern policing standards; and to carry out the work in such a way that the wider community had confidence in the outcomes. It was headed by a commander from the London Metropolitan Police and had an annual budget of £30 million.

Despite considerable success and popularity amongst victims' families, the HET was wound up in September 2014 following a critical report by Her Majesty's Inspectorate of Constabulary (HMIC). This found that HET had investigated cases where the state was involved with "less rigour" than others, and that its approach had serious shortcomings. As a result of this criticism and after closing down the HET, the PSNI prioritised security force killings, handing on some 300 Army cases to its successor, the PSNI's Legacy Investigation Branch (LIB), for reinvestigation.

Since then, the present PSNI Chief Constable, Simon Byrne, and his predecessor, George Hamilton, have tried desperately to evade their responsibility to address historic crime. Hamilton was adamant that this is not police work and must instead be "victim-focused". He proposed following the example of Operation Kenova. This was set up in 2016 under former Bedfordshire Chief Constable Jon Boutcher, originally to investigate alleged offences by "Stakeknife", a high-level British agent inside the IRA, and people associated with him, including IRA members, security personnel and civil servants. The PSNI subsequently passed other investigations to Boutcher following court rulings which criticised the PSNI for a lack of independence. Boutcher now has some 80 staff and a budget of about £5 million a year. He has told the NIAC that he would be willing to investigate all 3500 historic death cases, a proposal which has had wide support and has gone largely unchallenged. It would require a 25-year operation and a huge budget.

Ninety-nine percent of Troubles deaths have had inquests and were investigated by the police, as best as could be done in the often perilous circumstances of the time. Viewed out of context, the investigations are inadequate compared to what could be done today. But why should a murder case in 1970s Belfast be re-opened without credible and compelling new evidence if the same would never happen in Bedford? The answer is that only here do the victims' families determine the process within the new doctrine of "victim-centred justice".

A related problem that is not recognised, perhaps even by Boutcher, is that Kenova is dealing with a limited subset of victims' families. He famously told NIAC that "Every family wants to be a Kenova family." That is understandable in relation to the families of deceased agents or informants, who typically learn more from Kenova than they otherwise would: the state wisely does not reveal whether a murdered individual was on its books. Prior to Kenova, the relatives of informants who were killed in the Troubles were denied definitive information. The other group of families predominating in Kenova are of those killed by the Glenanne gang of loyalist terrorists operating in border areas in the early 1970s. These relatives are largely convinced of the collusion allegations against the Army and the RUC.

Boutcher has put 18 files before the Public Prosecution Service (PPS), which decided in October 2020 not to prosecute in four cases. The first of these concerned an individual's alleged perjury, two related to former members of the security services, and the fourth to a former PPS prosecutor. The alleged offence of the latter three was misconduct in public office around the decision not to prosecute the first individual in 2007. The PPS is still considering other files from Kenova on military and IRA personnel, and more will be submitted. Boutcher has recently extended his investigations to various deaths in the Republic, also linked to loyalists.

Policy initiatives

In June 2007, Secretary of State Peter Hain announced the formation of an independent "Consultative Group on the Past", led by Archbishop Robin Eames and Dennis Bradley, to advise him on how best to address legacy issues. They produced a comprehensive report with detailed recommendations, but it foundered over their proposal to offer a £12,000 "recognition payment" to victims of the Troubles. A series of policy initiatives followed in the Haass Report of December 2013, "A Proposed Agreement"; the Stormont House Agreement (SHA) of December 2014; Teresa Villiers's "Fresh Start" Agreement of November 2015; and Karen Bradley's draft Legacy Bill, issued for consultation in May 2018 under the title "Addressing the Legacy of Northern Ireland's Past". In July 2019 the Northern Ireland Office (NIO) published a summary of the consultation responses.

A controversial question emerged after Eames/ Bradley in relation to victims' pensions: what constitutes a "victim", and can a terrorist be one? The Victims and Survivors (Northern Ireland) Order 2006 equated injured perpetrators with their innocent victims, something the Victims Commissioner, Judith Thompson, stood over. When the legislation introducing pensions finally reached the statute book in January 2020, it stipulated that a person is not entitled to victims' payments in relation to a Troubles-related incident where the person has a conviction in respect of the conduct which caused that incident.[1] The Minister of Justice, Naomi Long, has indicated that the pension scheme could cost up to £800m. The question of who pays (Westminster or Stormont?) was resolved only after a judicial intervention, which forced the Sinn Féin Minister of Finance to agree to underwrite the funding. The scheme opened for registration in June 2020.

The Haass Report proposed four new institutions: the Historical Investigations Unit (HIU), a parallel police force for the past; the Oral History Archive (OHA); the grandly named Independent Commission on Information Retrieval (ICIR); and the Implementation and Reconciliation Group (IRG). The HIU was intended both to investigate and judge past crimes, a travesty of ECHR Articles 6 (fair trial) and 8 (right to a reputation). The justice system precludes police from adjudicating on criminal responsibility: their role is to investigate and pass their findings to the PPS for a decision. HIU would have combined the two functions, in particular when it came to the promised "truth reports" to victims' families. They would have apportioned guilt, in the most part regarding the conduct of the security forces, criminal or otherwise, and on "collusion". (There is no such crime as collusion and no statutory definition of it.) The Haass recommendations were rejected by the Alliance Party, the Democratic Unionist Party (DUP) and the Ulster Unionist Party (UUP). I was one of the two UUP representatives and saw how the parties operated. The Social Democratic and Labour Party (SDLP) had limited aims and pressed them home doggedly, seeking, successfully, to get "patterns and themes" (in other words "collusion"), into the new structures. The DUP had no visible aims and over the years has agreed many of the dangerous proposals currently under consideration, either through carelessness or in deals struck to enable it to get back into government. Its only legacy achievement in twenty years – and under serious pressure from grassroots activists – was to block the re-appointment of Judith Thompson as Victims Commissioner, although DUP leader Arlene Foster did eventually stand aside from the proposal to create the unique, retrospective disciplinary offence of "historic police misconduct". The UUP majored on the rule of law and the role of history.

In a dynamic process where law was sidelined, nationalism prospered within the alphabet soup of proposed new institutions. A year after the collapse of Haass, the DUP mysteriously agreed the Stormont House Agreement, despite it being "son" of Haass. SHA had by then been agreed by four of the political parties, but the UUP still dissented: it is not an international agreement like the Belfast Agreement, despite misleading statements from nationalist parties.

The Fresh Start Agreement of November 2015 endorsed the SHA but stated that "Despite some significant progress a final agreement on the establishment of new bodies to deal with the past was not reached".

The 2018 draft Legacy Bill silently added the iniquitous "historic police misconduct" aspect to the SHA at the behest of the Police Ombudsman for Northern Ireland (PONI) and the Alliance Party. PONI, in justified fear of this addition being abandoned, demanded in its "five-year review" of late 2020 that the Justice Minister should include such misconduct investigation in new PONI powers.

The "New Decade New Approach" deal of January 2020 was designed by Irish Foreign Minister Simon Coveney and Secretary of State Julian Smith to return Sinn Féin and the DUP to power. This was the nearest we have come since 1998 to joint authority. But Smith was swept aside shortly afterwards as Boris Johnson, emboldened by his December 2019 election victory, decided to exert the power he had, as opposed to what the civil service wanted him to have. The Tory manifesto had stated that "We will continue to seek better ways of dealing with legacy issues that provide better outcomes for victims and survivors and do more to give veterans the protections they deserve". This was in response to the emergence of the military veterans' lobby, which is wielding increasing influence in parliament and in the Conservative Party. Johnson appointed Johnny Mercer to be the veterans' minister, responsible for advancing legislation to address the problem of constant Iraq and Afghanistan war re-investigations. These had become something of a lawyers' industry in Britain with the disgraced solicitor, Phil Shiner, as its exemplar. The cost of these inquiries has run into hundreds of millions of pounds, and they have left many ex-soldiers in a legal limbo.

The next policy development was the Written Ministerial Statement of 18 March 2020 by Smith's successor, Brandon Lewis. Little detail was given, but the statement presaged a narrowing of the overblown SHA arrangements on criminal re-investigation, if not on "truth recovery". These were the NIO headlines: "A new independent body focused on providing information to families and swift examinations of all unresolved deaths from the Troubles; an end to the cycle of reinvestigations that has failed victims and veterans for too long; ensuring that Northern Ireland veterans receive equal treatment to their counterparts who served overseas."

The NIO tacked on a reconciliation aspect, but nobody will be reconciled by one-sided, victim-focused justice. The concept of truth recovery has been seriously damaged following the collapse of the Joe McCann murder trial in May 2021. The judge (predictably) ruled as inadmissible statements made by the soldiers to the military police in 1972 which were innocently repeated to HET in 2010 for the family who said it wanted "truth not retribution". In the event the family is now seeking a fresh inquest. The advice is already out from retired generals to squaddies: "Have nothing to do with anyone knocking your door wanting to talk about truth recovery and reconciliation".

The paramilitaries too have learnt their lesson, after being recorded on the Boston College tapes, resulting in police investigations and prosecutions. Nobody can risk believing that a no-prosecution policy today might not be followed by the opposite tomorrow. Nobody can surely believe that those involved in the 3,500 killings will record their actions for the sake of the families, even if no prosecution could ensue, as occurred in South Africa.

Since there were probably half a dozen people involved in every murder, there would be some 20,000 accounts of the truth to be registered.

The mantra of "truth, justice and reconciliation" is a false god. Impartial professional historians alone can retrieve whatever can be established of the truth, while lack of evidence for prosecutions means that formal justice for the 3,500 families is impossible.

The NIO's statement of March 2020 was published alongside proposals for the Overseas Operations (Service Personnel and Veterans) Act 2021, designed to limit prosecutions and re-investigation of alleged crimes by army veterans (Strasbourg had extended its reach to the acts of soldiers in wars outside the UK). That Act offered no amnesty: rather it put in place extra hurdles before a prosecution can start. They involve time limits, new evidence, the military context (stress and threat levels), the public interest in finality, and the level of previous investigation. It has vestigial elements of a statute of limitations. When the government failed to introduce equivalent provisions for the veterans of Operation Banner, as it had promised, Johnny Mercer walked out of his ministerial job and became the veterans' hero.

The view emanating from the NIO and elsewhere is that Northern Ireland equivalence would have to apply to terrorists as well as soldiers. Whether this argument is a cover to stave off criticism about an "amnesty" or a genuine concern about litigation is unclear. However, the ECHR jurisprudence may be now thought sufficiently open for the NIO to go ahead with equivalence and face down the wall of rage that would ensue.

Lawfare

Increasingly, throughout two decades of legacy recommendations, initiatives and proposed legislation, there has been an accelerating use of the courts to advance the republican narrative, assisted by legal aid. (Legal aid is not available to the reasonably well off, such as former police officers. The NI Retired Police Officers Association won key sections of their case against the Police Ombudsman over his Loughinisland report, but bizarrely were denied their six-figure costs.)

This development has come to be termed "lawfare", and its potential for expansion is limitless. It may be better than warfare, but it is politically debilitating for Northern Ireland. One wing of government, however, is not wedded to normal constitutional stability. We are told the Belfast Agreement brought peace, which is a myth that needs examined. The war ended because the IRA chose to end it, seeing a more promising path. Their demand for "all-party talks now" within a "peace process" proved to be remarkably perceptive. That process is continuing, and in their view can end only with the demise of Northern Ireland. Unionism, in contrast, is about maintaining the status quo and minimising concessions. This is conservative territory which is generally unappealing to the young and woke. Northern Ireland can only lose once. Republicanism for over a century has lost repeatedly but is currently feeling triumphant.

Only a minority of victims' families are in victims' groups. It may be that most families have accepted the fact of the death in question, have a good idea of who did the killing and why, and accept there is no extra truth or justice available. This applies more to the 2000 killed by the IRA, as state and loyalist deaths can be constantly re-examined for culpability and suggestions of "collusion". As to those killed by the security forces in the early 1970s, when the Army was facing an insurrection and the police had been disarmed, discredited and disbanded, there was little strategic policy guidance available: foolish and inaccurate statements from the Army's PR officers came to the fore as casualties mounted.

The families of those killed by republicans and loyalists are often motivated not by abstract concepts of truth, justice and reconciliation but simply by anger that their loved one died for no purpose and that their memory is now discarded and neglected as the media, academics and the criminal justice system focus on "state-sponsored killings".

The courts, especially in Belfast, remain open to judicial reviews, demands for the re-opening of inquests, civil suits for damages, challenges on convictions, requests for new public inquiries, all alongside PONI investigations and Strasbourg cases. The value and cost of all this activity needs to be questioned, but it would take a brave government to put in place legislation to curb, let alone stop the lawfare industry. It could, however, abandon the myriad institutions promised by the Stormont House Agreement, which will only compound the problem.

Reopened inquests have displaced public inquiries, going beyond their limited statutory powers. The Kingsmill massacre aside, most involve state killings or those where collusion is alleged. Haass refused even to consider incorporating inquests in his new bodies because of "Article 2 compliance" assertions, something that went unchallenged by the DUP. And it is ECHR Article 2 which is the motor for most of the reinvestigation. Indeed, a case can be made for almost every one of the Troubles deaths having a re-opened inquest: they may yet.

In this context it is worth quoting both parts of Article 2 in full, especially the second which seems rarely to be argued in aid:

1. Everyone's right to life shall be protected by law. No one shall be deprived of his life intentionally save in the execution of a sentence of a court following his conviction of a crime for which this penalty is provided by law.

2. Deprivation of life shall not be regarded as inflicted in contravention of this article when it results from the use of force which is no more than absolutely necessary:
   (a) in defence of any person from unlawful violence;
   (b) in order to effect a lawful arrest or to prevent escape of a person lawfully detained;
   (c) in action lawfully taken for the purpose of quelling a riot or insurrection.

Legal opinion on Article 2 differs, although that would be hard to notice in most public discussions, especially in the broadcast media. The Malone House Group (MHG) a recognised NGO at Strasbourg, has taken issue with the conventional wisdom in submissions to be found on the Council of Europe website.[2] As yet they remain a minority view. "Article 2 compliance" can be achieved in a dozen different ways if the Committee of Ministers can be brought through diplomacy to a better understanding of what is needed in Northern Ireland cases. There is no sign, however, that British diplomats at Strasbourg are working on the other 46 member states to achieve this. They have left the Republic of Ireland with the whip hand as one of the six countries on "the Bureau", which sets the Committee's agenda.

Four recent cases

The UK Supreme Court says on its website: "UK courts are not required, however, always to follow the decisions of the Strasbourg Court. Indeed, they can decline to do so, particularly if they consider that that Court has not sufficiently appreciated or accommodated particular aspects of our domestic constitutional position". That, however, has not prevented judgments in a series of cases going against that position. Four hugely important judgments in relation to the Troubles have been made recently in the Belfast courts, in two instances on appeal to the Supreme Court. They all require close analysis but suggest a new balance in how the local judiciary views the past – and indeed the future.

They are firstly the hooded men case where two consecutive Strasbourg judgments about torture (as opposed to inhumane treatment) of detainees in August 1971 were overturned in the Court of Appeal in Belfast in 2019 in a unique decision by the Lord Chief Justice, Sir Declan Morgan and Sir Ben Stephens (Northern Ireland's new judge on the Supreme Court), with Sir Donnell Deeny valiantly dissenting.[3] By a majority of two to one, the Belfast Court "was satisfied that the treatment to which Hooded Men had been subjected to would if it occurred today properly be characterised as torture, bearing in mind that the European Convention on Human Rights is a living instrument, but that the test had not been met to enable an Article 2 or 3 procedural investigation to take place given the passage of time." Overturning Strasbourg was a new departure for a UK court.

Secondly, the judgment of 13 May 2020[4] in the Gerry Adams custody order case at the Supreme Court, written by the late Lord Kerr. The violent context was ignored and the order overturned, reflecting a new legal, political understanding, especially on precedent.[5] MHG has published several articles about the judges' reasoning[6], and the think tank Policy Exchange has sought legislative action to restore the Carltona principle which Lord Kerr dispensed with: it concerns junior ministers and civil servants being able to take decisions on behalf of Secretaries of State.

Thirdly, in the Finucane case at the Supreme Court the judges concluded that there had not been an Article 2 compliant inquiry into the death of Patrick Finucane. "It does not follow that a public inquiry of the type which the appellant seeks must be ordered. It is for the state to decide … what form of investigation, if indeed any is now feasible, is required in order to meet that requirement". A general point about retrospectivity in all Article 2 cases is the Supreme Court's view that it does not apply to deaths before 2 October 2000, when the Human Rights Act 1998 came into force, incorporating much of the ECHR into domestic law. Why has the government not tried to effect or enforce that position?

The fourth key case, a coronial court judgment, was that by Mrs Justice Keegan[7] in her May 2021 findings relating to ten fatal shootings by soldiers in Ballymurphy, Belfast in August 1971. It will be the template for the future, with inquests becoming effectively tribunals of inquiry even though this goes beyond the limited role of a coroner when interpreting the four basic factual questions required by the Coroners' Rules. The fourth question, how the deceased came about their deaths, is being used to broaden inquests into investigations of culpability.

The way forward

A civil war was averted in the 30 years from 1969. No credit is given for that, certainly not to the security forces and their dead. Sadly, young people for the most part have little empathy for those families. Solidarity when shown is largely within the republican community who use law to achieve the ends once reserved to war.

The government's proposal for an amnesty or statute of limitations on police investigations may appease veterans in the short term at the expense of a great deal of outrage from all sides. However, without a serious attempt to limit lawfare, not least in relation to reopened inquests, the basic problem will remain. Without closing down new inquests, civil suits, private prosecutions, free legal aid for legacy cases in judicial reviews, etc., a no-prosecutions policy will do little or nothing to reduce the hurt over unfairness or the enormous cost. It can be done, but the NIO would have to steel itself.

The proposed alternative "truth recovery" bodies may subsume the HIU but have the potential to be as toxic as continued criminal investigations if there are no cost caps or time limits. The notion of reconciliation is a dead letter even if regularly touted by the NIO. What is possible is a narrowing process. It appears to be under way and has to be supported so far as it goes. From August 2021, a new

Protocol 15 will be attached to the ECHR. It encourages subsidiarity and gives states a heightened margin of appreciation. This surely can be called in aid in future Strasbourg cases.

Without a grand settlement, which is unlikely given the political nature of the process, the legacy debate will grind on. Nationalist lawfare cannot lose as the legal variants still remain limitless. Non-nationalist lawfare, in so far as it exists, can call into question conventional legal wisdom on Article 2, but will London risk the wrath of Dublin and new legal challenges at Strasbourg?

On a more positive note, veterans have for the first time created a counterweight to the human rights industry.

Agreement to differ, putting the past behind us, is a better policy than well-funded politically-motivated archival archaeology supported by generously state-funded lawfare.

Endnotes

1 The Victims' Payments Regulations 2020 6.—(1) A person is not entitled to victims' payments in relation to a particular Troubles-related incident where the person— (a) has a conviction (whether spent or not), and (b) that conviction was in respect of conduct which caused, wholly or in part, that incident.

2 Malone House Group MHG submissions on the Council of Europe website: Article 2 legal opinion by Austen Morgan DH-DD(2020)500 and SHA legal opinion by Peter Smith QC and Neil Faris DH-DD(2020)705

3 Hooded men judgment in Belfast Court of Appeal on 20 September 2019: https://www.judiciaryni.uk/sites/judiciary/files/decisions/Summary%20of%20judgment%20-%20In%20re%20Francis%20McGuigan%20and%20Mary%20McKenna%20(The%20Hooded%20Men).pdf

4 Adams custody judgment https://www.supremecourt.uk/cases/uksc-2018–0104.html

5 Adams custody judgment article by Jeffrey Dudgeon in the *News Letter* on 21 May 2020: https://www.newsletter.co.uk/news/crime/jeffrey-dudgeon-supreme-court-ruling-gerry-adams-ruling-didnt-reflect-violent-context-times-when-civil-war-was-imminent-2860821

6 Adams custody judgment by Austen Morgan in Conservative Home on 21 May 2021: https://www.conservativehome.com/platform/2021/04/austen-morgan-as-gerry-adams-seeks-compensation-for-his-unlawful-detention-a-legal-conundrum-could-get-in-the-way.html

7 'Introduction' by Keegan J to Ballymurphy inquest findings on 11 May 2021: https://www.judiciaryni.uk/sites/judiciary/files/decisions/In%20the%20matter%20of%20a%20series%20of%20deaths%20that%20occurred%20in%20August%201971%20at%20Ballymurphy%2C%20West%20Belfast%20-%20Introduction.pdf

The Scandal of Legacy

Ben Lowry

The distortions of legacy

It is hard to know where to begin when writing about the way in which the story of the Troubles has been largely conceded to the IRA. It is an immense scandal that has been building for more than 20 years, and one that has many elements and origins. For all its layers, though, the essence of what is happening on legacy is easy to grasp.

There is now a barely challenged version of the 1968 to 1998 violence as involving three main "actors", who were equally to blame for the violence: the British state, republican paramilitaries and loyalist paramilitaries. But the UK state was, by implication, worst of the three because it should have operated to a higher standard, when in fact it was a murderous enforcer of an apartheid unionist state.

The scathing nationalist assessment of the first 50 years of Northern Ireland, of a rotten society, is itself now only lightly challenged, and it leads to either the argument that violence was justified, or to a sense that those nationalists who rejected violence were following a noble course, given the provocations to which they turned the other cheek. Much of society is increasingly jumping to the first of those conclusions: that while the IRA might not have been pleasant it was on some level justified, because it resisted a brutal Britain.

I can think of at least seven broad reasons why this shocking distortion of what happened during the long years of terrorism has met so little resistance.

First, unionists show little tendency to defend or revisit the past, and London is even less inclined to do so.

Second, related to the first point, most mainstream unionist politicians and all the main Westminster political parties want to keep Sinn Féin, a party that wants Northern Ireland to fail, within Stormont – and sporadic SF-led crises are only resolved when the IRA is happy with the outcome of a resulting political negotiation.

Third, defenders of the UK state often fail to comprehend, let alone explain, elementary statistics as to either Troubles killings or historical investigations – and what those statistics tell us about the anti-state direction of legacy (more on that at the end of this chapter).

Fourth, while the number of people of influence on either side of the Irish border who support the IRA campaign is still small, the number of people who are neutral between it and the UK security forces, indeed more hostile to the latter, is vast – and growing.

Fifth, while unionists have been at sea on legacy, republicans have for decades plotted their legal and propaganda assault on the UK state.

Sixth, while the UK has reason to be proud of its overall record in Northern Ireland, its failure to shed light on its security blunders in the early Troubles was not only in itself wrong, but has at this late stage made it hard to bring context to those mistakes when they get the scrutiny that they need.

Seventh, the security forces are far more vulnerable to historic investigations because they kept records and state personnel can be traced.

There is space in this chapter to examine only some of those seven points.

Post-Troubles appeasement – I

Latterly the most prominent legacy problem has been trials of soldiers for historic killings, which are massively disproportionate in number to those of terrorists (see below). Elderly soldiers face investigation for single shootings which, even if proven to be reckless, in almost all instances lacked pre-meditation. Yet IRA leaders do not face trial, and were allowed to come off their calculated and sustained mayhem at a time of their choosing in 1994. Republicans were allowed to return to it in spectacular fashion in 1996, bombing Canary Wharf in London when political talks were not moving fast enough for them.

With hindsight we can see that the second IRA ceasefire, of July 1997, was perhaps an even more significant landmark in the Troubles than the first. That second cessation was the beginning of a period of unwavering British weakness towards republicans that persists to this day.

The August 1994 ceasefire had followed a long spell in which the UK had, for all its backdoor contacts with republicans, demonstrated that it was not going to be bombed into submission. But in summer 1997, weeks after two RUC men were shot dead at point blank range in Lurgan, the new prime minister Tony Blair rushed to hasten the pace at which Sinn Féin was brought into talks.

Since then, every contortion has been performed to avoid taking sanction against the republican movement, no matter how outrageous its conduct, from IRA spying at Stormont to breaking into Castlereagh police station in 2002.

Occasional penalties were imposed only on the basis that everyone suffered, rather than Sinn Féin alone. Devolution was suspended for all in 2002 and in 2005 all Stormont parties were dis-invited from the White House on St Patrick's Day, months after the Northern Bank robbery and IRA murder of Robert McCartney (even though Sinn Féin was singled out for criticism by the influential US politician Senator John McCain).

When direct rule was imposed in late 2002, amid tardy IRA decommissioning, Mr Blair continued to advance his secret On The Run scheme for fugitive republicans.

The trial of army veterans comes 20 years after that scheme got under way, and four years after the 2017 funeral of Martin McGuinness, which was attended by dignitaries including the (recently prior) DUP first minister of Northern Ireland, the director of public prosecutions, the PSNI chief constable, the Taoiseach, the Irish president, some of their predecessors and a former US president and former first minister of Scotland.

A nearly state occasion hardly encourages the idea that if Mr McGuinness had lived he would be in fear of a trial on a charge commensurate with directing terrorism. Or that other late IRA leaders such as Kevin McKenna, Billy McKee or Brian Keenan would have been charged for atrocities that they ordered from the IRA Army Council.

Despite this sense of two-tiered historic justice, there has been no political engagement with something Alan McQuillan, a former PSNI assistant chief constable, wrote in the *News Letter* in 2018. He said that future legacy investigators might face "political pressure, not least from the two governments, not to pursue those whose arrest might 'destabilise the peace process'". He said that "decisions made earlier in the peace process have utterly undermined, indeed destroyed, our real ability to deliver for victims". The obstacles to legacy justice cited by Mr McQuillan were obvious ones, but his comments were still sobering given his authority. But the media did not pick up on it, nor on any of the 2018 *News Letter* "Stop the Legacy Scandal" series of essays of which his article was a part.

The parameters for inclusion in the series were that contributors agreed that legacy was panning out in such an imbalanced way as to be scandal. Beyond that, authors approached the subject in different ways. There were articles from academics, politicians, commentators, lawyers, victims, churchmen, ex-security forces, intelligence personnel, and former paramilitaries, many of whom were so concerned about legacy that they jettisoned their reluctance to speak publicly on such a contested matter.

The collusion lie
My view is that the "collusion lie" is at the heart of this scandal. In 2016, after the (second) Police Ombudsman report into the 1994 loyalist massacre at Loughinisland (the first did not find collusion and was quashed), I wrote an essay, "The growing myth of loyalist collusion". I said that while of course there had been some collusion, it was clear that there was no systematic policy, unless collusion is defined so widely (to include running informers) as to be meaningless.

My labelling of collusion as a myth caused uproar. But my description was too mild, and I now refer to this conspiracy theory as the "collusion lie". It is a carefully cultivated and promoted lie about the role of the UK, disproved by a glance at the statistics of the Troubles dead, let alone close analysis of them.

Loyalist intelligence was poor. Of the 1,100 people that they murdered, fewer than 50 were republican paramilitaries. Yet Ulster Defence Regiment soldiers, who are smeared as being central to collusion, had significant information on what they called the "main players".

Hundreds of Provisional IRA terrorists were well known to the Ulster Defence Regiment and Royal Ulster Constabulary, and could have been killed by the security forces in an evening, yet were able to go about their murder over decades. Many terrorists were jailed, but few of them met a violent death.

The appalling loyalist murder of the lawyer Pat Finucane at home in February 1989 happened early in a period leading up to the ceasefires when loyalist killings became more targeted, suggesting better intelligence, and when state forces killed IRA gangs on murder missions, such as at Loughgall in 1987 and at Coagh 1991. But while the number of IRA losses in these years was striking, in absolute terms it remained small. Purely sectarian loyalist killings of Catholic civilians continued.

Twenty years ago the collusion theory of the Troubles pushed unionists into an early blunder on legacy. Talks between Northern Ireland politicians at Weston Park in summer 2001 led to a document which set the tone for how the past has been tackled ever since. As a young *Belfast Telegraph* reporter, I wrote an analysis of Paragraph 20 of the paper, which was a plan not to pursue IRA fugitives but which critics saw as a gateway to a wider amnesty. But Weston Park also set in motion an examination of various killings said to involve collusion, such as that of Mr Finucane.

Unionists sought balance by seeking scrutiny of republican killings in which officials had seemingly colluded, such as the killings of Mr Justice Gibson and Lady Gibson crossing the border in 1987. But this foolishly accepted the nationalist notion of collusion as a key feature of the Troubles, and so led to, among other inquiries, one into the prison killing of the loyalist Billy Wright. But the unionist wound with regard to Ireland's role in the violence was not caused by the small number of cases in which republicans got help from someone in authority, usually south of the border. It is from the utter lack of Irish resolve towards tackling the IRA, evident in the fact that from 1973 to 1997 the UK made 110 extradition requests from the Republic but only eight were successful.

County Fermanagh starkly illustrates the vulnerability of border Protestants to IRA killers who freely escaped the jurisdiction to safety in Ireland (to plot their next murder of an isolated farmer). The county also exposes the gross exaggeration of loyalist-state collusion. In Fermanagh there was not only no collusion, there was almost no retaliation. Of 116 people killed there in the Troubles, 100 were killed by republicans (99 of those by the IRA), five were killed by loyalists, five by army, one by UDR, one by RUC, one a terrorist by their own device, and three died of other causes such as drowning.

Still, to this day, when the UK is being hounded by Irish governments over its handling of the legacy of violence, including efforts by Dublin to humiliate Britain in Europe over cases such as Pat Finucane and the "hooded men", there has been no unionist demand for an examination of extradition refusals, which made easier so many rural murders.

The Finucane murder clearly deserved extra scrutiny because there was some state complicity, and it got that scrutiny. Millions of pounds have been spent on this one Troubles killing out of 3,600 dead, including the collusion probes by Sir John Stevens.

The UK tried to meet its 2001 Weston Park obligation in 2005, but the Finucane campaigners rejected as insufficient a public inquiry under the terms of the 2005 Inquiries Act. Amnesty International said only a "truly independent judicial inquiry" was acceptable. This rejection was why the murder was later given a review by the internationally admired human rights lawyer, Desmond de Silva QC, who found collusion in the killing but no over-arching conspiracy.

Incredibly, this spurning of an inquiry under the 2005 act terms, leading instead to de Silva, and the family's much later indication, after his report, that it would in fact accept such inquiry terms, was ignored in the deluge of media reports criticising the UK for its decision in late 2020 again to turn down an inquiry. The latest push to spend yet millions more on the Finucane killing got feeble press scrutiny, despite the fact that there is a mountain of unsolved terror cases.

Meanwhile, after unionists had acquiesced in the loyalist killer Billy Wright's death getting an expensive inquiry, one of those relatives of IRA victims, Anne Graham, got a letter from the Historical Enquiries Team saying that there was no new evidence on her brother Edgar's 1983 slaying. No report for Mr Graham, no new investigation, certainly no inquiry.

This murder of a 29-year-old lawyer, academic and politician at Queen's University where he was employed had far reaching implications. It was literal terror, instilling fear in bright young unionists. I believe that Northern Ireland's governance problems, at the hands of mediocre politicians, are linked to the IRA's success that day in scaring talent away from unionism.

Restraint under provocation
There is a theory that the brutal loyalist mix of random and targeted killings from the late 1980s, including some illegal help from elements of the state, and the state use of intelligence to ambush vicious IRA units, hastened the end of the republican campaign. But looking at the longer thirty year Troubles, the wider UK response to terror after 1973, of normalisation, clearly worked. By the end of that year the army, which killed many more people than did the RUC, was already more disciplined than it had been in those initial chaotic years. Half the 360 state killings happened between 1969 and 1973, and the other half happened over a far longer period, from 1974 until 1996.

We have heard much this year about the Ballymurphy killings by the Parachute Regiment in August 1971 but nothing about a turning point earlier that year: the PIRA honey-trap murders of three young Scottish soldiers. It had been possible for republican women to lure the trio to a pretend party and their roadside execution only because squaddies were in March still relaxed about their security. There had been a mere 58 Troubles killings by then, three of them soldiers who died in riots. By the end of that year a further 156 people would be dead.

The introduction of internment that August, based on bad intelligence, and the deployment of the Parachute Regiment at that time, and then in Londonderry in January 1972, were disastrous moves with tragic consequences, but there is almost no focus now on the circumstances of their deployment. The IRA had sought to shatter any remaining relationship between soldiers and the nationalist community that had welcomed them.

From 1974 until the late 1990s there were more than 2,000 terrorist killings and fewer than 200 state killings. It is hard to think of a powerful society in history that would have tolerated such an insurgency for so long, knowing all the ringleaders. The Spanish response to ETA in the 1980s, for example, while hardly ruthless by the standards of the civil war in that country only decades earlier, included greater law-breaking by elements of the state (such as Spanish operatives in the French Basque territory) than in Northern Ireland at the same time, even though the IRA killed twice as many people as ETA.

By 1974 the UK had learned from internment and Bloody Sunday, and there was no repetition of them. But that early security force wrongdoing was an unresolved and festering sore among nationalists. Both Tory and Labour governments had settled on a mild security response to terror, as the best way not to inflame it, but there was no will to investigate carefully preceding excess force by the state, given the context of inadequately trained young soldiers operating against serious terrorism.

The IRA went on to try every tactic to outwit and demoralise the UK. When its bombing campaign in

Belfast in the early 1970s was thwarted, it bombed the mainland. When its targeting of off-duty security force members got harder because such personnel got better at their own security, it tried to murder service members in places where they were less vigilant, such as England or Germany. The IRA ultimately targeted those in Northern Ireland who supplied the security forces. It murdered judges and lawyers, particularly those of a Catholic background. It later moved on to the civil service, blowing up Sir Ken Bloomfield's home in Co Down (no-one was injured but the bedroom of his daughter, who was not at home, was destroyed). It targeted politicians and royals, and ultimately the cabinet, coming close to murdering prime ministers in 1984 and 1991. Still the UK knew not to over-react and create martyrs.

A counterfactual scenario
Many people's memories of the phases of violence have become muddled. In the early 2000s, after Princess Diana died, I noticed a reputable media outlet implying that her 1992 Belfast visit had been brave, "at the height of the Troubles". The 1990s was in fact its lowest point. Even the hideous eruptions of killing and bombing in the 1980s came at least a decade after the worst days in the 1970s. Reginald Maudling's 1971 reference to an acceptable level of violence was mocked, but just such a level had been achieved as early as 1978, by when Troubles deaths were far lower than road deaths (81 killings in NI that year compared to 288 traffic collision fatalities).

Northern Ireland had been getting ever more prosperous, with the cross-party Westminster approach of improving housing and pumping money at the province (continued after 1979 by the supposedly frugal Margaret Thatcher) helping to curb any appetite for violence. My generation (born early 1970s) remembers well this normalisation because we were at an age when the revitalisation of Belfast seemed thrilling. By the time of the 1980 re-opening of the Grand Opera House and the launch of eateries such Capers Pizzeria, packed from its first night in 1982, the city centre was already a bustling space that did not feel unsafe to families or school groups.

By 1990, the various IRA tactics had failed. Security analysts say the IRA was riddled with informers and not getting recruits but even non-experts could see that it was only able to wage a low intensity campaign. In summer 1993, when I was a student working in Berkeley, California, I was struck by a San Francisco newspaper report about the murder toll in nearby Oakland for the first six months of that year, which I could see was higher than Northern Ireland. Oakland, with around 400,000 people, had less than a third of NI's population (years later I checked the homicide toll for Oakland for all of 1993, which was 154 killings, NI's Troubles toll was 84). Gun violence in Oakland meant that it had six times more violent killings per capita than NI, where there was apparently a "war" bad enough to attract the concern of US presidents. It was the IRA's last flourish, in the 1990s, that achieved the most for them. Not the bombing of the prosperous unionist towns of Coleraine and Banbridge and Bangor, but the targetting of mainland commercial targets in Manchester and London.

Consider a counterfactual scenario, in which the Conservative-Labour consensus from the 1970s, of not rewarding IRA terror, continues after 1994. In this alternative reality, the UK response to Irish republicans is closer to Spain's uncompromising response to Basque separatists. If the Provisional IRA had continued to decline, it might long ago have ended up little bigger than dissident republicans are today, almost devoid of support and barely able to carry out acts of terrorism.

Republicans might not have grown politically in the way they did after Sinn Féin entered government in 1998, and unionism would not have had to make concessions of an existential nature (such as accepting that a 50%+1 vote by the people of Northern Ireland alone will lead to our exit from UK, with no say in the matter for the rest of the nation).

Post-Troubles appeasement – II

But rather than taking such a robust approach to the IRA, Tory-Labour governments have since 1997, via the Northern Ireland Office, been consistent in their application of an appeasement strategy. The Conservative and Unionist Party has been no less craven in its approach to Sinn Féin than Labour. After 2017, when Sinn Féin pulled down Stormont and kept it down until their demand of an Irish language act was met, the Tory prime minister, Theresa May, then Boris Johnson, and their uninformed secretaries of state did not utter a word about this vandalism. When I interviewed Mrs May in February 2018, I was allowed a single question, so I posed this one: "Our readership is mostly unionist and there is a large feeling within unionism that Sinn Féin have been allowed to bring the process to a halt for 13 months. Do you have any thoughts on that nervousness that there is amongst many people in Northern Ireland?" She replied: "… I think both sides, both the DUP and Sinn Féin, have been working hard over the last 13 months…"

In October 2019, Boris Johnson was even worse. A man who had not even hinted at disapproval of Sinn Féin (no Tory leader would now dare), turned on Nigel Dodds in the House of Commons, the deputy leader of a DUP that had sustained them in power for two years, and ridiculed the North Belfast MP's plea for a cross-community vote on the Northern Ireland Protocol (which established an internal UK barrier). Mr Johnson had in November 2018 travelled to the DUP conference to undermine his party leader, Mrs May, and specify that her Brexit plan damaged "the fabric of the Union with regulatory checks and even customs controls between Great Britain and Northern Ireland". Months later, having supplanted her as prime minister, Mr Johnson betrayed his own pledge and agreed to both such controls in the Irish Sea. But when Mr Dodds recounted that 2018 commitment, Mr Johnson was not merely unfazed, he turned to backbenchers, to draw their support against the DUP, and said how regrettable it was that any one party would want a veto in NI against the protocol. The very veto that the PM had days earlier allowed the DUP to think he also supported, just before his sudden deal with Leo Varadkar.

This political cruelty towards Mr Dodds came from a prime minister whose party has done nothing to counter the long republican veto threat that hovers over Stormont. And Mr Johnson that day in late 2019 still had nothing to say about the sectarian veto Sinn Féin had actually implemented in the previous three years, leaving hospitals and schools rudderless until it got Gaelic laws.

Mr Johnson had also on becoming PM shown his ignorance of the crisis facing unionism by making a disastrous appointment as secretary of state, Julian Smith.

Mr Smith not only continued the culture of never criticising Sinn Féin, he too specified the DUP as the problem, and cited them as an obstacle to the return of a Stormont republicans were keeping down until the language ransom was paid.

But, faced with weak unionists and a weak Tory government, language was not the only republican demand. In the January 2020 deal to restore devolution, Mr Smith surprised Stormont, and delighted the IRA, by including legacy in the deal. He agreed with Dublin to bring forward legacy legislation, implementing the 2014 Stormont House Agreement, within 100 days. The Ulster Unionist MLA Doug Beattie, a fierce critic of Stormont House, said that shortly before the 2020 deal he heard Julian Smith say to Sinn Féin: "we need to talk about the specifics of legacy". It was extraordinary enough that the political party seen as inextricably linked to the IRA felt sure a legacy deal was good for them. But worse, a republican movement which had been made to account for so little of IRA bloodshed, was so unafraid of the mooted structures to deal with the past that it had become increasingly furious in its demand for their implementation.

A Tory secretary of state still seemed above all keen to want to placate republicans on legacy despite what had become an overwhelming investigative focus on state killings. In little more than a decade there has been the Bloody Sunday inquiry; the Ballymurphy inquest (in effect a major inquiry); a Police Ombudsman caseload of hundreds of claims of past police wrongdoing; multiple civil actions against security forces (funded by legal aid); approval for 90+ legacy inquests, almost all of which are killings by state forces; major police reviews into allegations of collusion such as with the loyalist Glennane gang; the Kenova investigation (which has become a vast probe with a disproportionate focus on the state).

Mr Smith was sacked as secretary of state for Northern Ireland, perhaps over legacy. In March 2020, his successor Brandon Lewis announced a retreat from the Stormont House plans. But I always thought that this was motivated by a determination to stop soldier trials, while keeping Sinn Féin happy. Sure enough in November 2020 secret legacy talks were held at Lambeth Palace, which excluded all the main critics of the pro-terror direction of legacy, but did include military representatives. Lambeth also included Judith Thompson, who had not been renewed as commissioner for victims that year after losing the confidence of many survivors of terror, who are by far the largest category of victims. The reasons for that loss of faith were many, but included her neutral response to the resignation of Jackie Nicholl (whose infant son was murdered in an IRA bombing) from the victims and survivors forum when he found that he had been serving beside a "victim" who had also been an IRA bomber.

As with so many of these surreal legacy scenarios, you wonder what the nationalist and media reaction would have been to a parallel situation – say if a British soldier who had been both responsible for illegal violence and a victim of such violence had then been chosen to sit on a victims body, but with his own violence kept quiet so that a victim of state forces was sitting alongside him, unaware of his history.

But it was the IRA victim, Mr Nicholl who left the victims forum, not the ex IRA bomber – and there was barely a word about it outside of the *News Letter*. Mr Nicholl told the newspaper: "To think that my son, my beloved son, was killed by an IRA bomb and I had been tricked into sitting alongside an IRA bomber … I wanted to help victims who had suffered like we had done. Instead I was sitting beside a boastful bomber. I had sympathised with him about his grandfather being killed but lost all sympathy when I heard he had turned to bombing himself. We never turned to violence. I became a trade unionist, working for everyone." Yet Judith Thompson was at the 2020 Lambeth legacy talks, as were republicans, It is not remotely surprising that republicans are unafraid of legacy. For 20 years they have seen that there is no desire, not even within unionism, to make legacy an uncomfortable experience for them.

The UK state suffers a blizzard of legacy assaults, including a verbal onslaught from Ireland, yet still it refuses to countenance a response that might actually scare those who bombed, shot and terrorised Northern Ireland to the brink of civil war, or the state that in effect harboured them. The only proposed balance in Stormont House to the focus on the UK state was a Historical Investigations Unit (HIU). While this would have in theory had a huge remit, it became increasingly clear that it too might turn against the state. Recent years have shown the vulnerability of state forces, who have records, compared to terrorists, who became skilled at covering evidence fit for a criminal court. State forces are being adjudicated in investigations where the burden of proof is the civil one of balance of probabilities, and so it is easier to find against them, while terrorists only face a possible criminal process, where the standard is beyond all reasonable doubt.

HIU was also due to adjudicate on allegations of past serious "police misconduct". Thus, the RUC alone would be examined over allegations that did not relate to killings, but paramilitaries would not be examined over the vast number of terror attacks in which people were maimed and businesses ruined but no-one actually died. The army, which has far more to answer than the RUC in terms of allegations that do not involve killing (beatings for example), would not be pursued for misconduct either. But the idea of systemic police misconduct fits the collusion lie.

Another concern was that the HIU director would have had large discretionary power, and that previous legacy investigators have rarely shown the zeal for chasing terrorists that some of them seem to show for state forces. It became clear to me years ago that even if the HIU was established, there was no prospect of more than a handful of prosecutions of low-ranking IRA men for historic murders, by which time all the other probes, funded at great cost by the ever generous UK, would have trashed the reputation of a state that prevented civil war, then normalised Northern Ireland.

Personally I fear that poring over the past reawakens division, but we seem determined to allow republicans to rake over things on their terms. Last year, London was so apologetic in turning down a Finucane inquiry that it made one almost inevitable at some point in the future. So be it. But if so, the UK should give up on an agreed approach with an Irish government whose legacy demands are indistinguishable from those of Irish republicans.

Grant the Finucane probe, yet another examination of UK-loyalism, and then take advantage of all the security experts who are still alive and who know who did what, and unilaterally announce a dozen or so major public inquiries into republican terror. Hold one into the worst IRA atrocities against civilians; one into the bombing of business targets; one into mainland bombing; one into IRA murders of legal figures; one into its attacks on politicians; one into the big attacks on government; one into Irish extradition; one into the role of Irish America; one into the use of informers (that is an examination of the huge successes of that programme, and how it might be improved, as opposed to one that ends up putting intelligence agencies in the dock).

And a final public inquiry, the biggest of all, into the IRA campaign itself – what it did and how, who led it, how it was defeated, and how we can respond in future if we ever see its like again.

Postscript on statistics

In 2017, the BBC said it had figures that "challenge claims" that Troubles investigations are unduly focused on security force killings. The PSNI legacy branch was then examining 1,188 deaths, of which 530 were carried out by republicans, 271 by loyalists and 354 by state forces. The BBC put this in a graphic, which it used repeatedly thereafter, to show that "only" 30% of the PSNI legacy caseload was security force killings. The statistic was seized on by some observers to show that there is no imbalance in legacy investigations.

The 30% figure might sound reasonable if legacy is seen to have involved three groups of "actors" of roughly equal culpability. But in fact the state was responsible for 10% of the Troubles killings, all of them tragic but most of them legal.

An exact breakdown of Troubles deaths is not possible because different lists include and exclude different cases, based on the exact circumstances of death. But the outline figures are not in dispute: republicans killed around 2,100 people, loyalists killed 1,100 people and the state 360 people.

There is no prospect of agreement on the status (justified or illegal) of security force killings. Republicans depict them as murderous, even such obviously legitimate killings as those at Loughgall in 1987, when the SAS stopped a heavily-armed eight-man IRA murder gang, implicated in scores of murders.

On the other hand, most defenders of the state would say that 80%+ of security force killings were legal. Even if we accept that 20% of state killings were unlawful, which would suggest that 70 or so killings were so (a figure that veterans groups would reject as far too high), it would amount to only 2% of the 3,600 Troubles deaths. Unionist politicians were late to seize on the fact that 10% of killings were by the state as a way of illustrating the investigative imbalance, but it seriously underplays the problem because it implies that all those killings were illegal, and that a 10% probe ratio would be fair.

Whatever way the numbers are crunched, it is a grievous imbalance for 30% of the PSNI legacy investigations to be into state actions. In any event, the imbalance is much greater than 30% because PSNI is only one part of the various investigations.

As to the trial imbalance, in 2020 I was concerned by Public Prosecution Service (PPS) figures on legacy prosecutions, which I felt were misleading (and which were uncritically reported by the BBC) because they referred to cases in which prosecutors had "taken decisions". Needless to say, that is less significant than cases in which the decision led to trial. So I did my own analysis of legacy charges post-2007. I could find nine republican charges (in cases that involve killing) and six soldiers.

Similar numbers of trials of security forces and republicans are cited by nationalists to show that there is balance, and if cases against republicans are ahead there is even an implication that the state is getting off lightly, when in fact it is a breath-taking imbalance given that the state was responsible for a tiny fraction of illegal killings.

Human Rights in Northern Ireland

Daphne Trimble

Human rights long predate the twentieth-century international declarations and conventions on human rights, going back through the American Declaration of Independence to Magna Carta and beyond. The concept of individual freedom has been central to the unwritten British constitution as it has evolved over centuries.

Following the carnage of two world wars there was an appetite to set out basic rights for individuals which would guarantee for every individual in a state certain basic minimum standards, giving us the Universal Declaration of Human Rights of 1948, followed in 1950 by the European Convention on Human Rights, with various protocols being added in subsequent years. The Convention created a European Court of Human Rights, having jurisdiction as between signatory countries, and jurisdiction to hear applications from individuals. The procedure for cases to be brought by individuals was complex and slow, and cases from Northern Ireland were few.

One notable case was far-reaching in its effect. Homosexuality remained unlawful in Northern Ireland after being decriminalised in England and Wales in 1967. Jeff Dudgeon brought his case to the European Court of Human Rights and in 1981 the court held that Northern

Ireland's criminalization of homosexual acts between consenting adults was a violation of Article 8 of the European Convention on Human Rights, a judgment that led directly to the decriminalising of homosexuality in Northern Ireland [*Dudgeon v UK* (1981) 4 EHRR 149]. But such cases were rare. When I was a young law student at Queen's University Belfast in the early 1970s, human rights law did not even feature as an option on the syllabus; it was part of other relevant areas of study, such as criminal or constitutional law.

However, rights were very much part of the political discourse of the time in American and Europe; here in Northern Ireland the language of human rights was adopted almost exclusively by the nationalist community and used by republicans to justify their campaign of violence. Then, as later, the public discourse exaggerated greatly what could ever have been achieved. Indeed, all the socio-economic grievances could have been resolved through legal and political channels without the loss of a single life.

The Standing Advisory Commission on Human Rights, created in 1973, published annual reports on human rights issues to government until it was superseded by the creation of the Northern Ireland Human Rights Commission (NIHRC) in 1998.

1998 was a pivotal year in Northern Ireland. That was when the Belfast Agreement was agreed. I know more than most how difficult it was to achieve, and how much discussion went into every single clause. Under the heading "Rights, Safeguards and Equality of Opportunity", the Agreement provided for the creation of the NIHRC, and charged it with the obligation:

To advise on the scope for defining, in Westminster legislation, rights supplementary to those in the European Convention on Human Rights, to reflect the particular circumstances of Northern Ireland, drawing as appropriate on international instruments and experience. These additional rights to reflect the principles of mutual respect for the identity and ethos of both communities and parity of esteem, and – taken together with the ECHR – to constitute a Bill of Rights for Northern Ireland. Among the issues for consideration by the Commission will be: the formulation of a general obligation on government and public bodies fully to respect, on the basis of equality of treatment, the identity and ethos of both communities in Northern Ireland; and a clear formulation of the rights not to be discriminated against and to equality of opportunity in both the public and private sectors.

Also in 1998, the provisions of the European Convention were incorporated into UK domestic law as the Human Rights Act 1998. Thereafter any alleged breach of human rights law could be decided by domestic courts. Human rights issues had become matters which could be argued and adjudicated in every court in the jurisdiction; consequently two separate bodies of case law now exist, those decided by the European Court of Human Rights and domestic cases.

By its nature, a bill of rights is intended to be a fundamental document, overarching all other legislation. The effect of this is that all other legislation must be human rights compliant and justiciable; that is, any person may bring a legal case to argue that a particular piece of legislation or a particular method of implementation of any legislation is contrary to any particular right. This shifts decision-making from elected members of the legislature to unelected members of the judiciary, although the judges do not rule on legislation as a whole: they can rule only on the particular facts of the case brought before them.

We know from experience that many cases involving human rights law are brought with the assistance of wealthy organisations and individuals, who seek out cases to forward their own political views and advance their interests. Overall, the effect of human rights legislation is to remove power from elected politicians, and give that power in perpetuity to unelected judges. And it follows that the funders, who have no democratic accountability, become more powerful. Meanwhile, people whose rights cases do not match the views of wealthy lobbyists are not supported and have more difficulty asserting their rights. It also follows that elected politicians find their ability to act is circumscribed, and consequentially the ability of the voter to decide what happens in the country is diminished. So it is that additions to human rights, even if desirable in themselves, tend to transfer power and influence away from elected representatives to the judiciary, and by extension to individuals and organisations with deep pockets. In other words, we diminish democracy by adding to human rights legislation.

The comments above apply to the current position, where human rights law is the same across the UK. Matters become more complicated when you seek to change it in only one part of a jurisdiction. The Northern Ireland Human Rights Commission spent ten years debating the issues before submitting their report to the Secretary of

State in 2010. He decided against implementing any part of it. It drew heavily on a report from the Bill of Rights Forum (2008) which comprised members drawn equally from the main political parties and civil society. But as the Forum's report noted, there were deep divisions between the representatives of the two communities on a wide range of issues: "At the end of the Forum's work there was still no consensus on what constituted 'the particular circumstances of Northern Ireland' or as to the handling of the issues of 'mutual respect' and 'parity of esteem'."

I was a member of the Human Rights Commission when it produced its report. Like the Forum, it fell into the trap of overenthusiasm: instead of sticking closely to its remit, it tried to address many societal problems not arising from the "particular circumstances" of Northern Ireland but common across the UK, Ireland and other countries: housing, poverty and deprivation are replicated in disadvantaged communities across the world.

The Commission made little attempt to restrict themselves to the wording of the Agreement, which set out constitutional, political and administrative arrangements intended to resolve decades of conflict between people divided on ethnic, religious and political grounds, with their mutual hostility leading to a near boycott of the "other" in political, economic and social life. That is the bitter division which the Agreement was addressing, and which the signatories had in mind when they asked the Commission to consider if there were any additional rights which could contribute to its alleviation. The report adopted a maximalist approach, with over eighty separate recommendations, and I found myself unable to agree with most of it.

One problem that we in Northern Ireland have had with human rights legislation is that it is designed to apply to state actors, while most of the rights abuses during the "Troubles" were committed by non-state actors. Readers will be aware of the thorny issues which persist in our community around legacy, victims, survivors and inquiries. These are "particular circumstances" that the Commission should have been addressing but failed to.

The Commission wanted to include socio-economic rights in a Bill of Rights. I will refer only to one of them, healthcare. The Commission proposed this: "Everyone has the right to the highest attainable standard of physical and mental health. Public authorities must take all appropriate measures, including legislative measures, to the maximum of their available resources, with a view to achieving progressively the full realisation of this right". In the UK all individuals who lawfully reside in the country are entitled to healthcare from the National Health Service (NHS) free at the point of delivery. It is not set out in any Human Rights Act or Bill of Rights, but it is the ethos that has underpinned government policy and healthcare legislation since the inception of the NHS. The NHS has become part of the fabric of society, almost a religion. Yet we all know in these pandemic days that the NHS is stretched as never before and has to make choices around delivery of planned healthcare which impact on individuals. Resources are finite. If the above health clause had been incorporated in current legislation, we would likely find the NHS, and possibly the Minister for Health, being sued by someone whose cancer operation had been cancelled. A judge would have to inquire into the allocation of resources leading to such a decision, and potentially give directions as to future allocation of resources.

Politicians are the ones who are elected to make these decisions. They know very well that if they don't do the job well enough, the electorate will give them their marching orders at the next election. That is the essence of democracy. Allocating resources and ensuring that they are used appropriately is the task of government. At the best of times it is not easy. Do we want to make that task even more difficult?

Consider also the effect there would be on our society of having different human rights laws in Northern Ireland from the rest of the United Kingdom, or indeed from the rest of Europe. Northern Ireland is not a large economic region. Do we want to become so different in these regards? The two communities in Northern Ireland have in general opposing views around human rights. Nationalists tend to be enthusiasts for developing and enlarging human rights, while unionists tend to be content with the status quo across the UK; nationalists advocate changes which pull us away from the rest of the UK, while unionists prefer to treat the UK as a whole.[1] It is this which has allowed nationalists to create the narrative that they care about human rights in a way that unionists do not. Unionists do care just as much about human rights; they simply take the view that our rights should be identical to those in the rest of the UK.

There are practical questions too. What would be the extra workload for our legal system? Would our courts have the capacity to cope? What would happen to decision making when a particular issue was awaiting trial? I don't have answers, but these practical outworkings all need to be considered in advance of any changes.

Over ten years on from the Commission's report, An Assembly committee is considering human rights again. They are taking evidence from a wide range of experts, both those who are enthusiasts for extending human rights law and those who are more cautious. The issues have not changed. It will be some time before they produce their report. I am not going to predict what it will recommend, but I hope they will take account of all the implications and difficulties of having human rights laws in Northern Ireland which differ from the rest of the UK, and indeed the EU.

Endnotes

1 There are, of course, some beliefs and principles which some unionists wish to uphold and practise differently from the majority of citizens in the rest of the UK, such as opposition to abortion and gay marriage. Abortion and gay marriage, however, are unmentioned in the European Convention on Human Rights and differ from human rights that derive from international declarations and conventions.

The Island Economies: Comparative Living Standards

Graham Gudgin

The Irish Government likes to claim that there is such a thing as an all-island economy, but this is almost the opposite of the truth. There are two radically different economic models on the island and surprisingly little trade between them. The South's economy is the world's largest tax haven. The North is a region fully integrated into the United Kingdom economic union. Currency, tax rates, social security systems and business law all differ across the border. Only 1% of the Republic's output of goods and services goes north. Only 6% of Northern Ireland's output is recorded as exports to the South and a third of this is goods like cars and oil passing through from Great Britain.

The view of the Northern Ireland economy from southern economists has always been jaundiced and self-serving, lacking a real understanding of how the UK economy works. John Fitzgerald and Edgar Morgenroth of Trinity College and ESRI in Dublin, for instance, describe the NI economy as lacklustre, lacking dynamism and held back by low productivity.[1] Living standards, they say, depend on payments from central government and are thus vulnerable to shocks. In their view Brexit leaves

Northern Ireland facing a serious negative impact.

The celebrity Dublin economist David McWilliams dines out on his view that 100 years ago most of the island's manufacturing was in the north-east while now the great majority is in the south. He provides no context and perhaps does not understand that this reflects UK-wide trends. Most large British cities shed all of their manufacturing before the beginning of this century. London shed a million jobs in manufacturing while converting itself into the world's leading financial powerhouse.

The necessary context is that the UK has become the world's leading exporter of services. Even if Northern Ireland has not fully shared in this transition, most of its inward investment is in services, including legal services, fintech, software and cyber-security. The UK economy is quite strong enough to pay for a uniformly high level of public services in those areas where financial and business services are not as well developed as in London and south-east England.

The whole question of subsidies for public services is poorly understood in Ireland. The background in Northern Ireland is an economy which grew at close to UK rates (even during most of the Troubles when employment grew faster than in GB). However, its population expanded much faster than the UK average leading to a shortage of jobs which was very largely met by outmigration to GB. The UK's response was to create many jobs in the public services, allowing more people to stay in Northern Ireland thus making the population larger than it otherwise would have been. This larger population then created a need for public spending greater than the taxes generated from Northern Ireland's private sector. At the same time services are generously funded, just as they are in Scotland. This is a state of affairs with which British public opinion is content. There is no real pressure to change it. It is not a vulnerable situation as Fitzgerald and Morgenroth imagine.

Nor does Northern Ireland lack dynamism. Over the last decade its economy has grown at exactly the UK average growth rate. Before that it generally grew faster, except for the years of the banking crisis when its construction boom was cut down to size with the loss of many jobs. It is true that the UK as a whole has had a problem of slow growth in productivity since then, but this problem is shared with the USA and much of the western world.

What of the Republic? Its official national accounts statistics paint a picture of rapid growth and the claim is regularly made, even on the BBC, that Ireland is now one of the world's richest economies. Would that this were true, but it is not. Ireland's economic statistics are close to meaningless. In the words of the American economist, Brad Setzer, they tell us more about the tax affairs of American corporations than they do about the Irish economy.[2] To Nobel prize-winning economist Paul Krugman, it is leprechaun economics.[3] No version of Irish GDP statistics gives a meaningful account of Irish living standards, as former Irish Central Bank chairman, Patrick Honahan, has recently written (see below).

All of this statistical nonsense is caused by the Republic's status as one of the world's largest tax havens. Huge proportions of the profits of global corporations slosh through Irish national accounts, although little of it ends up in the pockets of either Irish households or the government. If we use a well-accepted measure of living standards, spending by households and by government on behalf of households, then the data in the Republic is much more accurate.

Fitzgerald and Morgenroth used this measure to calculate that living standards were 20% higher in Northern Ireland in 2012 than in the Republic. When they updated their calculation using data for 2016 their figure was 4%. They did not, however, allow for lower prices in Northern Ireland, especially house prices, which mean that households in Northern Ireland get more goods and services for any given amount of spending.

This result is staggering. It means that after 60 years as a tax haven and 48 years inside the EU, the Republic of Ireland has not managed to raise the living standards of its people to Northern Ireland levels. If the Republic were to rejoin the UK, it would be as the UK's poorest region just as it was a century ago. While tax haven status and EU membership have worked for the Irish elite, the majority of Irish citizens have gained little.

Two versions of a paper by McGuinness and Bergin, 2020 and 2021, contested the conclusion that living standards are higher in Northern Ireland.[4] In an article for the QPOL website on this subject (reproduced in the *News Letter*) I wrote last February that a rigorous comparison would show Northern Ireland ahead and briefly dismissed their conclusions.[5] In March Professor John Doyle replied. Rather unusually he replied as editor of the journal *Irish Studies in International Affairs* in which the latest of the Bergin and McGuinness articles had appeared.[6] He particularly objected to my comment that Bergin and McGuinness used "discredited Irish Accounts" to make their case that living standards are higher in the Republic.

Doyle went on to say that "It would be extraordinary indeed if both journals [*ISIA* and *CJE*] were so poor in their peer-reviewing as to allow work to be published that relied on discredited accounts".

Professor Doyle obviously has more faith in journal reviewers than I do, especially in expecting reviewers for an English journal to understand the problems with Irish national economic accounts. In any event, let's examine the evidence. The full reference to Bergin and McGuiness in my February article was as follows: "Other authors [also] attempt to contest Northern Ireland's advantage in living standards. Adele Bergin and Seamus McGuinness try this using the discredited Irish National Accounts, ignoring Honohan's warnings about the data. They also use household incomes but again fail to adjust properly for price differences".

The reference to Honohan was to a recent article by Patrick Honohan, who was Governor of the Irish Central Bank from 2009–15 and is currently a Senior Fellow at the Petersen Institute for international Economics. Dr. Honohan wrote an article in February 2021 entitled "Is Ireland Really the Most Prosperous Country in Europe?" in the Irish Central Bank's journal *Economic Letters* (2021:1). This article made the same case that others, including myself, Krugman and Setzer, had earlier made that Irish measures of GDP are hopelessly distorted and provide a poor guide to either the size of the Irish economy or the living standards of its citizens

The table below compares the Irish and UK economies using official data from the Central Statistics Office (CSO) in Ireland and the Office for National Statistics (ONS) in Britain. The table shows the ratio of the Republic of Ireland to the UK for a range of indicators measuring the size of the two economies on a per capita basis. For instance, the top row shows that per capita GDP is 81–86% higher in the Republic than in UK. The first column shows the measures using the average exchange rate for 2018. The second column uses purchasing power parities – a measure of relative prices. The table indicates that per capita GDP in the Republic is almost twice as high as the UK. This is, of course, a fiction since the Irish data is hugely inflated by the profits of global companies which route their profits through Ireland to take advantage of the low and sometimes minimal profits taxes in Ireland. GDP is often used by the UN and other international organisations as a standardising measure to make comparisons between countries on such things as spending on education, health or the environment. Because Irish GDP data is hugely inflated, Ireland is typically an outlier in such comparisons which fail to measure its true comparative position.

Ratio of Ireland to UK in 2018

	Current Exchange rate	PPP
GDP per capita	1.86	1.81
GNI per capita	1.46	1.45
GNI* per capita	1.14	1.12
AIC per capita	0.93	0.91
Household Disp Inc	0.94	0.92

Sources of data: CSO (Ireland), ONS (UK), OECD (PPP measure). PPP or purchasing power parity adjusts the national figures for differences in prices. Irish prices in 2018 were 15% above the UK. AIC is actual individual consumption, a combination of what consumers spend on themselves and what governments spend on their behalf. "Household Disp Inc" is disposable income per capita of the household sector.

The traditional way of adjusting GDP to record who owns the income rather than where it is produced is to remove what are called net factor incomes from abroad. This involves subtracting the profits of foreign corporations and wages of foreign workers earned in Ireland and adding in the profits and wages of Irish companies and workers earned abroad. If EU subsidies and taxes are also subtracted, the result is Gross National Income (GNI) which measures the incomes accruing to Irish companies and workers wherever these are earned. In 2018 the CSO in Ireland calculated that net factor incomes to be subtracted from headline GDP amounted to a huge €70.6 billion, or just under €15,000 per head of population. By 2019 this figure had risen to €17,000 per head. As a result, Irish GNI was 23% smaller than GDP whereas in most advanced economies the two would be similar in magnitude. For OECD countries, the GDP and GNI differ by less than 2%.

Even this adjustment greatly exaggerated the true size of the Irish economy and the CSO was led to make a further adjustment unknown anywhere else in the world. Following a massively distortionary and wholly implausible 35% increase in Irish GDP in 2015 the CSO introduced a measure termed GNI* (Gross National Income star). This measure subtracted the profits of "redomiciled companies", i.e. firms which moved their headquarters to Ireland without any real activity in Ireland. This removed a further €5 billion from the national accounts. A much larger reduction of €54 billion (€11,000 euros per head) was made to remove the depreciation on foreign-owned intellectual property and aircraft leasing. Multinational companies had registered much of the value of their brands and intellectual property in Ireland, again for tax reasons, reflecting Ireland's very low corporation tax rate of 12.5% and its lenient taxation of intellectual property. These registered assets are capital and do not count as GDP or GNI, but international rules determine that the depreciation of these assets does count. For instance, the decision of the global aircraft leasing industry to register its assets in Ireland led to the huge increase in GDP in 2015. There is no equivalent of GNI* in the UK (or in most other countries) since there is no need for such an adjustment except in tax havens.

There can be no doubt that GDP or GNI are discredited as measures of living standards. The use of GNI as a benchmark for some EU payments means that mismeasurement will involve a real fiscal cost for Ireland for instance in payments to the EU. Some regard GNI* as a reasonable measure of the size of the Irish economy, and hence of living standards, but a consideration of "actual individual consumption" (AIC) suggests that this is not so. AIC adds together consumer spending by households and current spending by government on behalf of households on things such as health and education. It is thus a measure of what is spent by or on behalf of households.

Professor Doyle says that AIC "is not a standard measure of living standards". However, it is used by Fitzgerald and Morgenroth (2020) in their papers_on the Northern Ireland economy. Even Bergin and McGuiness say that it is "a useful indicator of the level of goods and services that individuals enjoy". Also, Patrick Honohan states that AIC is "an alternative aggregate national indicator of household welfare used in international comparisons" The conclusion to Dr. Honohan's article is worth repeating in full:

Ireland is a prosperous country, but not as prosperous as is often thought because of the inappropriate use of misleading, albeit conventional statistics. There is less consumption per capita than in the UK, and on this metric we are closer to New Zealand, Israel and Italy, than to the United States, Switzerland or Norway (which is where the GDP comparison would put Ireland). *The same conclusion is drawn if GDP is replaced with the Ireland-specific GNI* indicator* [my italics]. Using GDP as a measure can mislead analysis of such matters as debt, carbon-intensity and inequality.

While GDP or GNI must be regarded as discredited measures of living standards, there is little reason to suggest that AIC is not an eminently sensible measure. After all, it measures what is spent by and on behalf of households. In the case of the Republic it is doubly appropriate since both household consumption and government spending do not include any distorting effects from multinational company profits. This measure suggests that living standards in the Republic are 6–8% below those in the UK when price differences are taken into account (see table above).

Anyone who uses any GDP measure is thus using statistics which are not creditable measures of relative living standards. Do Bergin and McGuiness use GDP measures? Well yes, they do. They mention two. The first is per capita GDP where they conclude that Northern Ireland has living standards 50% lower than in Ireland's Southern and Eastern region (which contains three-quarters of Ireland's population) but slightly above the rest of Ireland in the poorer Border, Midland and Western region. The second is household disposable income, which they found to be $3000 a year higher in Ireland than in Northern Ireland. This measure was criticised in my own QPOL article for not taking into account the fact that consumer and housing prices were lower in NI compared to the national UK price index which they used.

In their second article McGuinness and Bergin mention the flaws in the per capita GDP measure but still use it, and GNI, in their table 1. They say that per capita GDP in the Republic is 232% higher than in Northern Ireland! (This appears not to use the correct value for GDP in Northern Ireland.) They also say in this article they prefer GNI★ which they regard as having removed the FDI-related distortions. They say that per capita GNI★ in the Republic is 51% higher than per capita GDP in Northern Ireland, but they wrongly compared current price GNI★ in the Republic with constant price GDP for Northern Ireland. The correct figure for this comparison would be 41%. We might notice that none of these points were picked up by those who reviewed the article for the journal, just as the inappropriateness of using Irish GDP figures was apparently not picked up by the *CJE* reviewers.

As Patrick Honohan suggests, although GNI★ removes the most obvious distortions it does not remove them all. Elsewhere in the paper McGuinness and Bergin discuss north–south differences in trade without apparently recognising that exports in Ireland are equivalent to 122% of GDP and imports are 94% of GDP. In other words, Ireland exports more than its total output of goods and services. In the UK, an economy without the Irish distortions, exports and imports is a more normal 30% of GDP. The distortions in Ireland's account clearly stretch well beyond the profits of multinational companies.

McGuinness and Bergin reject the AIC measure in favour of household disposable income on the grounds that consumption is affected by savings. In other words, for any given income a household will spend less if it saves more. This is true in principle, but current living standards depend on spending not on saving. Most saving takes the form of pension contributions and capital repayments on mortgages. In areas of high house prices, including Dublin and London but not Belfast, mortgages are necessarily larger and capital repayments greater. This means that there is less to spend on current consumption. The upside of course is that households own more valuable housing assets, although the value may accrue to their descendants rather than to themselves.

McGuinness and Bergin calculate that household disposable incomes were 12% higher in the Republic in 2017 than in Northern Ireland. This is based on consumer price differences at *national* level. However, prices are lower in Northern Ireland than the UK average and hence money buys more goods and services. The ONS calculated regional consumer prices excluding housing for 2016 and it is assumed here that the ratio of Northern Ireland prices to UK prices remains the same in 2018. The ONS calculation is that consumer prices in Northern Ireland are 2.4% below the UK average. Housing costs are 30% lower and combining the two (with a 20% weight for housing) gives aggregate prices in Northern Ireland at 8.1% lower than the UK average.[7] Allowing for this price difference gives household disposable income in Northern Ireland in 2018 at 2.8% below that in the Republic. Using the same price adjustments for Northern Ireland, my calculation is that in 2018 NI had higher consumer spending than the Republic by 1%. The difference between the income and expenditure figures is due to differences in saving.

These calculations do not include spending by government on behalf of households on health, education etc. Government current spending per head at national PPP prices in Northern Ireland was 18% above that in the Republic in 2018. No allowance is made here for lower NI prices since most wages in the NI public sector are at national UK levels. Combining consumer spending with government current spending results in Northern Ireland having actual individual consumption 5% higher than in the Republic.

The standard of public services in Northern Ireland does not always fully reflect the higher spending and NI's advantage may not be as large as 5%. McGuinness and Bergin discuss aspects of service provision including in health where the NI Assembly has long failed to drive up standards to national UK levels in face of resistance from the medical profession. In education their analysis is less secure, being based largely on inputs and not outputs including international Programme for International Student assessment (PISA) scores. The 2018 PISA scores show NI above the OECD (Organisation for Economic Co-operation and Development) average for all three subjects. For science and maths there is no significant difference between NI and the Republic although the latter was as always clearly better at literacy.

There is no time here to support my claim that "the view of the NI economy from southern economists has always been jaundiced and self-serving", which Professor Doyle describes as unsubstantiated. Two examples may however give a flavour. McGuinness and Bergin (2020) say that "In Northern Ireland employment in manufacturing fell over the 1970s ... this performance was much worse than the wider UK". This is partly true, but employment in manufacturing fell fairly consistently throughout the UK from 1970 right through to 2010 as the UK became a service-oriented economy. Northern Ireland did a little worse than the UK average in the 1970s but much better in the 1980s. Manufacturing employment in NI then actually expanded in the 1990s up to the Belfast Agreement in 1998 while it fell in GB. After the Agreement, decline set in again, but more slowly than in GB. Over the whole period of the Troubles, 1970–98, manufacturing employment declined significantly less in NI (34%) than in GB (44%). This can be put down to a lower cost base and government financial support especially for new foreign direct investment (FDI). None of this good story is mentioned by McGuinness and Bergin (2020) who reference only the 1970s, using as evidence a 40-year-old article.[8] As in other studies, an arbitrary time-period is selected which shows NI in a negative light and overlooks favourable performance.

The second example is the statement by McGuinness and Bergin (2020) that "the nationalist, mainly catholic, population were geographically concentrated into poorer areas and suffered from economic and social discrimination". The only evidence cited is the same 40-year-old article. No later work is cited including those which show that Catholics were actually over-represented in state-owned housing and not under-represented as generally believed or argue that high Catholic unemployment had structural causes.[9] This level of superficial comment should not be acceptable in academic journals. Neither this, nor the example in the previous paragraph, appears to have been questioned by the referees for the *CJE*.

Conclusions

All of this is, of course, relevant to the issue of a border poll on Irish unity. Some have pointed out that voters rarely vote to become poorer. This is not quite right in national questions where sovereignty or national identity are at stake, but nevertheless living standards will always be of some relevance. The fact that the Republic of Ireland has not managed to overtake living standards in one of the UK's poorest regions, even after 60 years as a tax haven, is likely to be at least one reason why half of Northern Ireland's Catholics regularly tell the Life and Times survey they would prefer to remain in the UK rather than join a united Ireland. It may also explain why Sinn Féin has made such strong progress among the Southern electorate.

As long as living standards remain higher in Northern Ireland we can expect the case for Irish unity to have little traction in the North. Irish living standards would need to be far above those in Northern Ireland for economic issues to become a decisive factor in any border poll. This is unlikely to happen because the best is almost certainly past for the Republic's economy. President Biden is at last putting American weight behind a global reform of profits taxes paid (or more often unpaid) by multinational companies. The EU will gladly join in a campaign to prohibit tax havens like Ireland. At the same time Ireland has ceased to be a beneficiary of EU largesse and is now a net contributor to EU funds. The Northern Ireland economy is unlikely to lose much from Brexit and there is little reason to believe that it will receive less from the UK than it has in the past. All in all, economics is unlikely to help the cause of Irish unity.

Endnotes

1 John Fitzgerald and Edgar Morgenroth, "The Northern Ireland Economy: Problems and Prospects," TEP Working Paper 619, July 2019. https://www.tcd.ie/Economics/TEP/2019/tep0619.pdf

2 Brad W. Setser, "Ireland's Statistical Cry for Help," Council on Foreign Relations 100, posted 1 November, 2019.

3 Paul Krugman, "Leprechaun Economics with Numbers," *New York Times* Blogs, 11 November, 2017.

4 Seamus McGuinness and Adele Bergin, "The Political Economy of a Northern Ireland Border Poll," *Cambridge Journal of Economics*, vol. 44, no. 4 (July 2020).

5 "Who is Better Off, Northerners or Southerners," QPOL, 16 February, 2021, reprinted in the *News Letter*, 24 February 2021.

6 John Doyle, "Comparing Living Standards: North and South," QPOL, 23 March 2021.

7 "Relative Regional Consumer Price Levels of Goods and Services, UK: 2016", ONS.

8 R. Rowthorn, "Northern Ireland. An Economy in Crisis," *Cambridge Journal of Economics*, vol. 5 no. 1 (1981).

9 See my chapter, "The Northern Ireland Labour Market", in Heath, Breen and Whelan, "Ireland North and South: Perspectives from Social Science" (British Academy, 1999).

Ditch the Protocol:
the EU Threat to Northern Ireland

Lord Trimble

Twenty-three years ago along with John Hume we finalised what became known as the Good Friday (or Belfast) Agreement. It was intended to end the 35 years of terrorist violence that had cost thousands of lives in Northern Ireland and beyond, and to deal with the sectarian community divisions that had allowed terrorism to fester.

For the Ulster Unionist Party, of which I was then the leader, there were unpalatable compromises to swallow. Terrorists were released from prison under a very generous release scheme. Those who had taken part in terrorist activities were encouraged to participate in democracy and indeed some leaders of such terrorist groups became members of the Northern Ireland Assembly and even ministers in the Executive.

Political structures were set up for North/South cooperation – a development of which many unionists were suspicious, believing with some merit that they could be used to lever Northern Ireland away from the United Kingdom.

Such structures had led to the collapse of the Sunningdale agreement in 1973 between the British and Irish governments. But this time we got the wholly transparent, bottom-up structures, including all the major Northern Ireland parties, right.

Massive changes were embedded into the police which had borne the brunt of the terrorist campaign – changes which have proved difficult to absorb.

Despite all these compromises, the majority of people in Northern Ireland endorsed the Agreement.

They did so on the basis that Northern Ireland's constitutional position within the UK could not be changed – a commitment I had secured at great political and personal cost from the British government, the Irish government, nationalist leader John Hume, and the leadership of Sinn Féin. All the parties agreed that any such change would require the consent of the people of NI in a referendum. The declaration at the very top of the Agreement stated clearly that it would "be wrong to make any change in the status of Northern Ireland save with the consent of the majority of its people".

Despite strong opposition within my own community who resented the concessions to those engaged in indiscriminate killing, I campaigned for a Yes vote in the referendum on the Agreement, arguing that it made the Union safe and that the future of Northern Ireland was totally in the hands of its people through the ballot box.

They put their trust in my assurances and gave me and the Agreement their backing.

That is why I feel betrayed personally by the Northern Ireland Protocol, and it is also why the unionist population is so incensed at its imposition. The Protocol rips the very heart out of the Agreement, which I and they believed safeguarded Northern Ireland as part of the United

Kingdom and ensured that democracy not violence, threat of violence or outside interference, would or could ever change that. Make no mistake about it, the Protocol does not safeguard the Good Friday Agreement. It demolishes its central premise by removing the assurance that democratic consent is needed to make any change to the status of Northern Ireland. It embodies a number of constitutional changes that relate to Northern Ireland.

Firstly, every EU law, regulation and directive made in respect of agriculture, manufacturing, environment, work practices, and other matters will continue to apply to NI even though the rest of the UK is now free of them. The list of EU laws with which NI will have to comply runs to 70 pages and contains hundreds of thousands of regulations.

Secondly, any future laws made by the EU in respect of these areas (covering nearly 70% of our economic activity) will also apply to NI. No Northern Ireland input into these laws will be allowed, so even if the content of EU laws is damaging to us, we will not be able to make representations or to have them changed.

Thirdly, regardless of how damaging future EU enforced laws might be, they will have to be obeyed – otherwise the European Court of Justice will be able to enforce sanctions on the United Kingdom. In other words, a court based in a foreign jurisdiction will supersede courts in Northern Ireland and the United Kingdom.

Fourthly, as the UK decides how it wishes to exercise its new freedom from the EU in order to make its economy more competitive in global trade, any new laws it makes to achieve that competitiveness will not apply to Northern Ireland because of the requirement to abide by EU law.

This massive change in the constitutional position of NI is already manifesting itself in economic disruption through physical checks on trade between Great Britain and Northern Ireland, extensive bureaucratic requirements, a serious escalation in the cost of doing business between GB and NI, and time delays in receiving goods to the point where many GB firms have simply stopped supplying goods to NI.

This political betrayal and these economic costs have already raised tensions in Northern Ireland. So, far from keeping the peace, the Protocol risks a return to violence despite claims from its supporters that it is all about protecting the Agreement. To those who make such claims I respectfully say, "Read the Agreement and then tell me what part of the Agreement is protected by the Protocol".

The sad fact is that the threat to peace and economic prosperity in Northern Ireland as a result of the Protocol is totally unnecessary. The EU has nothing to fear from the minuscule level of trade that crosses into its territory from NI, and even that trade could be regulated without any need for checks on the border between NI and the Republic.

Through the Centre for Brexit Policy I have already put forward an arrangement that would require the UK and the EU to put in place a system for the mutual enforcement of each other's regulations that would apply to the small number of firms currently involved in cross-border trade. This would mean that firms selling into the Republic from Northern Ireland, or vice versa, would have to declare on their export documentation that they had adhered to the regulations in the other jurisdiction. If spot checks when the goods arrive or subsequent inspections at the point of sale discovered that the declaration was false, the business would be pursued by the authorities in the country in which it was based, and stiff mandatory penalties would deter any incentive to act unlawfully.

There are these and other mechanisms for dealing with cross-border trade. The question is, does the political will exist to introduce them or is the European Union intent on playing fast and loose with peace in Northern Ireland, damaging its economy and undermining the very basis of democratic decision-making, in order to punish the United Kingdom for voting for its independence from the European Union?

Back to the Future: The Constitutional Challenge Revisited

Arthur Aughey

The specific concern of my chapter on "The Constitutional Challenge" in the first edition of *The Idea of the Union* (1995) is now mainly of historical interest. And yet Irish history has a tendency to repeat itself and unfortunately not in a good way. So this revised version requires some historical reflection to establish the character of the present challenge. It can begin in 1995, the year in which the original book was published. Its publication loosely coincided with an important essay written not by a historian or by a political scientist but by a literary critic, Edna Longley. The essay "From Cathleen to Anorexia" in her book *The Living Stream: Literature and Revisionism in Ireland* (1994) was a key intervention into the tired political debates of the time and it continues to have important things to say about choices on the island, south as well as north.

Fleshing out accommodation

The Irish nationalist dream, Longley suggested, "may have declined into destructive neurosis" allowing ethnic assertion "to punch above its weight" and to set a universal tone

–the politics of the worst threatening to marginalise the possibility of the best. She cited the view of the playwright Robin Glendinning (who was a founder member of the Alliance party) that nationalism is always "finding novel ways of saying the same damned things", something Longley thought also applicable to traditional unionism (hence her later proposal that they should both be treated with "parity of disesteem" as no longer fit for purpose). Progress, she thought, must admit complexity, and institutionally such complexity "requires an intricately engineered four wheel drive" adequate to the challenge of securing and maintaining stability on the island of Ireland.

Attention has focused on the subsequent tortuous course of the so-called "peace process" of the 1990s – Hume-Adams, Downing Street Declaration, Framework Documents, Belfast/Good Friday Agreement – but in the background was an interesting intellectual engagement to find novel ways to change the same damned things or at least to draw their destructive sting. Without wishing to overplay the importance of that engagement, it is still worth recalling its value and, more importantly, what it signified. For want of a better term, this period can be called "the Mary Robinson years", not to stress the direct *political* contribution of the Irish President (1990–97) but to capture the indirect *symbolic* opening up which her presidency represented. There was an attempt to release the grip of what Longley called "ideological clamps upon the imagination" which she defined as the unionist object of cutting off Northern Ireland from the rest of the island and the nationalist objective of cutting off Northern Ireland from the rest of the United Kingdom. She cited the conviction of the late Maurice Hayes that it was only when people ceased to be fixated on these end states "that the possibilities become infinite for organic growth at a rate to which all the constituent elements can adjust and accommodate themselves". Both Longley and Hayes wanted politics to shift towards Northern Ireland (as Longley put it) relaxing into "a genuinely diverse sense of its own identity", and the 1990s provided the opportunity to move towards that relaxation.

Without wishing to romanticise or to idealise this era or to paint it in nostalgic colours, it involved an attempt – particularly in the Republic – to understand the unionist position and not to reduce it to an "Afrikaaner mentality" or to "false consciousness" or whatever other formula was appropriate to non-acknowledgement of its legitimacy and of Northern Ireland's existence. This engagement took place at a number of open forums (the Cultures of Ireland conferences being one) and at a number of discreet meetings. It wasn't a matter of persuading others of the "truth" of the unionist position or convincing those who did not share its premises or beliefs of unionism's unassailable logic. To claim that effect would be to put words into the mouth of history. Rather, unionist views were listened to respectfully and the sincerity of arguments accepted, even if agreement was not required. In other words, mutual understanding and not winning an argument were judged the ways to promote change and this was because a convergence of cultural criticism, historical revisionism and political necessity promoted opportunities (and a willingness) to get beyond anorexic nationalist demands – that there should be a date for British withdrawal (in the Hume-Adams document there was actually a space left blank for the date to be added), that the two governments should plan and prepare for Irish unity, that the UK Government should remove the unionist "veto" and then "persuade" unionists to accept unity.

In many ways the intricate and interlocking machinery of the Belfast/Good Friday Agreement of 1998 resembles that "intricately engineered four wheel drive" Longley had argued for (of course, without attributing "ownership" of the Agreement to her) rather than the clapped out rhetoric of national destiny. Equally, the Agreement established the rate by which all the constituent elements could adjust and accommodate themselves to change as Hayes also hoped, and that rate was determined by the principle of consent. Looking back to those years and to the substantial intellectual weight given to the principles of accommodation, recognition and complexity, it is difficult not to conclude that things have gone backwards.

Back to the bare bones
What is the constitutional challenge today? My original chapter argued that the challenge was a question of language as a measure of political intent. Let's take the intent first. In Chapter XVII of his *History of the Peloponnesian War* Thucydides put that famous line of crude political realism into the statement of the Athenian delegation – "you know as well as we do that right, as the world goes, is only in question between equals in power, while the strong do what they can and the weak suffer what they must". Nationalism – particularly its articulation in Sinn Fein intent and expressed from the north – now believes that, as the world goes, the balance of power no longer requires equality (or parity of esteem or even consent) but puts nationalists in the position of strength to do what they want. Unionists,

now weak, have to suffer what they must (or "own it") from the Northern Ireland Protocol to Bobby Storey's funeral. Ranged against unionists, "advanced" nationalists now consider they have a formidable set of allies to be lined up, from the US to the EU (and perhaps soon a Sinn Féin dominated Irish state). And the calculation is a simple one informed by all the implicit logic of Carl Schmitt's *The Concept of the Political* (1932). If the appropriate distinction in morality is between good and evil, in aesthetics beautiful and ugly, in economics profitable and unprofitable, then for Schmitt the specific "distinction to which political actions and motives can be reduced is that between friend and enemy". It is irrelevant, he thought, whether one finds this criterion barbaric or atavistic. It is the fundamental truth of power politics and it is the logic of Sinn Féin's position. Nationalism can mobilise its friends and unionism has few or no friends and, in the text of the current post-Brexit Protocol, has been betrayed once more by those it believed were its friends. That is why Brexit is now assumed to be the "game changer" and one which will usher in unity.

As a consequence, the changed power balance requires the concession of a border poll on Irish unity, and agitation for it has become increasingly insistent, almost as if the Mary Robinson years had never happened. Arguments for a border poll remind one of 1990s and the anorexic neurosis Longley diagnosed. The demands look like the same damned things expressed in a novel way and stripped of their 1998 flesh – that the UK should set a date for a border poll (premised on the assumption of Irish unity), that in advance of a vote the two Governments must plan and prepare for Irish unity, and that the two Governments (but above all the UK) should encourage unionists to "engage" with the process. In short, the complexity of the B/GFA is reduced to only *one* idea and that one idea only requires 50%+1 (the only part of the Agreement that remained faithful to the simple majority principle was the provision for a referendum on Irish unity). One of the many ironies of recent constitutional arguments is that the simple majoritarian principle – the principle against which nationalism campaigned for generations in Northern Ireland – makes its return as an unimpeachable democratic necessity.

Another irony is that the case for this strategy is predicated on that supposed nationalist game changer of the 2016 EU referendum and its aftermath. The argument runs that the EU poll was called without any plan or preparation and with no consideration for the consequences of Brexit, hence the years of chaos and confusion which followed. The supposed lesson to be learnt is that an Irish border poll requires both Governments to plan and prepare now such that voters will be able to make an informed choice between Union and Irish unity.

Of course, there is another lesson of Brexit and it is that an issue which was rarely a priority for either voters or politicians was made the *only* priority. In the present iteration, Irish unity is inevitable (of course) so we need to prepare for it now. And since the answer is known already, the conversation can only be framed with a set of questions delivering the correct answer. The policy agenda and political language will be determined by only one issue, how to achieve unity. It's the old politics of transition, working back from the end (Irish unity) to present means – set a date, begin preparations, make unionists engage. *Qui vult finem, vult media quoque.*

One of the old political slogans used to be "if you are not part of the solution then you are part of the problem", a slogan which carried with it an obvious threat. Today that slogan has been revised such that those not signed up to the new agenda are dismissed as "border poll deniers", in denial of reality, in denial of necessity, in denial of democracy and (ultimately) in denial of their own self-interest (and as a consequence they will have to "own" the consequences or forced to be free). However, it is noticeable how little of the tactful exchanges, respectful listening and reflective exchanges now inform this sort of nationalist thinking (unlike the Mary Robinson years) and how little effort is thought necessary to persuade unionists of anything. A significant part of the problem with so-called unionist political "inarticulateness" was that for 50 years it let power – majority will, right of possession – do the talking for it. Today that relationship has been reversed.

Patrick Murphy asked perceptively in the *Irish News*: "Is nationalism the new unionism?" He thought its sectarian success wasn't surprising, but its triumphalism was a shock, concluding that the "shift in sectarian power is just different, not better". Reviewing Murphy's question, Mick Fealty (2021) summed up the argument by observing how Sinn Féin's "politics of inevitability has taught them they need not compromise".[1] Why take unionism seriously when history has put them in the dustbin already? Here, unionism has returned as an ideological obstacle to progress and that return to basics cuts with the grain of some thinking which emerged after 2016 in the Republic of Ireland (what Murphy called the "post-Brexit demonisation of unionists by Dublin and Brussels"). A further irony in these times of intellectual "de-colonisation" is that nationalism appears to have adopted the tone of the old coloniser's "civilising mission" and "enlightenment project", presenting itself as liberal, secular and progressive, while unionism is portrayed as reactionary, sectarian and incapable of improvement *from within*. It needs to be transformed *from without* (the shorthand for which is a united Ireland).

The constitutional challenge can be stated another way: "Let's substitute the complex and consensual *modus vivendi* of 1998 with the simple, binary, absolute choice and assume a consensus can be delivered from that profound division". The tribal drum is the beat of back to the future because no positive case need be made apart from the promises of a Sugar Candy (united) Ireland. After all, electoral demographics will sort it all out. It is the (re)proclamation of a never-ending story which is always a new story (as Glendinning saw) and it is that the future belongs to us. It is a return to the politics of the desert island, not, of course, in the sense of an idyllic, paradisiacal, existence. The meaning is the very opposite, a vision of people trapped in Northern Ireland by malign historical circumstances in a hostile landscape. The resources of the place are depleting and the future is bleak. The only possibility is to prepare for the day of delivery when the rescue ship SS United Ireland appears on the horizon. Thereafter the narrative involves a state in which all old facts become new, all old obstacles removed and all present limitations overcome as we sail into the new dawn. It is idealism of the imagination which can only see fact or evidence as an intolerable imposition which explains why ideologues within Sinn Féin and without continue to believe unionists/loyalists have no ideas, no imagination, can't engage and are an obstacle to progress. We are back to the rhetoric of "stupid unionism" (and nationalist reason can only "engage" with unionist "stupidity" by defeating it). Eventually unionists will come to see the writing on the wall (an assumption with a pedigree of at least a century and a half) and if they don't, too bad for them. Border poll tribalism, the expectation that in a few years there will be a nationalist majority, is the same damned thing all over again.

A healthy alternative to living on hot air

There is an assumption that "most Unionists will admit to the inevitability of a united country" and that "the search for agreement should begin now". There is little point in evading "any further the inevitability on which all are agreed". This was said back in 1971 – by John Hume. Later Hume changed his language and approach to accept an "agreed Ireland" rather than a "united Ireland" and to advocate uniting people and not territory.

Today the claim is that all is changed and changed utterly because of Brexit. It would be foolish not to accept that there is a post-Brexit temptation to accept the lure of Irish unity as an escape from present discontents. But where is the evidence of an irresistible march towards Irish unity because of Brexit, or because of the Protocol? Scholars, via robust polling and surveys, show that a border poll delivering a majority for Irish unity is *not* imminent. Support for Northern Ireland's present status remains consistently strong. Insistent and bullying advocacy of a border poll ignores evidence. Most people do not think it is a priority and much of the uptick in public expressions of Irish unity *conceivably* happening is a response to a possibility at least twenty years hence. Much was made of a LucidTalk poll showing 43% of those who responded favouring Irish unity. That finding was seriously out of line with academic studies (for example the Liverpool Study and Life and Times Surveys) which show sustained support for Northern Ireland staying in the UK. Neither the UK nor, significantly, the Irish Government is in favour of a poll.

For example, when he launched the Shared Island initiative, Taoiseach Micheál Martin spoke of "the genius of the Agreement is that we do not need to be defined or dominated by constitutional questions, as we were in the past." He noted that because no outcome is *pre-ordained* under the B/GFA, everyone could work together "for a shared future without in any way relinquishing our equally legitimate ambitions and beliefs – nationalist, unionist or neither." And it was refreshing to hear Martin speak of the "need to probe some of the simplistic narratives about what we have all come through, which have emerged on both sides of the border." This was proper "Mary Robinson years" language. His refusal to make a commitment to a border poll acknowledges the potentially destabilising consequences of the process. Old hands like Fergus Finlay, Bertie Ahern and the late Seamus Mallon have all been cautious about simple majoritarianism, obviously recognising a destructive neurosis when they see one. This is positive albeit with reservations. Longley, considering the discourse of thirty years ago, argued that while talking of Ireland "as an island is an improvement on Ireland as nation, it omits the totality of relations in the archipelago". Her point was that the singular "island" remained a "political word and map game with specific origins in Northern Irish politics". It is so today as well.

The problem with the Protocol is that it takes the East-West, UK dimension out of the picture (substituting the EU dimension instead). This omission must be addressed – by London, Dublin and Brussels – to re-balance the 1998 Agreement and to secure stability on the island. It is the way to really engage with unionism.

Intellectual pessimism is a recognisable characteristic of unionist thinking but it must avoid becoming a suicide cult of self-defeating self-pity. As Lord Bew (2021) noted, there is no historic train steaming along the one way track to unity: there is, "instead, as there has always been, a big task ahead for those who want to make the case for Irish unity by consent."[2] They aren't doing a very good job of it. In the 1990s the UK and Irish governments "accepted that there were two functioning economies on the island of Ireland". Furthermore, a single Ireland economy is not mandated post-Brexit and "the rhythm of economic and social life between north and south will be quite distinct." In short, Brexit or no Brexit, the fact of the Union still means that the economic "facts of life" remain in favour of the UK. Unionists need to celebrate the truth that Northern Ireland *does* work and commit to politics making it work better for everyone. That is the evidence-based exposition of the pro-Union case which needs consistent re-stating, reaching out to those "neithers" who are more instrumental in their political allegiance. For "middle Ulster" (not only unionists) and for "middle Ireland" (not only nationalists) there is a common purpose in the prosperity, stability and welfare of Northern Ireland, north south, east and west. This is true whether you want unity or whether you want the Union. Here is the choice and the challenge. Reduce the B/GFA to one and final purpose –

a border poll – and return political culture to exclusive symbolic identifications, as if nothing has changed since 1990 (or even 1969). Or – promote a collective interest in making Northern Ireland work – employment, health and welfare – and engage seriously in the project, defined by Seamus Mallon, of making Northern Ireland a "shared home place" where uniting people is more important than uniting territory.

Endnotes

1 Mick Fealty, (2021) https://sluggerotoole.com/2021/04/11/nationalisms-sectarian-success-is-not-surprising-but-its-triumphalism-is-a-shock/
2 Paul Bew, "No Poll on united Ireland yet, but don't take the northern province for granted", *Sunday Times*, 24 January, 2021.

Reaching Out: Reimagining Post-Centenary Unionism

William J.V. Neill

While some unionists in 2021 are fixated on commissioning a rock in the Stormont estate to mark one hundred years of Northern Ireland's existence, such affirmation could better be extended to revising what unionism in broad terms stands for and not casting in stone a lazy representation of a polity and reality that are long gone. The pen in this respect is mightier than the chisel. Here unionism, since justifiable protest, inept management and neglect overwhelmed the Stormont era in the early seventies, has been more preoccupied in asserting what it is not (for example, soft on the prospect of Irish unification) as opposed to articulating a vision of what it is and aspires to be.

This challenge is now acute. People in Northern Ireland stoically resisted and said NO to a campaign of republican violence and mayhem. The reasons, however, for such an understandable hunkering down and introversion are long gone. The battlefield is now a cultural one in a constitutional chess game which unionism is losing. I speak from the starting-point of someone from a working-class, state-educated background, born 67 years ago in the then predominantly Protestant environs of south Belfast.

I had no notion of the divided society into which I was positioned until at the age of six my playmate Patrick accused me of cheating him in a game of marbles because he was Catholic. Things were never the same again and my loss of innocence with words I could not understand at the time still stirs feelings of guilt and regret. My entrance to the world also overlapped with the coronation of Queen Elizabeth II. For this accident of birth I received a half crown from the British government deposited in the Belfast Savings Bank . Having lived outside Northern Ireland for half my working life in university environments and policy advisory roles in the United States, England and Scotland, and having now returned home to retire, sentiment and affection for the Union and its possible post-Brexit loss, prompts me to write. The half a crown gesture of solidarity and celebration across the entire United Kingdom at the start of the Elizabethan age seems to beckon for a response across the years as its days draw in.

Northern Ireland and the Union
Whilst it is fashionable in some quarters of "woke" academia to belittle the Union flag as a negative emblem of empire, this is because the case for the Union too often goes by default. This applies to the United Kingdom in general despite the wake-up call of the 2014 Scottish referendum. While no one indeed, to quote John Hume, can eat a flag, neither do people exist by bread alone. Passions matter. Here cultural affinity with place is crucial. To me Northern Ireland represents the corner of the Union which is both Irish and British. My cultural identity is bound to a feeling for the place and its symbolically endowed landscape which incorporates both these dimensions alongside in particular

a strong Scottish link through a metaphorical open-ended "cultural corridor". Indeed while working in Aberdeen, I often found the local accent close to that in Ballymena.

Sticking with Edna Longley's fecund image of the corridor in Andy Pollak (ed.), *A Citizens' Enquiry* (1993), this space of the imagination and real cultural interaction remain potentially fluid and permeable and open to new possibilities. While political unionism is still too associated with puritan-like religious dogma most noticeable in the backward-looking Democratic Unionist Party, such influences are not the core values of unionism. The essence of Unionism is not defined by what John Wilson Foster in the 1995 *The Idea of the Union* calls "immoderate Unionism" in its various manifestations. Rather, unionism for me identifies with a British sensibility, shared experience and unfolding story or narrative. It is to state the obvious that to be out of step with the thrust of liberalising currents in this wider whole is to invite embarrassment and dismissal as the peculiar relative in the attic of the Union, a Union without which unionist identity ceases to be. The argument by one academic expatriate from these shores, Norman Porter, in *Rethinking Unionism* (1996), that neither unionism nor nationalism can transcend rootedness in culture is a telling one. Any attempt to distil the essence of Unionism in more neutral, dry constitutional/legal relationships, obligations and rights or even economic interest, important as these may be, does not get to the more visceral cultural factors generating broad group identity. Like Foster I would endorse the sentiment that "I am a unionist because unionism is my culture", a constituent part of a broader British culture which I unapologetically embrace. Genuine unionism has no truck with discriminatory sectarian practices. That unionist culture is shallow, based on economic supremacy and related to a hangover from a colonial presence, is still a view with currency. It met with short shrift from the respected political scientist John Whyte whom I had the good fortune to be lectured by as an economics and politics undergraduate at QUB. In his influential book *Interpreting Northern Ireland* (1990) he warned not "to place too little weight on cultural factors". Illustrating his observation, he pointed out that: "if economics outweighed culture, one might have expected the Protestant farmers west of the Bann, whose material interests were much closer to those of their Catholic neighbours than they were to the workers and industrialists of the Belfast area, to have been drawn to nationalist Ireland, but in fact they were quite as staunch unionists as any other Protestants in Ulster" .

The Good Friday/Belfast Agreement of 1998, of course, acknowledges the centrality of culture with the institutionalized recognition of differences between the two major cultural traditions in Northern Ireland. These are to be treated on the basis of due recognition or parity of esteem. However, the hoped-for dialogic generation of an emergent civic culture bridging the ethnic divide has after over twenty years of gestation failed, until perhaps recently, to come forth. Brexit may have enhanced the ethnic divide but it is not the source. As was pointed out at the time by Brendan O'Leary the reasons for this are partly structural in that the GFA/BA "rests on a bargain derived from diametrically conflicting hopes about its likely long-term outcome".[1] While unionism on the whole pragmatically saw the deal as the best available, republicanism saw the Agreement as a transitional step towards full Irish political unification. The result has been what Jennifer Todd and Joseph Ruane in *A Shared Future* (2010) call a difficulty in moving beyond institutionally encouraged cultural trenches in a war of attrition with "a reification of cultures which pushes change into the future and loses sight both of the positive potential and of the dangers of the present". The inherent potential fluidity of cultural identities has been semi-frozen, attenuated in part by recent growing support for the non-aligned Alliance Party. Rather, what is needed is a notion of cultural identities embedded within a civic culture of openness, dialogue and honest communication which is not closed to the potentially novel and perhaps unexpected.

Unionism in reimagining itself must think beyond and through a presently asymmetrical cultural erosion from Sinn Féin. Here narratives of the past in particular are in sharp contrast between republican and unionist protagonists. This reinforces territorial politics and transforms the conflict, as Sara McDowell says, especially for republicans, into "war by other means".[2] This is a phenomenon recently alluded to by Peter Shirlow and Colin Coulter (in *Studies in Conflict and Terrorism*, vol. 37, 2014), as a "discursively constituted proxy war" where "the war of narratives", as Nolan puts it,[3] has replaced the war of weapons . Even so-called symbolic handshakes by former Sinn Féin Deputy First Minister, Martin McGuiness and Queen Elizabeth in June 2012, by Sinn Féin leader Gerry Adams and the heir to the British throne three years later, or the Sinn Féin speaker of the Assembly issuing condolences on the passing of the Duke of Edinburgh go some way towards normalising relations between the British state and Irish republicanism. It cannot elide what is perceived by unionists as a cool reception to the tolerance of British-Irishness on the island of Ireland. The perception of a cultural war waged against unionist symbols and identity was not assuaged by the reported comments of Adams in late 2014 positing that an equality agenda, rather than being justified for its own sake, was in fact viewed by Sinn Féin as part of a broader strategy: "the Trojan horse of the entire republican strategy is to reach out to people on the basis of equality" (Adams, quoted by the BBC, 25 November 2014).

To engage this cultural politics unionism needs to have a strategy involving more than ad hoc reaction. In short, moderate unionism must as a last line of defence reassert itself. I am old enough to remember the "Ulster at the crossroads" television address almost 50 years ago by Northern Ireland Premier Terence O'Neill. He pointed out the writing on the wall. The only future for unionism was to be inclusive. The failure to follow this path in the first half of Northern Ireland's existence helped to open a Pandora's box which remains to be shut. David Trimble as leader of the UUP in his Nobel speech in 1998 acknowledged, echoing O'Neill, that Northern Ireland had been a cold house for Catholics. While the Ulster Unionist Party has been eclipsed by the more extreme DUP, it remains the case that staunch political unionist adherence to a past resistant identity has far outlived its sell-by date. In a recent Fodor 2018 travel guide, for example, murals in unionist areas are derided as "comic-book like" while those in republican areas are "Sistine Chapel-lite". More specifically, Republican artwork is portrayed as carrying themes of freedom from oppression, and a rising nationalist confidence that romantically and surreally mixes and matches images from the Book of Kells, the Celtic mist mock-heroic posters of the Irish artist Jim Fitzpatrick, assorted phoenixes rising from the ashes and revolutionaries clad in splendidly idiosyncratic sombreros and bandanas from ideological battlegrounds in Mexico and South America. By contrast, loyalist murals had a "grimmer air" with typical subjects including wall-eyed paramilitaries perpetually standing firm against increasing liberalism, nationalism and all the other -isms Protestants see eroding their stern, Bible-driven way of life. Such is the image-mountain unionism faces and not just in the wider world but within these islands. A narrow-minded, constipated, socially conservative image so often projected by political unionism in uncompromising rhetoric and backward-looking policy has no future. It is an image to which unionism must react soonest and lay to rest for good or face extinction. With the hands ticking, unionism is already in extra time.

Moderate Unionism: challenging the Janus faced character of a "New Ireland"

The present call by Sinn Féin with a hand stretched out to Unionism to join in building a "new Ireland" (as opposed to the harsher "united Ireland") consisting of a rainbow of identities is a velvet touch in relation to which unionism has cause to be sceptical. That political republicanism cannot acknowledge "Northern Ireland" as the name of the British jurisdiction which the "new Ireland" seeks to subsume is already to unionism a longstanding cause of irritation. However, the Janus face is more stark. The denigration by republicans of a unionist tradition characterised as a stereotypical sectarian monolith is now the subject of frequent critical comment by seasoned political commentators and academics sympathetic towards a liberal unionist position. In the *Irish Times* of 23 November 2017, the commentator Newton Emerson sees Sinn Féin as having pitched its latest manoeuverings at Stormont as though it were a battle for inalienable rights against intractable unionist bigotry. Further, according to Alex Kane, "an Irish language act will not resolve the political crisis, because, if it could, unionists would happily endorse one. If it could be resolved by more space being provided for statues of republican icons in the grounds of Stormont or Belfast City Hall, unionists would go the distance on that, too. If it could be resolved by curbing the number of Orange parades and Union Flags in July and August, I'm pretty sure most unionists could live with that. But the fact is this: no amount of trying to provide "parity of esteem" for Sinn Féin's agenda would result in a moment being reached at which Sinn Féin would say; "OK, that's fine. That's all we wanted. Let's get on, now, with building a new era'" (*News Letter*, 25 September, 2017). Ruth Dudley Edwards is harsher: as the Provos realised that they had to abandon their failed military strategy, they set about undermining unionist culture, and refashioned history to render perpetrators as victims, victims as perpetrators, and all unionists as bullies and bigots (*Belfast Telegraph*, 27 November, 2017). As Connal Parr pointedly expresses it in *Inventing the Myth: Political Passions and the Ulster Protestant Imagination* (2017): "culture functioned as an integral path for Irish Republicans to move away from physical force methods with culture not decommissioned by republicans but rather 'militarised'".

Challenging the Janus face of the "new Ireland" will

involve unionism setting out its own stall and resisting the enticements of the spider to encourage the fly into its nationalist web of assumed superiority. Specifically that political offer should involve claiming title to Irishness on its own terms, recognising the Republic of Ireland's movement in the direction of a prosperous and liberal secular state, connect to current British preoccupations with identity matters, seek to think beyond the present cultural war of attrition, make the case for the Union to moderate nationalism and adopt a less belligerent and defensive response to issues regarding the symbolic recognition of identity.

Unionism on the window ledge of the Union
The prominent cultural geographer and founder of the Institute of Irish Studies at Queen's University Belfast, Estyn Evans, observed with bemusement over 30 years ago that unionists "still obstinately refuse to call themselves Irish" (*The Common Ground*, 1984). Here he alluded to the conjuring up of Celtic mists populated by warrior heroes that formed part of the romantic business of Irish nation-building. This left little room for those of "planter stock" especially when that romanticism is used as a badge of identity worn by republicans. With those mists now clearing the way is open for unionists to assert their own brand of Irishness which is shot through with Britishness as well. This involves the belated appropriation and internalising of Irishness as a constituent part of unionist identity.

Nothing brought this failure to claim common roots in Irish soil home to me more than the absence of any representative of political unionism at the funeral of the Nobel poet Seamus Heaney. Rootedness in place was also central to the search for identity by the poet John Hewitt whom Heaney described as "the conscience of the Planter tradition". Famously, Hewitt in 1943 expressed his identity ambivalence thus:

> This is my home and country.
> Later on perhaps I'll find this nation is my own;
> But here and now it is enough to love
> This faulted ledge, this map of cloud above
> And the great sea that beats against the west
> To swamp the sun.

However, such yearning does not preclude the resting of primal desires of the heart within the wider context of the United Kingdom. Symbolic landscapes can connect and interweave with cultural narratives and affinities over long distances, let alone the 13-mile wide North Channel either with or without a bridge. Connecting meaningfully to current debates about identity and belonging in Brexit Britain is a substantial but vital challenge for unionism where the record, on past performance, has been poor. A harsh view would be that Northern Ireland has and always will be regarded as "a place apart", an expendable appendage as demonstrated in the creation of the Northern Protocol and the ensuing Irish sea border. The English-born poet and critic Tom Paulin brought up in Belfast often paints a picture of Ulster Protestants clinging to a British identity when nobody in Britain wants them. Yet the mirror of cultural recognition casts back images of other bonds of feeling forged through history, events and shared experience which stir the blood. *Titanic* is a reminder of Irish/British industrial culture, the Somme of blood spilt in common. The praise of Winston Churchill for Northern Ireland's World War 2 efforts in armaments output (bringing down the wrath of the Luftwaffe), military personnel and protection of the life-line of the Northern convoys, would be another dramatic case in point. The reading of the list of the fallen pupils from my old school, Methodist College Belfast at the yearly remembrance service leaves a deep mark. British comedy, film, popular music and so forth weave a web of common acknowledgement of a way of seeing, experiencing, interpreting and forging meaning no doubt shared in both jurisdictions in Ireland as part of a close two-way cultural exchange.

While shared memory is important in group identity it risks being overly static if it's not open to flux as new generations and challenges make their way on to the historical stage. Here unionism has not adapted well and risks survival like the proverbial frog in the gradually increasing heat of the water in which it squats. In short, unionism must engage with present debates over the character of Britishness as it is reworked and mutated to meet an increasingly diverse society with the consequent stresses and strains involved. With the possible secession of Scotland, the Union is in jeopardy. Unionism cannot be a neutral observer from the crow's nest of the *Titanic*. The auguries for such progressive engagement are not encouraging, however. The reality that the United Kingdom can be a cold house for Ulster unionism does not excuse the failure to make a positive and much less defensive case for the Union. This was not in evidence when Britishness was the subject of vigorous debate during New Labour's flirtation with a multi-cultural Britain, with the weight of exhortation and policy emphasising diversity over integration. The flagship Parekh Report at that time called for a conception of Britain as a "federation of cultures held together by common bonds of interest and affection and a collective sense of belonging". The fact that unionism accepted the exclusion of Northern Ireland as "a place apart" from the deliberations of the report is to say the least unfortunate.

Northern Ireland has a lot to bring to the debate on the negative fall-out of parallel societies on social cohesion. Almost 20 years later there is a widespread acceptance of the importance of Britishness as a civic glue creating space for intercultural communication and social bonding. Difference can be celebrated and respected but it must be accompanied by values that are shared. Foremost here would be a pluralistic tradition of tolerance. Simple multiculturalism can elide the reality that groups and regional identities need to have a relationship with one another. It is left to a recent writer, Afua Hirsch, born of Ghanaian parents in the United Kingdom and author of *Brit(ish): On Race, Identity and Belonging* (2018), to highlight the obvious that the UK has four nations each with different relationships to a sense of self. Her quest to find a sense of belonging by engaging with what Britain has been as a colonial power, and reimagining Britishness for future use, warns against the protection of a carefully curated notion of Britishness which remains closed and susceptible to cultural "othering". The author makes a forceful case that Black and British are not mutually exclusive identities . The argument that British and Irish are likewise not mutually exclusive categories needs strong voices not least because a siren call from the Republic of Ireland enjoins unionism in uncertain Brexit times to throw in its lot with an evolving updated nation on a different European trajectory.

The spectre conjured up by David Trimble in 2002 of the Republic of Ireland as a "sectarian mono-ethnic, mono-cultural state" as opposed to the more inviting United Kingdom as "a liberal multi-national state" is no longer sustainable, but it does not follow that a case cannot be made for the advantages of the continuance of the Union. This must go beyond saving the Union for unionists because Britishness would surely atrophy inserted in a different polity and animating ethos. Rather, political unionism in particular must make a case to the middle ground of Northern Catholic opinion, a ground which carelessness and lack of vision has let almost slip away.

Belatedly reaching out to the broader Union
Unionism remains embroiled in the slow and sapping drip of a culture war. This was outlined in dramatic fashion in a report authored by the present British Minister for the Cabinet Office, Michael Gove, when Home Editor of *The Times*. His commentary shows the mountain faced by Ulster unionists in making a case to continue belonging to the UK association of nations and ethnicities. According to Gove, the hollowing out of Northern Ireland's Britishness is a progressive process, whereby the British state divests itself of responsibilities and strips the Province of evidence of its British character. Whether or not the IRA's military war is over there is a culture war raging in Ulster and in this war Britain is at best neutral, and much more often, an objective ally of republicanism … the [Belfast] Agreement is not a settlement, merely a staging post. A staging post on a motorway without an exit. On a motorway which leads

to the separation of Northern Ireland from the United Kingdom ... with peace equated with the dilution of Ulster's Britishness.[4]

The background is the lessening appetite of British elites since 1945 to remain in Ulster. The cutting loose of Northern Ireland, now subjected to an internal UK economic border, is a sacrificial offering greasing the wheels of Britain's Brexit deal. It is consistent with Gove's summation. It puts Northern Ireland in a place described by the commentator Brian Rowan in *Political Purgatory: The Battle to Save Stormont* (2021), referencing the leader of the Ulster Unionist Party, as "the window ledge of the Union". It is a bitter irony that Gove the politician overcame his own analysis and voted in concert to make Ulster expendable to the Union. In truth, however, the greater guilt lies with unionism itself for failing over the years to tackle the image of "a place apart". Bartering for more chips at the poker table of the Union and heeding empty assurances that Northern Ireland in Brexit talks would be treated the same as Finchley, have proved calamitous to the unionist cause. The lack of spade work over many years to align with UK mainstream concerns and conversation in the broader "family of nations" has come home to haunt. Nevertheless, there is a lot still to play for.

Unionism must think beyond the imposed frame of Gove's culture war analysis, difficult as that is. The republican vision energised by Brexit is not withering away anytime soon. The play is heating up for a New Ireland. The competitive offer of a secular, plural prosperous Europhile Republic of Ireland is a strong one . The watchwords of any counter offer must be courtesy, due recognition of cultural difference, and reasonableness and compromise even in the face of provocation. These are words that come more easily from the growing voice of the non-aligned Alliance Party which is managing to reach out beyond tribal tram lines. Unionism in putting to rest Brexit misadventures must be more generous. For unionism circling the wagons is not an option. The Union will more likely survive through kind words than belligerent defiance. On a personal note, returning recently to Ireland from a foreign trip, I presented my British passport to a border official at Dublin Airport. He took a perfunctory look and said "Welcome home, sir". Those three kind words did more to waken in me my Irish roots than three decades of armed IRA struggle. Disputes over flags, marching, and naming are, of course, emotive. But the high ground does not promote parades or display bunting when not welcomed. It does not seek to insult. It contemplates compromise on language rights and so on. It points to aspects of culture like the National Health Service held solidly in common and which got us through the pandemic, and the advantages of attachment to the rich tableau of multiple cultures making up the United Kingdom including both Irish Catholics and Protestants and those of a more secular hue.

However, Irish nationalism is powerful and the middle ground of those open to a plural UK pitch is in danger of shrinking further depending on the outworking of Brexit and the illiberal approach by some in the DUP to major social issues as abortion, same sex marriage and homosexuality. Whether attempts to try and make up ground belatedly and slowly will be enough to lead on to a necessary repositioning of unionism remains to be seen. It is a necessary vision which is pressing. The seasoned political commentator Alex Kane expresses frustration: "the continuing 'rise and rise' of Sinn Féin is not unstoppable. Irish unity is not inevitable. That won't, of course, stop Sinn Féin's relentless propaganda and repositioning. And nor should it stop unionism from relentless deconstruction of Sinn Féin's arguments; or of kick-starting their own major, thought-through, broad-based, pro-Union campaign. Put bluntly, stop whingeing about Sinn Féin and, instead, counter their various strategies, policies and narratives."

The address by Arlene Foster in May 2018 to a symposium on reimagining the wider UK Union, including Northern Ireland, post-Brexit was a small sign of intellectual engagement with a wider family of nations debate. The First Minister's attendance at a GAA match final was symbolic and welcomed. Yet such unionist political thinking remains too marginal and in danger of becoming more so. If there is a long overdue case to be made for the United Kingdom before Scotland is lost, the case for Northern Ireland's membership of that alliance of interest and affinity is even more pressing . Given disunity amongst the unionist political class, the signs are not hopeful. Two things, though, are clear. Any association with violent resistance to the Irish sea border while wrong in itself would be self-defeating, reinforcing the idea of "a place apart". Secondly, while Sinn Féin and others scramble for unionist participation in "conversations" on a new, agreed and shared Ireland, unionism is best served by reaching for a conversation with the rest of the UK on reinvigorating the plural Union we already share.

With the resignation of Arlene Foster as First Minister

as a casualty of Brexit in late April 2021, Ulster unionism is again at a crossroads. Trenchant resistance to the Irish sea border by any successor while shoring up a core fundamentalist unionist vote is unlikely to be in the long-term interests of the Union itself. Seeking reasonable mitigations of the Northern Ireland Protocol carries less risk of self–harm to political unionism and Northern Ireland's place in the Union. While the "peace process", as Michael Gove conceded, still has inbuilt aspects of a culture war, a new fluidity identified by Brian Rowan in his recent book has opened up in Northern Ireland politics. The non-aligned Alliance Party could now be conclusive in any border poll on the continuance of the Union or any modified sympathetic constitutional outcome. If the Belfast Agreement were based on a binary, a new space has opened up in which political unionists must engage or prepare to leave the historical stage. Rowan quotes Stephen Farry, Alliance Party deputy leader: the party has proven that in a political context usually framed around the constitutional question and a clash of identities a liberal and cross community party can not only survive but flourish. If unionist political diehards cannot measure up to basic values of reconciliation and an integrated Northern Ireland based on fairness and equality it is time for moderate civic unionism, for too long muted, not to cede ground to extremism, and speak up or lose the Union. Civic nationalism is active on the constitutional chess-board. An equivalent response from unionism is long overdue. It is time to stop being embarrassed to be a unionist, not least, it must be said, among the ranks of academia.

Endnotes

1 Brendan O'Leary, "The Nature of the British Irish Agreement," *New Left Review* 233: 66–96 (1999).

2 Sara McDowell, "Selling Conflict Heritage through Tourism in Peacetime Northern Ireland," *International Journal of Heritage Studies* 14: 5 (2008): 405–421.

3 P. Nolan, Northern Ireland Peace Monitoring Report, no. 3 (Belfast: Community Relations Council, 2014).

4 Michael Gove, "The Price of Peace: An Analysis of British Policy in Northern Ireland", Centre for Policy Studies (2000).

Making Northern Ireland Work

Mike Nesbitt

Let me start by introducing myself. I have always liked the way J.D. Salinger opens *Catcher in the Rye*: "If you really want to hear about it, the first thing you'll probably want to know is where I was born, and what my lousy childhood was like, and how my parents were occupied and all before they had me, and all that David Copperfield kind of crap." I was born in Belfast in 1957, just in time to grow up through what we so euphemistically call our "Troubles": three decades in which we lost over 3,500 fellow citizens, while tens of thousands of others suffered, and continue to suffer, physical, mental and psychological injury.

My home was a detached, four-bedroom property in the leafy suburbs of the east of the city and my schooling was at Campbell College, a fee-charging voluntary grammar. Even as I type this, I sense the reproach of readers for whom working-class roots are the only acceptable credentials. I would rebuff that simply with the thought that Making Northern Ireland Work means embracing everyone's right to belong, whatever their socio-economic class, constitutional preference, or point of difference from your own worldview, including how they want their children educated.

A good starting point for political analysis is to recognise no one is going away. You and I can get ourselves cryogenically frozen for five, fifteen or fifty years; when we re-emerge, there will still be British unionists and loyalists, Irish nationalists and republicans and those who are non-aligned on this little postage stamp on the world map. So, we have to find a way to rub along together. If we can do that, maybe we can do even better and actually prosper together; turning the negative of a divided society into the positive of a diverse one.

Making Northern Ireland Work requires respect for the dignity of all. That includes my family. Middle class as we might be, we were not immune from the conflict. My paternal grandfather, Alfred Nesbitt, founded a linen business in Belfast city centre, "A Nesbitt & Company Limited, Linen Manufacturers". On the company invoices, below that masthead, was a statement I find quite extraordinary. It reads: "Deduction of odd pence not allowed." Really? Hang in there for the last penny, Grandad? Evidently so, as he was not prepared even to pay the printers to include the definite article ("*The* deduction …") or add a two-lettered verb ("… *is* not allowed").

Grandfather had two sons, my father Charles and his elder brother Jack, over ten years Dad's senior. The age gap was to prove highly significant. On 25 January 1973, the Provisional IRA blew up A. Nesbitt & Co. Ltd. My father was 49 years of age. In that moment, every certainty in his life disappeared but all responsibilities remained. He still had a wife, three young children, a car, a house; the whole nine yards of adulthood to fund, but suddenly with no regular income stream. It took the government two and a half years to pay out the compensation. By then, Uncle Jack was retired. He had no interest in investing his half of the compensation in reviving the business and Dad could not do it alone. His life was not over, but his lifestyle was, along with his dignity, self-esteem, social standing.

For my family, that January day was what Charles Dickens calls a memorable day. In *Great Expectations*, Pip says: "That was a memorable day to me, for it made great changes in me. But, it is the same with any life. Imagine one selected day struck out of it, and think how different its course would have been. Pause you who read this, and think for a moment of the long chain of iron or gold, of thorns or flowers, that would never have bound you, but for the formation of the first link on one memorable day".

The trouble with our long conflict is that too many of our fellow citizens have experienced memorable days that have wrapped them in chains of iron and thorns. Politicians tend to talk of dealing with the past in terms of truth and justice for those families who suffered lost lives. But what about the surviving victims and survivors who suffered lost opportunities, in education and employment, in social inclusion and family life? In my time as a Commissioner for Victims and Survivors, I was struck by the fact that victims are not a homogeneous group with uniform needs. That said, there are two characteristics that are all too common. The first is they had a reasonable expectation that on becoming a victim or survivor, the state and the state's agencies would form the wagons in a circle, but that did not happen. No one was there to take their children to school, do their food shopping, or complete the paperwork associated with death. The second was the huge number suffering poor mental health because of what happened.

Making Northern Ireland Work requires a fresh, less political approach to the legacy of the Troubles. Every political negotiation of the last quarter century, from the Belfast Good Friday Agreement (1998) to the Stormont House Agreement (2014) has been conducted within the maxim "nothing is agreed until everything is agreed". I do not think legacy can be addressed that way. As Leader of the Ulster Unionist Party (2012–2017), I argued and argued that we could work on improving people's mental health, notwithstanding our disagreement on truth and justice issues. If you agree mental health is a massive burden blighting so many citizens' lives (which all the parties to the negotiations from Haass O'Sullivan, 2013, to Stormont House did), how cruel have we been to fail to act on mental health and wellbeing, because we cannot agree on other aspects of legacy?

If we address mental health and wellbeing, we not only transform lives, we transform our society and our economy. Think of all those people who wake up every morning with no sense of purpose in their lives, no reason to get out of bed and get on with it. It is not because they are lazy, it is because they do not have the mental capacity. They are on welfare benefits, not because they want to be, but because we have failed to equip them with the energy and tools to do what the rest of us take for granted.

It is not my intention to dwell on the past, but dealing with the "Legacy" is essential to Making Northern Ireland Work, so it cannot be ignored. Throughout my leadership, I was keen that every party leader, together with the Prime Minister and Taoiseach of the day (and preferably the President of the USA) would stand shoulder to shoulder and make acknowledgement statements. I was thinking I could say that as leader of the party that ruled Northern Ireland for its first fifty-one years, we could have done better, especially in creating a warmer house for non-unionists. It is in the ballpark of David Trimble's speech accepting his Nobel Peace Prize. No government can navigate a single mandate without making mistakes, be it deliberate or accidental. Therefore, over half a century, it is a given that we got it wrong at times. I believe the truth is that it was not as bad as nationalists like to think, but worse than unionism is normally prepared to concede. Such an acknowledgement does not affect my belief that nobody had to die for us to get where we are today. If the Civil Rights movement was intent on reforming Northern Ireland, while the Provisional IRA was out to destroy it, I acknowledge one as legitimate, but not the other.

My offer was to make a statement reflecting those sentiments, concluding that none of us can change the past, but we can all commit to building a better future. In response, I wanted the late Martin McGuinness to stop telling me that I (unionism) left him no choice but to join the Provisional IRA. My response was that if you pick up a gun, you choose to pick it up. If you press the detonator on a bomb, you choose to press that button. Martin's reply was to tell me I had not grown up in the Bogside as he did, suffering the prejudice and sectarianism inflicted upon his community. He told the story of seeking a job with the local butcher, who asked him how he spelt McGuinness. When he told him, the butcher sent him packing. It is true I did not have Martin's lived experience in Derry/Londonderry. However, John Hume did and John never chose to pick up a revolver or plant a no-warning device. I would argue John achieved much more than Martin. In this centenary year, John's Social Democratic and Labour Party can reflect on how our politics is founded on the famous three strands of relationships, internal to Northern Ireland, north–south on this island, and east–west between the isles. Republicans must reflect on a century of failure. Whether it was with the Armalite alone, in combination with the ballot paper, or through the politics of Stormont, they are no nearer their goal than when they began.

I understand republicans will disagree with that analysis. They will argue they have the wind of history in their sails. It would serve unionists well to heed their optimism and understand that, despite my belief that we are nowhere near constitutional change, we have travelled a long way from the environment of 1921. The business commentator from Kildare, Charles Handy, in his book *The Age of Unreason* (1989), tells a story: "I like less the story that a frog if put in cold water will not bestir itself if that water is heated up slowly and gradually and will in the end let itself be boiled alive, too comfortable with continuity to realize that continuous change at some point may become intolerable and demand a change in behaviour".

I am concerned unionism could be that frog. Our environment is changing. Firstly, the demographics of Northern Ireland are shifting, with no political group representing a majority any more. Rather, we have a number of minorities. Secondly, Brexit has unsettled many, putting the constitutional question back on the political agenda. Thirdly, there is the rise of other nationalist movements beyond the Irish brand: Scottish nationalists want Indyref II, believing success is in reach; English nationalism is an unquantified danger, but perhaps best characterised by Boris Johnson's willingness to throw Ulster unionism under the bus.

None of the above is necessarily fatal to our future place

in the United Kingdom - not if unionism reacts strategically to actions and positions within our control. Simply put, if the demographic that represents our traditional base is no longer sufficient to secure a majority, we must reach out to the other minorities.

The day of the Brexit result, 24 June 2016, coincided with the US Consul General hosting her annual Independence Day garden party at Ardnavalley in south Belfast. Two young men approached me and asked for a private word. They were in their thirties, describing themselves as business people from the nationalist tradition. Their sense of nationalism, though, was not absolute, in that if you asked them if they would like to see a united Ireland sometime, they would say yes; but if you asked them to sign up as an activist to make it happen, they would say no. The reason for the reluctance is explained quite simply. They were too busy, earning good money, having their children well-educated and enjoying their quality of life, to be bothered striving for change. That is the attitude unionism should be striving to spread as deeply as possible into the minorities that are our nationalist and non-aligned brothers and sisters. If Northern Ireland is working for them, why would they be concerned about effecting change? Why would anyone?

I believe Irish republicans have made many strategic errors, one of which is to deride Northern Ireland (a name, like Harry Potter's Voldemort's, they dare not speak). We are, in Sinn Féin-speak, a "failed statelet". This defies the first rule of marketing, which states that whatever you are selling, you should make it easy to buy. Come a border poll, how do they explain to the Irish electorate why they should vote to adopt a "failed statelet" of 1.8 million people, a significant minority of whom want nothing to do with constitutional change, and all of whom require a significant annual financial subvention to keep our public services operational?

Irish nationalists and republicans have a shared interest with unionism to Make Northern Ireland Work. We may differ in the question of why we want to make NI work, with unionists focused on cementing our place within the United Kingdom, and Irish nationalists and republicans wanting us to be more attractive to Dublin. That does not preclude or prevent a joint effort to improve our lot. Colum Eastwood gets that and said so when he assumed the role of Leader of the SDLP in 2015. I heard him use the language of "making Northern Ireland work" and in conversation with him, I confirmed we were defining success in the same way: the quality of our public services; the prosperity of our people, measured in terms of not only their finances, but also their sense of wellbeing. Given that our devolved system of government is a consociational model, framed by a multi-party Executive, this is what all politicians should be doing as of right. But it also makes sense whatever your constitutional preference.

At speaking engagement these days, conducted by virtual communications of course, I have condensed my analysis to what I call Four Ironies and a Paradox. Irony Number One is that the greatest obstacle to a United Ireland for people of my age and background was the IRA. Their bombs and bullets were a crude attempt to coerce unionists into something they did not want. Not only was it always destined to fail, it was sure to leave a legacy that will take many years to heal in terms of community relations, mutual respect and the building of trust.

Irony Two is that the group doing more than any other to ensure the constitutional question is back on the political agenda, long after the 1998 Agreement took it off the table, is the DUP, the Democratic Unionist Party. I cite their support for Brexit, undertaken without any real consideration of the consequences for Northern Ireland; their short-term tactical thinking (demanding money as the price for their confidence and supply arrangement with Theresa May's government); and their attitude to nationalists (Arlene Foster's famous "crocodile" comment of 2017, which energised nationalism in a way Gerry Adams could only dream of).

Irony Three is that most unionists fail to realise that the biggest brake on any drive for a border poll on reunification is applied by people like Micheál Martin, the Taoiseach. Irony Four is that after centuries of unionists looking over their shoulders at Irish nationalists as the great threat to our place in the Union, in the early 21st century, the Irish barely make a podium finish, coming third behind Scottish nationalists, with English nationalists taking gold.

The paradox is that any unionist giving serious thought to lessons to be learned from the Brexit Referendum debate to be applied to a border poll is that you should not think of going to the people until you have thought through the implications of change to the nth degree. That means starting with what happens when you wake up and open your curtains in the morning; is the post box still red, or is it now green, and if it's green, is that important to you? From there, you work your way through to the biggest ticket items, like the National Health Service and pensions. Yet, paradoxically, the same unionists will berate you if you try to engage in that sort of debate, on the basis that the more you talk about it, the more you contribute to making change happen. Four Ironies and a Paradox.

So, what is the way forward? For me, it is to change the narrative. Irish republicans believe the remedy for this "failed statelet" is constitutional change, as if that act in itself is the panacea that cures all ills. That is patent nonsense – just as it is clear that membership of the United Kingdom is not a fix for all our problems. Rather than an endless, unproductive debate about constitutional preference, I would like a collective effort to define the sort of society we want to create for all of our people. In this centenary year, what is our Vision for the future? What values do we want to embed in our politics?

It may be open to the accusation of "motherhood and apple pie" but my desire is to build a society that is truly at peace, where every citizen has their dignity respected, has as good a chance as the next person of having a successful day and feels prosperous in their financial, physical and mental wellbeing.

Currently, as stated, those seeking constitutional change see a united or new Ireland as the aim, from which ill-defined benefits flow. Agreeing a vision and associated values for all our people changes the dynamic. If the vision becomes the aim, then the constitutional status of Northern Ireland becomes part of a strategy to achieve that aim, no longer an aim in itself. This takes constitutional change to a new place: away from that misty-eyed belief that all will be well if only we were united, to a hard-nosed debate on the facts of UK membership.

In re-framing the debate, it might be useful to address the vexed question of identity and a transforming first step would be to accept there are precious few pure Gaels or pure Brits to be found on these islands. I am a Nesbitt, which signifies French Huguenot roots. My mother was a Hay, which is Ulster Scots. As stated previously, father made his living as a linen trader in Belfast. Henry Joy McCracken of the United Irishmen was a leader of the 1798 Rebellion against the British Crown. His parents, like mine, were a mixture of Ulster Scots and French Huguenot, and like mine, traded in linen in our capital city. There you have a leader of the Ulster Unionist Party and a republican icon, spectral opposites politically, yet with identical origins. We are inextricably intertwined, not just on this island. Acknowledging that would make a good start in recalibrating relationships.

In 2014, I had the pleasure of participating in the first state visit by a president of Ireland to the United Kingdom. My highlight was not the state banquet, nor Her Majesty Queen Elizabeth and Uachtaráin Michael D. Higgins welcoming guests to Windsor Castle. It was the celebration of Irish culture in the Royal Albert Hall. The performers were Irish, the audience largely Irish men and women who had lived in England for decades; some, like host Dermot O'Leary, were born there. As the event began, all were asked to greet the guest of honour as he entered the royal box. That guest was the President of Ireland. It was a moment that gave visual and aural meaning to our connection.

There is, of course, the infamous slogan "No Irish, No Blacks, No Dogs", but there is another narrative of the Irish in Great Britain. It is of escape from oppression, the opening up of opportunities, building better lives. I commend the fine BBC Radio 4 series "How the Irish Shaped Britain", presented by BBC broadcaster and Irishman, Fergal Keane.

Fergal concludes the final programme with these words:

"I am one of those who settled here, was welcomed and given opportunity, and I know we cannot escape our geographical closeness, our cultural connections our shared history, or our mutual responsibility to protect peace, that greatest prize of our long journey together."

Think also of the many Irish living in the Republic who support English football teams, watch *Coronation Street*, download British music and are as immersed in British culture as they are in Irish. It is not just about the British on this island, although I would welcome an explanation from those who seek constitutional change how "Brits Out!" has become "Brits In".

Meanwhile, unionism must concentrate on producing a vision of life in Northern Ireland that appeals to more than unionists, a vision that inspires confidence that their interests will be best served by it, that there will be political delivery of a lifestyle that is so appealing that no alternative is up for consideration. It is a vision for Making Northern Ireland Work.

Letter to *The Irish Times*

C.D.C. Armstrong

Dear Sir,

In speculating about the position of unionist parties and unionist voters in a united Ireland, both Newton Emerson and Jim O'Callaghan are labouring under a misapprehension (Opinion, March 25th.).

Unionism is, strictly speaking, a political allegiance to the integrity and membership of the United Kingdom of Great Britain and Northern Ireland. It is neither a synonym for Protestantism nor a term denoting fondness for flute bands and bonfires; it does not refer to entitlement to a British passport – a right which can be enjoyed by an expatriate in Paraguay or Thailand – nor does it mean membership of the Commonwealth, an institution in which the United Kingdom is just one member among many others.

In a united Irish republic unionism would be nothing more than an unrealistic aspiration to the reversing of the result of a border poll. Those who claim to be unionists would do better to think about arguing for their case than dreaming about how they might be accommodated in a united Ireland.

Yours sincerely, C.D.C. Armstrong
(27 March 2021)

The Idea of the Union

Postscript:
The Practice of the Union

William Beattie Smith

Ulster at the crossroads?

It is over fifty years since the critical Stormont election of February 1969, when Prime Minister Terence O'Neill addressed the electorate: "Ulster stands at the crossroads... . For more than six years now I have tried to heal some of the deep divisions in our communities. I did so because I could not see how an Ulster divided against itself could hope to stand. I made it clear that a Northern Ireland based on the interests of any one section, rather than on the interests of all, could have no long-term future...".

His audience was not impressed. Although the Unionist Party gained two seats in the 52-seat parliament, the campaign divided it into two factions, for and against O'Neill. His "hardline" opponents attacked him for yielding to pressure from Westminster for reform. The pressure increased, and two months later they forced him to resign.

On Northern Ireland's hundredth anniversary, Ulster unionism again stands at a crossroads. In May 2021, both main Unionist parties, the Democratic Unionist Party (DUP), with 27 Assembly seats, and the smaller Ulster

Unionist Party (UUP), with 10 seats, replaced their leaders in anticipation of a challenging Assembly election, conditionally scheduled for May 2022. Whilst the UUP changed leaders without visible rancour, the brutal nature of Arlene Foster's ousting opened up a deep and long-standing division in the DUP. Foster told the *Financial Times* that she would not only be standing down as Leader, but also leaving the Party because "I think we are regressing and becoming more narrow... If the Union is to succeed, we need to be a bigger tent." If Foster is right, or if the main party of unionism fragments, how will this impact on Northern Ireland's long-term future?

The Unionist parties can't credibly argue that their participation in the devolved administration has strengthened the Union, improved the governance of Northern Ireland, or attracted popular enthusiasm. Only 20% of respondents to the 2015 NI Life and Times Survey thought the Assembly offered good value: 42% said "definitely not". The Assembly has operated for only twelve of its twenty years. Since its last reincarnation in January 2020, garlanded with the myriad strategies and promises listed in the "New Decade, New Approach" document, it has struggled with straightforward administrative decisions, such as appointing a new head of the Civil Service, let alone tackling controversial policy issues like segregated education. In a LucidTalk survey conducted in January 2021, the only one of eight Northern Irish political leaders to be given a positive rating was Robin Swann, the UUP health minister, whose performance was rated "good/great" by 75% of respondents, compared with 24% for Foster: this perhaps reflected his skilful non-partisan response to the Covid crisis.

As a mechanistically formed mandatory coalition, the Executive lacks an essential element of democratic accountability: there is no official opposition. The five largest parties in the Assembly – DUP, Sinn Féin, SDLP, UUP and Alliance – are all entitled to ministerial posts, and the two largest (DUP and Sinn Féin) effectively control the government agenda. Ministers from both parties have been embroiled in financial scandals with impunity: they oversee their own conduct through their control over the Assembly's committee system. The Executive is highly unstable: by withdrawing from it in 2017 and threatening to do so again in 2021, Sinn Féin have reminded the world that IRA bombs are no longer needed to bring down Stormont.

Although it is too soon to predict outcomes with any accuracy, recent surveys suggest that Sinn Féin will be the largest party in the Assembly after the next election. If so, in line with the 2006 St Andrew's Agreement (which amended the 1998 Belfast Agreement) they would select the First Minister. This would be another symbolic scalp for them, and another milestone in unionism's decline. The surveys also suggest that the Alliance Party will gain from the DUP's losses; the LucidTalk Tracker poll for May 2021 (taken before the rupture in the DUP) found that 16% of respondents would vote DUP, down from 28% in 2017; while 16% would vote Alliance, up from 9%. If this trend continues, the DUP could be knocked into third place.

Changes in the ranking of the five parties would have major consequences for political stability, sufficient to require a more in-depth review of the devolved institutions than has yet been attempted. The intention of the two governments in drafting the 1998 Agreement was that Unionists would have to share power with Nationalists. But if it became the second largest party, Alliance – which has self-designated as "Other" – could reasonably claim the right to select the deputy First Minister. Although formally designation applies only to Unionists and Nationalists, in political terms to deny the second largest party an entitlement which it could have had as a single-community party would be inconsistent with the principles of reconciliation and equality which supposedly underpin the Agreement. On the other hand, as an early and enthusiastic proponent of powersharing, how could Alliance credibly argue for the exclusion of a Unionist or Nationalist as First Minister just to create a space for one of its own? In either case, the shifts within unionism and the rise of Alliance bring into question the practicality and desirability of requiring powersharing exclusively between Unionists and Nationalists.

Three broad options lead away from today's crossroads: to do nothing and continue to act as if Stormont were fit for purpose; to proceed towards a single-state "united Ireland" (the exclusive nationalist option); or to make Stormont work for most voters (the inclusive unionist option).

Option One: do nothing
The obvious advantage for the two governments and the main political parties (although not the people of Northern Ireland) from doing nothing is that nobody can take offence, nobody will be blamed, there will be few risks and no nasty surprises. Many unionists are comfortable with this, particularly those in office. They can argue that radical

initiatives have in the past left unionism worse off: and that it is better to muddle through quietly than risk losing more ground. This conveniently enables them to hold on to their salaried posts, media opportunities and status.

In due course, events will likely force the British government to review the 1998 Agreement seriously, rather than continuing (as in January 2020) to stick plaster over wounds that require surgery. The Executive may well collapse again in the not-too-distant future under the weight of its own internal contradictions. Or, as suggested above, the results of the next election may bring into question the whole sectarian apparatus of designation, cross-community voting and mandatory coalition. Until then, the people of Northern Ireland will continue to suffer from a dystopian regime characterised by minimal trust between party leaders who have no collective commitment to the constitution or to Northern Ireland; increasing polarisation in society; and a political agenda orientated towards deepening rather than healing O'Neill's deep divisions.

Option Two: United Ireland

Arguments for a single-state or "united" Ireland outside the United Kingdom are readily accessible online. I mention them here only to clarify what it is that unionists dissent from and why. The traditional nationalist case is rooted in the conviction that the Gaelic-speaking Catholic Irish were chosen to have dominion over the island. Similar ideas were common across Europe in the 19th century, have caused great harm, and tragically haven't gone away. A second, equally illogical, idea is that because Ireland is an island it must be run as a single jurisdiction. This misconception appeals to the concrete mind, but has no relevance to anyone who recognises that in the organisation of human affairs it is social, cultural, economic and political associations which matter, rather than the vagaries of prehistoric geology.

As a teenager I was briefly stirred by the 1916 Proclamation of the Irish Republic, with its promise to "cherish all of the children of the nation equally, and oblivious of the differences carefully fostered by an alien Government which have divided a minority from the majority in the past." But for the IRA's violent campaign against my community and the institutions which kept us secure, I might have continued to overlook the futility of the Easter Rising, and ignore how the Irish state has since 1969 exploited the threat of IRA violence to advance its selfish political agenda. I have heard its leaders advance an ideology which depicts the unionists of Northern Ireland – me, my family and community – as England's stooges, Ireland's oppressors, and comparable with Nazis. Nationalists then wonder why unionists – on the receiving end of IRA violence for the past fifty years – persist in withholding their consent to a collective act of violation.

In happier circumstances, the Republic's claim to Northern Ireland might have faded from salience during the 1960s. Throughout Ireland the influence of the Catholic church declined, social values progressed, and people prospered. Taoiseach Seán Lemass and Prime Minister Terence O'Neill broke the ice, opening up opportunities for practical cross-border co-operation. But in 1969 obsessional republicans decided to hurry things along, so instead we have suffered fifty years of political regression. Now that the IRA have morphed into Sinn Féin and replaced the Armalite with the ballot-box, unionists have suffered a different kind of barrage — of deceitful and defamatory arguments intended to demoralise and unsettle us.

A superficially less reactionary case is made by the well-funded organisation *Ireland's Future*, which claims to be independent of all political parties. It maintains that a united Ireland is inevitable (without explaining how it has managed to remain inevitable for over a century). It asserts that demographic and other developments — such as Brexit and Scottish independence — will nudge it on its way. It depicts the 1998 Agreement (which like Moses' tablets it maintains cannot be altered by mere mortals) as the delivery vehicle for a united Ireland, implying that all the other stuff in it is there only to serve that single higher purpose — as in republicans' heads it is. In a pre-emptive strike against pragmatic nationalists like Séamus Mallon, Ireland's Future insists that voting in any border poll must be by simple majority. (Register that, reader: voting on small but potentially controversial things in the Northern Ireland Assembly must be cross-community to protect nationalists' interests; voting irreversibly on what has been the core issue in Irish politics for the past century must *not* be cross-community to protect nationalists' interests.)

Arguably the most promising pathway to successful Irish unification would be by first making Northern Ireland work. As Catholic public servant Maurice Hayes wrote in his memoir *Minority Verdict* (1995), "What more than anything is needed in Northern Ireland as a precursor to political activity is a build-up of trust. Too much energy is squandered in a search for great and complete constitutional constructs that will solve all problems at once and for all time."

Only when nationalists and unionists in Northern Ireland have learned to share the place they both call home in a spirit of mutual respect without constantly trying to change each other will it be possible for them both to join the rest of Ireland together painlessly and peaceably.

Option Three: make Stormont work

The third option may seem aspirational, and republicans will depict it as a vain effort to hold back destiny's tide. We believe otherwise. As Dennis Kennedy put it in the previous edition of *The Idea of the Union* (1995): "What is needed now is not a political process but a stable settlement. Irrational fears on one side and unrealistic hopes on the other are the greatest obstacles to a settlement, and potential ingredients for a return to violence. One does not have to be a Unionist, or even a unionist, to see that the best hope for such a settlement lies in the continued Union of Great Britain and Northern Ireland as the basis on which to build a more liberal pluralist Northern Ireland". In making Stormont work, the unionism of equal citizenship will expect its leaders to make early tangible progress on a range of strategic tasks. Here is a subset of six, all linked to the principled implementation of the Belfast Agreement.

Task One: ditching the Protocol

The most urgent strategic task is to resolve the constitutional impasse and impediments to free trade between Great Britain and Northern Ireland generated by the EU's insistence on the "rigorous implementation" of the Northern Ireland Protocol to the EU Withdrawal Agreement.

Small companies are facing bankruptcy, and consumers are having to pay higher prices for a more limited range of goods. Bad though this is, the damage to the Union is worse. Lawyers representing the British government have shockingly argued in court that by writing the terms of the Protocol into UK law, Parliament "implicitly" repealed provisions in the Act of Union 1800, the constitutional bedrock of the Union between Britain and Northern Ireland. In other words, without bothering to introduce explicit legislation, a Conservative and Unionist government invited Parliament to terminate the UK internal market, to subject the people of Northern Ireland to a swathe of EU regulations over which they have no say and from which Britain is now free, and to reorient Northern Ireland's trading links away from Britain and towards the EU.

The European Commission, the Irish government and the US administration have all contended that a "hard border" between the Republic and Northern Ireland would undermine the 1998 Agreement and risk provoking renewed violence (from republicans): yet none of them has shown any concern for the damage being done to the Agreement by the creation of a border between Britain and Northern Ireland – international border controls within a supposedly integrated nation state.

The leaders of three Unionist parties (DUP, UUP and the small but feisty Traditional Unionist Voice) have initiated a judicial review, which is likely eventually to be decided by the UK Supreme Court. If this fails to remedy the Protocol's harms, there will still be grassroots pressure to act. Only the UK government can resolve this: until it does, popular anger in Northern Ireland will increase in line with the damage that the Protocol is causing (and not just to unionists). This issue will undoubtedly influence the outcome (and perhaps also the date) of the next election. The prospect of electoral gains for "hardliners" will hopefully stiffen whatever resolve the UK government brings to its continuing negotiations with the European Commission.

Despite what their detractors say, unionists and their allies in Britain have come up with a range of alternative means to safeguard the EU's protectionist regulatory regime, avoid intrusive border controls whether on land or sea, and reduce trade friction. The problem is not that there is no alternative to the Irish Sea border: there are many. Rather, it is that the EU wants only one solution, on its terms, namely that the UK in its entirety must continue to comply with EU regulations covering food, plants and livestock. The people of Northern Ireland are pawns in a greater negotiating game.

In the context of efforts to improve relations across these islands, it is tragic that the Irish government and non-unionist parties in Northern Ireland have sided with the EU, bizarrely blaming the damage being inflicted by the EU on those who voted for Brexit, rather than on those who conjured up difficulties over a "hard border" (which nobody had proposed) in a failed attempt to derail Brexit altogether.

Task Two: moving beyond binary politics
The second task facing unionist leaders is finding ways of moving beyond binary politics. The toxic combination of community designation, cross-community voting, mandatory coalition and border poll has rendered the Executive unstable and unsustainable. Under the "Validation, Implementation and Review" section of the 1998

Agreement, any change in the arrangements for a border poll would have to be agreed by the two governments. However, the Assembly may itself initiate a review of its own operation.

Neither the DUP nor Sinn Féin has had any interest in doing so, since they both benefit from the current unsatisfactory arrangements. As Dennis Kennedy observed in his contribution to Roche and Barton's *The Northern Ireland Question* (2020): "The system has resulted in pressure on each community to concentrate politically on one party in order to command most seats in the Assembly, and thereby gain maximum strength in the Executive. With the background and the legacy of the troubles … there were more votes for parties pushing harder for often narrowly defined unionist or nationalist interests or ambitions, and increasingly fewer for any party reaching out to some middle ground and thereby committing the unpardonable sin of splitting the vote".

The next election (or the collapse of the Assembly) could bring matters to a head. The Alliance Party is already committed to replacing the process of community designation with a requirement for weighted majorities on defined votes; and to replacing the current system of mandatory coalition with one of voluntary coalition through negotiation between the parties. Initially, such changes could increase Alliance's power at the expense of Unionist parties. But there is a broader pro-Union argument to be made, that the reorientation of political discourse is an essential first step in building an inclusive Northern Ireland which will work on a stable basis for (almost) everyone.

Although a serious review of the Assembly and Executive

may be some time coming, unionists should get ready to initiate it when the time is ripe, grip the agenda, know what they want and have a strategy for getting it. Even if it doesn't suit their party's immediate electoral prospects, they should commit themselves to ending the current form of binary politics, recognising that it suits ethnic nationalism but manifestly does not suit the inclusive ideal of unionism which is rooted in the principle of equal citizenship.

The ideal case for the Union rests on equal citizenship and respect for diversity. It stands in opposition to the ethnic singularity of Irish nationalism, with its reactionary nineteenth-century roots. Unionist parties' message to the electorate should be that Northern Ireland has grown beyond a squabble which republicans seem determined to perpetuate, and that unionism is confidently leading the way towards maturity.

Task Three: securing outside support
Unionists need to maximise their impact in London, and especially in Westminster. Northern Ireland's enemies continue to exploit the British government's reluctance to endorse the Union unambiguously – even, on occasions, to betray it. In 2000, Michael Gove wrote in his pamphlet *Northern Ireland – the Price of Peace* (2000) that "the best guarantee for stability is the assertion by the Westminster Government that it will defend, with all vigour, the right of the democratic majority in Northern Ireland to remain in the United Kingdom." As I argued previously in this volume, upholding the constitution hardly seems too much to ask of a sovereign government. Gove is now Minister for the Cabinet Office, with special responsibility for protecting and promoting the Union. If he has changed

his position since 2000, he should explain why. If not, he should act on it.

In principle, Northern Ireland would be less of "a place apart" if the Conservative and Labour Parties put as much effort into fighting elections here as they do in the UK. As Prime Minister, David Cameron formed a partnership with the Ulster Unionist Party to fight the 2010 general election. This flopped: for the first time in over a century, the Unionist Party won no seats, leader Reg Empey resigned, and the partnership was dissolved. One failure is no reason to give up, however, and to their credit Conservative candidates have continued to stand for election in Northern Ireland. In contrast, the British Labour Party has to its shame failed to support the Northern Ireland Labour Party since the time of Harold Wilson, finally abandoning it in 1987.

Beyond party politics, it is vital, as Owen Polley says in his contribution to this book, for unionists to participate fully in the political, cultural and economic life of the UK: to develop relationships and secure support across influential networks, including social media, activists, departments, and the mainstream media. The British state is not a monolith as the term suggests, but a living community made up of official and unofficial networks, and open to outside influences.

Further afield, unionism (unlike nationalism) has neglected the USA, where there is a huge untapped pool of potential support, in particular around the cultural tradition celebrated by Senator Jim Webb in his *Born Fighting – How the Scots-Irish Shaped America* (2004). The Irish consular network lobbies for the nationalist perspective; British diplomats do not lobby for unionism; and the Office of the

Northern Ireland Executive in Washington is controlled as much by Sinn Féin as by the DUP. Much could be done by a small determined team at little cost, and the UK government's recent appointment of peace activist Trevor Ringland as unpaid Northern Ireland envoy to the USA is at least a welcome small step in the right direction.

Task Four: promoting east-west cooperation

As unionists, we would love to see Ireland reunited, within a bigger and better Union embracing the British Isles. The people of these islands have so much in common: language, culture, political and judicial systems and values, family ties, trading relationships. In Britain and the United States, people of British and Irish heritage mingle freely without acrimony. It makes no logical sense to separate them artificially in this archipelago merely for the purposes of political administration.

After a century of Irish national independence we would not expect to reconstruct the old Union which ended in 1920. But it is realistic to expect Britain and Ireland to repair and regenerate their relationship, which has deteriorated greatly since the European Commission instructed Ireland not to negotiate directly with Britain over Brexit, lest the two nations amicably resolve difficulties which it suited the Commission instead to inflate. Except to the extent that Ireland uses its influence with Britain to weaken the Union (which alas is frequently), we want to make Northern Ireland work within the framework of a strong, revitalised partnership between Britain and Ireland. After Brexit, there is a whole new agenda to be addressed between them. Many southern politicians, including Taoiseach Micheál Martin, share Unionists' antipathy towards Sinn Féin. Unionists should work with them whenever it strengthens the Union to do so.

It is hard to predict how the EU and the UK will fare relative to each other after Brexit; there are many imponderables, and unpredictable events (such as Covid) will intervene. But it is at least possible that the UK will thrive; and that Ireland, having shed its uncritical attachment to the EU, will follow the UK out (as ex-ambassador Ray Bassett has advocated in this volume), just as it accompanied the UK in. If so, it would clearly make sense for the UK and Ireland to form their own customs union and single market, building on the Common Travel Area which already guarantees the free movement of people around these islands, residency and even voting rights. Even if Ireland stays in the EU, its relationship with the UK will be transformed over the next few years, as it takes on the status of an EU external border region. It is in this broader European context that the future Union of Britain and Northern Ireland will evolve.

Task Five: standing up for unionists' rights

As several contributors to this collection have demonstrated, aggressive nationalism has generated a narrative about its deprivation of rights and equality which is fundamentally untrue. John Hume observed that none of the discrimination which Catholics suffered in Northern Ireland (matched by equivalent Protestant suffering in the Republic) justified the taking of a single life. Both communities have been on the receiving end of the IRA's 30-year terror campaign aimed at the destruction of the institutions which shielded them. Both have undergone murder and maiming, destruction of their property, security, family life and freedom of expression.

Under the European Convention on Human Rights, everyone in the UK has the right to life and legal protection of their life, including fair and consistent arrangements for law enforcement and criminal justice, free from political interference. For all the people of Northern Ireland this right was degraded by the concessions granted by Prime Minister Tony Blair to members of terrorist organisations during secret negotiations. If British soldiers can still be prosecuted in relation to events fifty years ago, why is it too late now to challenge Blair's interference from 1998 to 2006 with legal due process? The terrorists' victims still want justice. As Ben Lowry and Jeff Dudgeon have demonstrated, it is a scandal that members of the security services who risked their lives to defend others continue to face the prospect of prosecution in their old age while retired terrorists nominated by IRA leaders enjoy the benefits of early release from prison, immunity from prosecution, and the fruits of public office.

Secondly, on behalf of all the people of Northern Ireland, unionism should insist on equal citizenship within the UK, as Arthur Aughey argues in his essay "The Idea of the Union". The Union embodies rights and values which must not be bartered away without our willing consent. Everyone in Northern Ireland – whether they identify as British, Irish, or whatever else – has the right to be treated as full and equal citizens of the UK. This is a vital principle. It is withheld and degraded when the British state treats Northern Ireland like a colony, fails to protect its borders, dilutes its constitutional status, or permits it to be subjected to regulation by a foreign power.

Thirdly, following various international conventions, unionists are entitled to recognition as a double minority (in both the UK and Ireland), under attack since 1920 and intensively during the period from 1971 to 1997. We have been the target of a sectarian campaign of violence operating both internally and from the territory of a hostile neighbouring state. The people who orchestrated that campaign have since developed a new strategy of political activism and defamation, likewise directed at divesting unionists of the limited protections we retain as citizens of the UK. Unionism will never be secure in an Anglophobic nationalist Ireland, and we should not be manipulated into one without our collective consent, duly given through an open and legitimate process of joint consent.

Task Six: preempting a border poll
In any polity, peace and stability (whether for individuals, institutions or investors) require that fundamental constitutional changes should be introduced steadily and supported by all major groupings in society – the more so in a deeply divided society like Northern Ireland. It follows that any border poll should be conducted on the basis of parallel consent, as Seamus Mallon and other wise nationalists have argued. From a unionist perspective, "unification" of the territory without the express consent of the unionist electorate would be a moral absurdity. More than that, it would likely provoke intense resistance. Would the outcome really justify the risks of reigniting disaffection and political violence, with loyalist paramilitaries as the insurgents?

Unionists' preparations must include a strategy for reaching out to pragmatic voters who may not describe themselves as unionists (indeed they may identify as nationalists), but who will support the Union because they want to continue to enjoy its practical advantages. In fact, Unionist parties should be reaching out to these voters already, but the possibility of a border poll (however distant) adds another reason to do so. The University of Liverpool's Survey of the NI General Election 2019 indicates that Unionist parties are failing to attract pro-Union voters relative to nationalist parties and pro-unification voters. It will be for each party to decide for itself how best to do this, but it is worth noting that the survey respondents identified their two most important issues as Brexit and the National Health Service (rather than, say, abortion and the Irish language).

Conclusion

The chapters of this book have, each in its own way, set out arguments which accumulate to make a strong case for the Union. Their authors include experts in geography, history, economics, cultural studies, politics, government, law, human rights and more.

The thrust of their case is that unionists need to reconnect with the Idea of the Union as an honourable cause rooted in the principles of equal citizenship, national sovereignty, the rule of law, and upholding the constitution; to counter the defamatory narrative peddled by imperious republicanism; and, in the words of Nobel Laureate David Trimble to "raise up a new Northern Ireland in which pluralist Unionism and constitutional nationalism can speak to each other with the civility which is the foundation of freedom".

Most of our contributors do not identify with any political party, and we are not in the business of writing political manifestos. We have emphasised the importance of authentic narrative because we believe that politics and public policies should be rooted in a society's culture and values. George Orwell famously wrote that the most effective way to destroy people is to deny and obliterate their own understanding of their history. The republican movement has been trying to do that with unionism, to the extent that a great illusion has corrupted political life in Northern Ireland. Republicans have wrested control over the historical narrative of their thirty years' war against Northern Ireland, influencing others against us and distorting our understanding of our own history.

In some quarters, they have succeeded in depicting their sectarian campaign as a "just war". As historian Liam Kennedy has described in *Who was responsible for the Troubles?* (2020), they have twisted language to whitewash their crimes: the murder, injury, trauma, destruction, mayhem and demoralisation which they inflicted on a civilian population and its institutions. They depict terrorists as passionate campaigners for peace and justice. They maintain that because the murderers killed for "Ireland", their crimes were "political". The British state has failed to correct these distortions, and indeed has acted as if they were true by conceding concessions offensive to morality and the proper administration of justice. An overarching task for the leaders of unionism, including advocates, activists and academics, must be at every opportunity to challenge both the republican illusion and the flawed public policies which have been built upon it.

Many factors have contributed to the apparent decline of political unionism over the past 50 years, and some are beyond its leaders' control. But it has clearly suffered from its diminishing capacity to counter its opponents' unwarranted presumptions and falsehoods. The republican narrative - a polarising tale of chronic discrimination, prolonged oppression and unbearable humiliation - continues to reinforce third parties' negative assessments of unionists, their motives and actions.

Looking into Northern Ireland's next century, unionists need to be bold, calm, consistent and reasonable: firm on the Union, insistent on historical accuracy, and inclusive in our policy proposals. When the British and Irish states fail in their fundamental duties, we should call them out and see that those responsible are held to account. We should no longer tolerate ministers' setting the law aside for political expediency, exalting the perpetrators, blaming their victims, and defaming those who devoted their careers and in some cases risked their lives to keep the rest of us safe. The Union is still a fact. The cultural, practical and economic realities remain in its favour.

The Idea of the Union

Notes on Contributors

C.D.C. Armstrong was educated at Portora Royal School Enniskillen and Trinity College Dublin. He has written extensively on early modern and modern English and Irish history, including the *Oxford Dictionary of National Biography* entries on Lord Moyola and Sir Robin Chichester-Clark. He is a Visiting Research Associate in History at Queen's University, Belfast.

Arthur Aughey is Emeritus Professor of Politics at the University of Ulster. He was born in Banbridge, Co. Down and grew up in Lisburn where he attended Friends' School. He is a graduate of Queen's University Belfast and the University of Hull. He is the author of numerous scholarly articles and his books include *Nationalism, Devolution and the Challenge to the UK State* (2001), *The Politics of Northern Ireland: Beyond the Belfast Agreement* (2005), *The Politics of Englishness* (2007), *The British Question* (2013) and *The Conservative Party and the Nation* (2018). He is a former Leverhulme Senior Fellow (2008–2011) and served on the Northern Ireland Committee of the British Council. He is a Fellow of the Academy of Social Sciences.

Brian Barton's B.A. and Ph.D. degrees in History were from Queen's University Belfast and his M.A. degree from the University of Ulster. He tutored at the Open University, 1995–2013, and held research fellowships at Queen's

University and Churchill College, Cambridge. He is the author or editor of more than a dozen books, most recently *The Secret Court Martial Records of the Easter Rising* (2011), *The Easter Rising* (2011) and *The Belfast Blitz* (2015). He has co-edited with Patrick Roche four collections of essays on Northern Ireland, the latest being *The Northern Ireland Question: Perspectives on Nationalism and Unionism* (2020). He is a Fellow of the Royal Historical Society.

Ray Bassett was born in Dublin and educated at the O'Connell School, the oldest surviving Christian Brothers School in Dublin (established 1829). He attended Trinity College Dublin where he earned a Ph.D. in biochemistry. In an abrupt career change, he entered the Irish diplomatic service and served in Belfast, London, Canberra, Copenhagen and Ottawa. Dr Bassett was part of the Irish Government Talks Team during the Belfast (Good Friday) Agreement negotiations. He was later Irish Joint Secretary to the British Irish Intergovernmental Conference in Belfast, 2001–2005. He thereafter headed up the Irish Consular Service and the Irish Abroad Unit. During his last six years in the diplomatic service he was Irish Ambassador to Canada, Jamaica and the Bahamas. Since his retirement in 2016, he has become a columnist with the *Sunday Business Post*, Senior Fellow for EU Affairs at the Policy Exchange think tank, and the author of *Ireland and the EU Post Brexit* (2020). Last year, Dr Bassett was made a Poynter Fellow by Yale University.

Jeffrey Dudgeon was born and bred in Belfast. He was a pupil at Campbell College and then a student at Magee University College, Londonderry and at Trinity College Dublin. In 1981 he was the successful plaintiff at the European Court of Human Rights in Strasbourg, the judgement of which led to the decriminalisation of male homosexuality in Northern Ireland. He is the author of *Roger Casement: The Black Diaries – With a Study of his Background, Sexuality, and Irish Political Life* (2002, 2019). Jeff was awarded an MBE in the 2012 Honours List for his services to the LGBT community. He served as a Belfast City Councillor for Balmoral from 2014 until his defeat by the DUP in 2019.

John Wilson Foster, Professor Emeritus, University of British Columbia, Canada, was born in Belfast and educated at Annadale Grammar School and Queen's University Belfast (B.A., M.A.). He earned his doctorate at the University of Oregon. His books are on natural history and ornithology, RMS *Titanic*, and Irish literature and culture. The latter include *Colonial Consequences: Essays in Irish Literature and Culture* (1991), *The Achievement of Seamus Heaney* (1995), *Nature in Ireland: A Scientific and Cultural History* (sen. ed., 1997) and *The Cambridge Companion to the Irish Novel* (ed., 2006). He has been Senior Research Fellow, Institute of Irish Studies, QUB since 2009. His recent books are *Pilgrims of the Air: The Passing of the Passenger Pigeons* (2014, 2017) and *The Space-Blue Chalcedony: Earth's Crises and The Tyler Bounty* (2020). He was the inaugural National University of Ireland Visiting Professor (Maynooth, 2001) and a Leverhulme Visiting Professor to the UK (University of Ulster, 2004). He is a Fellow of the Royal Society of Canada.

Arthur Green died in 2006 at the age of 78. He was born into a Quaker family and educated at Friends School, Lisburn and Leighton Park School, Reading. He graduated from Lincoln College Oxford with a B.A. in Modern History and from Haverford College, Philadelphia with an M.A. in Philosophy. He joined the Northern Ireland Civil Service in 1952 and rose to be Assistant Secretary in the Department of Finance, 1972–1978, Secretary to both the Cameron Commission and the Scarman Tribunal, and Under Secretary in the Department of Education, 1983–1987. He served for a period as Head of the Northern Ireland Court Service. In retirement he served on the Council of the British Council, 1993 to 2000, and was an active member of the Irish Association for Cultural, Economic and Social Relations. He was a founder member of the Cadogan Group, where his contributions on cultural identity, education and related matters were particularly valued. He appeared on the BBC's Mastermind programme where his chosen subject was John Buchan.

Graham Gudgin was born in Aberdeen with strong Scottish maternal connections. A father in the RAF meant a peripatetic childhood and his attendance at ten different schools in England, the Far East, and a troopship. Post-war housing shortages meant his family lived in a caravan before being allocated a council house. He attended three grammar schools and went on to earn a first-class degree at London University. He was awarded an economics fellowship at Selwyn College Cambridge and became a member of the Cambridge Economic Policy Group. He was headhunted for the directorship of the new Northern Ireland Economic Research Centre and moved with his family to Belfast. He was Special Adviser to Northern Ireland First Minister David Trimble, 1998–2002. Dr Gudgin is now Honorary Research Associate at the Centre for Business Research in the Judge Business School at the University of Cambridge and is Chief Economic Adviser at Policy Exchange think tank. Together with the distinguished historian Professor Robert Tombs, he co-edited Briefings for Brexit, a pro-Brexit academic website out of Cambridge University which has since become Briefings for Britain.

Edgar Haslett was born in 1916. He joined the RAF in 1939 and was a pilot with Coastal Command, later being posted to India. On his return to Northern Ireland after the war he became a schoolteacher and taught at Belfast Model School. After a spell of teaching at Stranmillis Teaching College, he became the first headmaster of Larkfield High School. In 1960 he published a pamphlet for schools, *A Social History of Northern Ireland*. He later joined the Campaign for Equal Citizenship, the anti-devolution advocacy group begun in 1986 which promoted the full integration of Northern Ireland into the United Kingdom and of which Robert McCartney QC (and later MP) was a prominent member. Edgar edited its journal, *The Equal Citizen*. He died in October 1996.

Henry Hill is the News Editor and Home Nations correspondent of ConservativeHome, one of the UK's pre-eminent political websites. He was born and raised in Berkhamstead, Hertfordshire and holds dual British and Irish citizenship, his father being from Britain and his mother being from County Roscommon in Ireland. He was a pupil at Chesham Grammar School before reading History at the University of Manchester and Modern Irish History at Trinity College Dublin (M.Phil., 2013). Henry Hill is one of the most prominent opponents of the Blair-era devolution project in the British press as well as a respected radio and television commentator on broader constitutional issues. Henry also runs his own communications consultancy.

Catharine (Kate) Hoey, Baroness Hoey, was born in Mallusk, County Antrim in 1946, and educated at the Belfast Royal Academy, Ulster College of Physical Education, and London Guildhall University. She was Vice-President of the National Union of Students. At the age of 20, she was Northern Ireland high-jump champion. From 1985–89, she worked as educational adviser to Arsenal Football Club, moving on when elected as Labour MP for Vauxhall. In 1999 she was appointed UK Minister for Sport. Throughout her Parliamentary career, Kate has fiercely protected her independence of thought, criticising Labour's policies on issues including the war in Iraq, Trident, EU membership and Northern Ireland. Describing the EU as anti-democratic, she campaigned for Leave during the 2016 referendum. Kate retired from the Commons in 2019 and was created Baroness Hoey of Lylehill and Rathlin in September 2020.

Ben Lowry is Deputy Editor of the *News Letter*, the world's oldest surviving English language newspaper and now the only regional daily in Ireland which unambiguously supports the Union. Ben was born in Portland (Maine) in the north-eastern USA. He describes himself as "a man of the north Atlantic", with his heart both there and in Northern Ireland. He was educated Sullivan Upper School, Holywood, and Campbell College, Belfast. He regularly writes opinion pieces and articles on the political history of the Troubles for the *News Letter*, and is an active radio and television commentator. He has a particular interest in legacy issues and in the republican movement's misrepresentation of historical events to legitimate its campaign of violence.

William J.V. Neill is Emeritus Professor of Spatial Planning at the University of Aberdeen where he was appointed to a Sixth Century Chair in 2006, having previously held academic appointments at the University of Manchester and Queen's University Belfast. Having graduated from Queen's University, he completed a Master's degree in Urban Planning at the University of Michigan followed by a Ph.D. at the University of Nottingham. He worked as an urban planner for the State of Michigan in the 1970s and 1980s. His research interests revolve around the expression of identity in the city and how this is spatially contested and affirmed. He is editor of the book *Relaunching Titanic: Memory and Marketing in the New Belfast* (2013). His other books include *Migration and Cultural Inclusion in the European City* (co-ed., 2006); *Urban Planning and Cultural Identity* (2004); and *Reimaging the Pariah City: Lessons from Belfast and Detroit* (1995). He is a former Council member of the Royal Town Planning Institute and was a recent member of an EU URBACT expert group on the future of European cities. In 2018 he was appointed Visiting Research Fellow at the Institute of Irish Studies, Queen's University Belfast.

Mike Nesbitt is a prominent Unionist MLA. He was born in Belfast and educated at Campbell College and Cambridge University. His first career was in broadcasting as a radio sports reporter, then as a well-known reporter and news anchor with Ulster television. In 2008 he was appointed as one of Northern Ireland's four Victims' Commissioners. He resigned from this post in 2010 to pursue a career in politics with the Ulster Unionist Party. He was elected to the Northern Ireland Assembly as a representative for Strangford in 2011, then re-elected in 2016 and 2017. He served as Party Leader from 2012–17. In 2016, he negotiated with the SDLP to form an official Opposition, which meant declining the Ministerial posts to which the two parties were entitled: this arrangement ended with the collapse of devolution in January 2017 and was not renewed in 2020. Mike Nesbitt has served on a range of Assembly Committees, including those on the Executive Office (as Chair), Bill of Rights and the Economy.

Owen Polley is a journalist and commentator who has written for a variety of newspapers and magazines, including *The Daily Telegraph*, *The Times*, *The Guardian*, *Standpoint*, *The Critic*, *The Irish Times*, the *News Letter, The Article* and *CapX*. He is an Orwell Fellow, having been shortlisted for the Orwell Prize for political blogging, though he maintains his proudest professional achievement is writing a 3,500 word feature on Northern Ireland's "Green and White Army" for the football magazine *FourFourTwo*. He co-hosts the podcast PoliticalOD. From 2011 to 2015 he managed the Conservative Party's Northern Ireland campaign office in Bangor. Owen Polley was born in Antrim and brought up in Ballymena where he attended Ballymena Academy. He was educated at the University of Dundee.

Patrick J. Roche was born in Ennis, County Clare but when an infant his family moved to Northern Ireland. He attended Belfast High School, followed by nine years with the Belfast Banking Company. He graduated with a BA in economics and politics from Trinity College Dublin (1970) and an MA in political philosophy from the University of Durham (1972). He was a lecturer in economics at the University of Ulster (1974–1995). As a member of the UK Unionist Party, he was elected in 1998 as an MLA for Lagan Valley to the Northern Ireland Assembly and served until 2003. He has published numerous articles on Northern Irish politics in journals, including the *Salisbury Review*. He has co-edited with Brian Barton four collections of essays on Northern Ireland, the latest being *The Northern Ireland Question: Perspectives on Nationalism and Unionism* (2020).

Geoffrey Sloan is an Associate Professor in the Department of Politics and International Relations at the University of Reading. Formerly, he was Head of the Strategic Studies and International Affairs Department at Britannia Royal Naval College, Dartmouth. He has also been a Visiting Professor at the United States Naval Academy, Annapolis, and a Defence Fellow at St Antony's College Oxford. He served as a Seaman Officer in the Royal Naval Reserve for nine years. To date he has published three books on Geopolitics. His latest is entitled *Geopolitics, Geography and Strategic History* (2017), published in both the United States and the United Kingdom. It won the Stratfor Prize for geopolitical analysis in October 2017. The translation rights were sold to China in 2019. In 2021 the book was published in India in both hardback and paperback editions. He is currently researching a book on the British Army's campaigns in Ireland in the twentieth century.

William Beattie Smith was born in north Belfast and educated at Royal Belfast Academical Institution. He earned his B.A. in American Studies from the University of Sussex in 1971 and his doctorate in Political Science from Stanford in 1986. From 2003 to 2014 he was a Senior Research Fellow in Governance and Politics at Queen's University Belfast. The US Institute of Peace published his book *The British State and the Northern Ireland Crisis 1969–73* in 2011. His latest publication is *Early Years, Crossing Boundaries*, a biography of the Early Years Organisation. During his 30-year career in government, he worked for the Northern Ireland Civil Service, Northern Ireland Office and European Commission. He also served as Principal Private Secretary to First Minister David Trimble. Since leaving government in 2004, he has held ministerial appointments as a member of the Parliamentary Boundary Commission and Chair of the Ulster-Scots Academy Advisory Group, and has chaired or served on committees of the Human Rights Commission and Belfast City Council.

Daphne Trimble, Baroness Trimble practised as a solicitor in Belfast for 12 years before changing career to run her husband David's constituency office from 1990 until 2005. She was a member of the Equality Commission for Northern Ireland for two terms prior to becoming a member of the Northern Ireland Human Rights Commission from 2007 until 2010, when she resigned to contest the Parliamentary election in Lagan Valley for the Ulster Unionist Party. She departed from the advice on a Bill of Rights for Northern Ireland given by the Commission to the Secretary of State, and submitted her own Note of Dissent. She was a member of the board of the Northern Ireland Memorial Fund from its beginning in 1999, pioneering the work of supporting individual victims and survivors of the troubles, until the fund ceased in 2013, when its work was mainstreamed. She currently sits on the boards of the Ulster Youth Orchestra (Chair 2007 to 2017), Lagan Navigation Trust and the Goliath Trust. She remains an active member of the Ulster Unionist Party.

David Trimble is a Conservative peer. He grew up in Bangor, Co Down where he attended Bangor Grammar School. He graduated from Queen's University Belfast with a first-class honours degree in law and qualified as a barrister in 1969, after which he taught law at Queen's University until elected Unionist MP for Upper Bann in 1990. He was Leader of the Ulster Unionist Party from 1995–2005, in which capacity he negotiated the Belfast Agreement. He was awarded the Nobel Peace Prize in 1998, the Institute noting that he had shown "great political courage". He served as Northern Ireland's First Minister from 1998–2002, when the devolved administration collapsed as a consequence of republicans' bad faith. In 2006, he was created Baron Trimble of Lisnagarvey, and in 2007 he joined the Conservative Party. As a member of the Lords' EU scrutiny committee he witnessed the inner workings of the European institutions, and supported the Leave side in the 2016 referendum. His publications include *To Raise up a New Northern Ireland* (2001), a collection of articles and speeches, 1998–2000.

Graham Walker is Professor of Political History at Queen's University Belfast. His previous academic experience included spells at Manchester, Strathclyde, and Bristol universities. Among his books are *Intimate Strangers: Political and Cultural Interaction between Scotland and Ulster* (1995), *Scotland and Northern Ireland* (1998), *A History of the Ulster Unionist Party: Protest, Pragmatism and Pessimism* (2004) and *The Labour Party in Scotland: Religion, the Union and the Irish Dimension* (2016). He is the author of numerous scholarly articles and chapters, and these have included the subjects of popular culture, the politics of sport, and even Rangers Football Club. He was born, raised and educated in Glasgow and has lived in Northern Ireland for over thirty years. He is a Fellow of the Royal Historical Society.